The Firebird in Russian folklore is a fiery, illuminated bird; magical, iconic, coveted. Its feathers continue to glow when removed, and a single feather, it is said, can light up a room. Some who claim to have seen the Firebird say it even has glowing eyes. The Firebird is often the object of a quest. In one famous tale, the Firebird needs to be captured to prevent it from stealing the king's golden apples, a fruit bestowing youth and strength on those who partake of the fruit. But in other stories, the Firebird has another mission: it is always flying over the earth providing hope to any who may need it. In modern times and in the West, the Firebird has become part of world culture. In Igor Stravinsky's ballet *The Firebird*, it is a creature half-woman and half-bird, and the ballerina's role is considered by many to be the most demanding in the history of ballet.

The Overlook Press in the U.S. and Gerald Duckworth in the UK, in adopting the Firebird as the logo for its expanding Ardis publishing program, consider that this magical, glowing creature—in legend come to Russia from a faraway land—will play a role in bringing Russia and its literature closer to readers everywhere.

The Russian Symbolist Theatre

An Anthology of Plays and Critical Texts

Translated from the Russian and Edited by
Michael Green

ARDIS PUBLISHERS
NEW YORK, NY

This edition first published in paperback in the United States and the United Kingdom in 2013 by Ardis Publishers, an imprint of Peter Mayer Publishers, Inc.

NEW YORK:
The Overlook Press
141 Wooster Street
New York, NY 10012
www.overlookpress.com
For bulk and special sales, please contact sales@overlookny.com, or write us at the above address.

LONDON:
Gerald Duckworth & Co. Ltd.
30 Calvin Street
London E1 6NW
info@duckworth-publishers.co.uk
www.ducknet.co.uk

Library of Congress Cataloging-in-Publication Data
Main entry under title: The Russian symbolist theatre
Includes bibliographical references.
Contents: Against naturalism in the theatre / Briusov—The dictatorship of the director; For a theatre of action; Vera Komissarzhevskaya; The puppet show; The rose and the cross / Blok— |etc.|
1. Russian drama—19th century—Translations into English. 2. Russian drama—20th century—Translations into English. 3. English drama—Translations from Russian. 4. Theater—Russian S.F.S.R.—History—20th century—Addresses, essays, lectures. 5. Symbolism in literature—Addresses, essays, lectures.
I. Green Michael.
PG3245.R84 1985 891.72'08'015 85-20104

Printed in the United States of America
ISBN US: 978-1-4683-0635-4
ISBN UK: 978-0-7156-4580-2

2 4 6 8 10 9 7 5 3 1

CONTENTS

To anthologize is to exclude, and sometimes to exclude reluctantly. In making the present selection of plays, I will confess to a bias in favor of poetry, ambiguity and surprise—qualities that characterize the Russian Symbolist theatre at its most original and interesting. The possession of these qualities rather than formal adherence to a literary faction has been my main criterion for inclusion or rejection.

I wish to thank Dr. Neil Granoien, who prepared the first drafts for the translations of two plays in the present volume: *The Rose and the Cross* and *The Triumph of Death*.

I owe a special debt of gratitude to Professor Vladimir Markov, of whose generosity with his time and knowledge I have taken full advantage. My thanks are also due to Professor Robert Cohen, the late Professor Peter Colaclides, Professor Simon Karlinsky and Professor Thérèse Lynn for their kind help and advice.

My translation of Kuzmin's *The Venetian Madcaps* first appeared in *Russian Literature Triquarterly*, No. 7.

INTRODUCTION

The late nineteenth century was a period of rebellion and renewal in the European theatre. Discontent with the mediocrity of the commercial stage with its "well-made plays" and comfortable moral assumptions had given rise to the New Drama. Less a unified movement than a useful banner to which all those who wished for change in the theatre could rally, the New Drama looked toward both Symbolism and naturalism—a dualism embodied in the work of such dramatists of the period as Ibsen, Strindberg, Hauptmann and Chekhov. Poets and philosophers too had their vision of the theatre of the future. Nietzsche dreamed of returning the theatre to its origins in Dionysian ritual and sweeping away the barrier between actor and spectator. Wagner had looked back to the Athenian theatre and seen in it a profound union of poetry, music, drama, dance and design, the spirit of which he hoped to recapture in the modern *Gesamtkunstwerk*. In France, Mallarmé too called for a theatre that would lay all the arts under tribute to create a drama of mystery on a stage reduced to its barest elements. Maeterlinck announced that external action was dead and pleaded for a theatre of stillness and inner drama; his plays began to be taken up by the avant-garde as a sacred cause.

This ferment did not leave Russia untouched. With the first translations of Ibsen and Strindberg in the 1880s, the New Drama began to filter into the consciousness of cultured Russians; Maeterlinck and Hauptmann followed in the 1890s, and in the 1900s appeared a whole galaxy of new names that included Przybyszewski, Hofmannsthal, Wedekind, Hamsun, Schnitzler, D'Annunzio, Wilde and Shaw.

To a striking extent, the development of the Russian theatre at the turn of the century ran a similar course to that of the French theatre ten years earlier. In France, the naturalistic excesses of Antoine's Théâtre Libre (founded in 1887), which had specialized in painstakingly realistic productions of Ibsen and Hauptmann, had brought about a reaction in the shape of Paul Fort's Théâtre d'Art (1890) and its successor, Lugné-Poe's Théâtre de L'Oeuvre (1892), which introduced the dramas of Maeterlinck and staged Ibsen in a stylized "Symbolist" manner, bringing in artists of the Nabi school (Vuillard, Sérusier, Maurice Denis) to paint decorative backdrops. In Russia, the naturalism of Stanislavsky's Moscow Art Theatre (founded in 1898), which found effective vehicles in the plays of Ibsen, Hauptmann and Chekhov, was succeeded by the stylized theatre of Meyerhold, who produced plays by Maeterlinck, Ibsen and a number of Symbolists, both native and foreign, turning for decor to brilliant young painters from the ambience of the *World of Art*. There is, however, a factor that disturbs the neatness of the parallel—the ambiguous genius of Chekhov, whose relationship to the Symbolist theatre deserves some examination.

Chekhov has always been closely associated with the Moscow Art Theatre, which achieved its first significant success with its revival of *The Seagull* in 1898 and gave the premieres of all his major plays thereafter. Although Chekhov himself had reservations, the Art Theatre's naturalistic approach seemed ideally suited to Chekhov's plays, with the result that Chekhov has often been identified with naturalism in the theatre. Yet if Chekhov was a realist, he was a realist of a special kind who refined realism to the point where it threatened to become something else. Both realists and Symbolists sensed this in Chekhov. "Do you know what you're doing?" Gorky had expostulated, "You're killing realism." While in the opposite camp, Andrei Bely expressed the view that "while remaining a realist, Chekhov became the secret enemy of realism," and wrote the brilliant Symbolist exegesis of *The Cherry Orchard* included in the present volume.

Chekhov's later plays convey a mysterious sense of something pressing beyond words to find expression in the multitude of pauses that Chekhov, unlike most dramatists, is wisely content not to fill with stage directions. Dialogue seems to rise out of a profounder silence and to sink back into it. It is here that we sense a kinship between Chekhov and Maeterlinck, whose writings on the theatre are full of observations that, in a curious way, seem even more applicable to Chekhov's dramas than to Maeterlinck's own. "It is idle," wrote Maeterlinck, "to think that, by means of words, any real communication can ever pass from one man to another." He had argued that "psychological action" was "infinitely loftier in itself than mere material action," maintaining that "side by side with the necessary dialogue" there was "another dialogue that seems superfluous," but really determines "the quality and immeasurable range of the work."

Chekhov was drawn toward Maeterlinck, just as he was repelled by Ibsen. A whole bouquet of uncomplimentary remarks about the great Norwegian may be gathered from Chekhov's conversation and correspondence: "Listen, I tell you Ibsen is no dramatist," he wrote to Stanislavsky; to Andreyev he was even more unceremoniously dismissive—"Ibsen is an idiot." Ibsen, being, as Bernard Shaw admiringly observed in his *Quintessence of Ibsenism*, "a moralist and a debater as well as a dramatist," had invented the play of discussion. Ibsen belongs to the old drama of communication, Chekhov to the new drama of non-communication, which is perhaps why he seems so "modern" to us today. No doubt it was just this polemical quality in Ibsen that Chekhov found unappealing. In Maeterlinck, however, he took a warm interest. In 1902 he attempted to persuade the Art Theatre to stage an evening of Maeterlinck's short plays, and when at last in 1904 Stanislavsky did decide to produce *Les Aveugles, Intérieur* and *L'Intruse*, Chekhov, although mortally ill, took a keen interest in the project, demanding to be kept up to date on the progress of rehearsals. The plays were premiered on October 2, 1904—exactly three months after Chekhov's death.

It is tempting to speculate on the direction Chekhov might have taken had he lived longer. *The Cherry Orchard*—"almost a farce," as Chekhov insisted—anticipates the harlequinade of the pre-revolutionary years. Stanislavsky tells in his memoirs of a projected play that suggests that Chekhov was moving toward a decisive break with the manner he had brought to such perfection. The play was to deal with two friends in love with the same woman who journey together to the North Pole; the set for the last act was to represent an enormous ice-bound ship, and the play was to end with the two friends having a vision of the ghost of the woman (who had died in the meantime) flitting across the snow. The icy remoteness of the setting recalls that of Ibsen's last and most "symbolic" play, *When We Dead Awaken*, while both action and decor curiously anticipate Apollinaire's surrealist verse drama *Couleur du temps*. A jotting in Chekhov's notebook gives another hint of new departures: a play about a group of people waiting for someone who never arrives.

Appropriately, it was Meyerhold, then a youthful member of the Art Theatre, who had created the role of Treplev, the advocate of "new forms," in the Theatre's production of *The Seagull,* and the director was later to speak with pride of Chekhov's affection for him. Of the correspondence between the two, only one letter of Chekhov's survives, as against seven written by Meyerhold between 1899 and 1904; it is clear enough, however, that Chekhov was sympathetic to Meyerhold's increasingly critical attitude toward the Art Theatre, and that each tended to confide in the other his discontent with Stanislavskian naturalism. When Meyerhold, a founding member of the Art Theatre, was excluded from the list of shareholders when the Theatre became a joint stock company at the beginning of 1902, Chekhov was much concerned.

1902 was a year which saw the unmistakable emergence of new forces in the Russian theatre. In his article of that year, "Unnecessary Truth," Valery Briusov, the leader of Russian Symbolism, for the first time called into question the achievement of the Moscow Art Theatre, then at the height of its success, and wondered whether naturalism was not opposed to the very nature of the stage. In 1902 Meyerhold resigned from the Art Theatre to form a company, eventually to take the name of "The Fellowship of the New Drama"; with the young Aleksei Remizov as literary adviser, the troupe toured the provinces, including in its repertoire such unfamiliar names as Maeterlinck, Przybyszewski, Schnitzler and Hofmannsthal. In the same year the most popular actress of her generation, Vera Komissarzhevskaya, left the Alexandrinsky Theatre (where, in 1896, she had created the role of Nina in the original prodiction of *The Seagull*), dissatisfied with the entrenched routine of the Imperial stage; by touring the provinces she raised enough money to open her own theatre in St. Petersburg in 1904. The later conjunction of these two searchers—Meyerhold and Komissarzhevskaya—was to bring about the brief flowering of the Symbolist theatre in Russia.

Stanislavsky's 1904 productions of Maeterlinck, though generally agreed to be disappointingly unimaginative, had shown him to be not unaware of the need for a change of direction if the Art Theatre was to retain its leading position. Deciding that the time was ripe for experiment, and even for "novelty for novelty's sake," in 1905 he invited Meyerhold to take charge of an experimental "Theatre-Studio" attached to the Art Theatre. Briusov himself was to be in charge of the new theatre's literary section, and two native Symbolist dramas, Briusov's *The Earth* and Viacheslav Ivanov's *Tantalus*, were planned for inclusion in the repertoire. For the Theatre-Studio's opening production, however, Meyerhold chose Maeterlinck's *La Mort de Tintagiles*. Under the influence of the Belgian dramatist's own theory of "static theatre," Meyerhold matched the play's deathward drift and languid, hypnotic rhythms with a style of sparse, deliberate gesture that suggested the carefully composed groups of an antique bas-relief; formalized movement was complemented by formalized speech, each syllable falling, in Meyerhold's own memorable phrase, like a pebble into a deep well.

The Revolution of 1905 and Stanislavsky's dissatisfaction with the dress rehearsal of *Tintagiles* combined to bring about the premature demise of the Theatre-Studio, which never opened its doors to the public. Nevertheless, it had demonstrated during its brief, sequestered existence that a Symbolist theatre could exist outside the dreams of impractical poets. Moving now to St. Petersburg, Meyerhold became a frequenter of the famous Wednesday gatherings at the apartment of the erudite Symbolist poet Viacheslav Ivanov, where all that was liveliest in the artistic and intellectual life of the capital was to be encountered; apart from the host and his wife, the writer Lidia Zinovieva-Annibal, there were Blok, Bely, Sologub, Briusov, Berdiaev, Chulkov, Gippius and Merezhkovsky. The theatre of the future was a favorite topic of conversation at the Wednesdays. Imbued with Nietzschean ideas, Ivanov preached a theatre of religious communion and Dionysian ecstasy. The mood was one of expectancy. "The idea of a symbolist theatre hung in the air," wrote the poet, dramatist and critic Georgii Chulkov. "All that was lacking was a man of the theatre who would venture so risky an experiment. In those days only one director dreamed of a revolution in the theatre." That man was, of course, Meyerhold; together with Chulkov, he attempted to organize a new theatre: to be called "Torches," it would—so went the gossip in theatrical circles—"be something like a Petersburg version of the ill-fated Moscow Studio." Although "Torches," for want of financial backing, came to nothing, it did create conditions for an alliance between the new playwright and the new director, effectively bringing the poet into the theatre. It was for "Torches" that Blok, at Chulkov's suggestion, developed one of his lyrics into a short play of the same name--*The Puppet Show*.

In 1906 Komissarzhevskaya moved her theatre to new premises on Ofitserskaya Street and invited Meyerhold to be her director. An actress of great spiritual intensity who communicated to her roles something of her own tragic personality, Komissarzhevskaya won the hearts of poets (as Blok's touching obituary bears witness) no less than those of the theatregoing public; in the words of an admirer, "all the restless longing of a catastrophic epoch found its expression in her, all the vague reaching out, the satiety with the visible material world, the thirst to penetrate the undiscovered secrets of the universe and of life." Her adherence to the cause of the Symbolist theatre helped to broaden its appeal and make it less of a coterie enterprise.

The very appearance of the theatre on Ofitserskaya Street made it clear that radical departures were to be expected. The keynote was a chaste and severe restraint: walls and columns were painted a stark white and the curtains were of a plain dark material. The only color was provided by Bakst's drop-curtain, on which a Greek temple in the depths of a mysterious forest suggested the theatre's aim of returning the theatre to its ancient ritual origins.

Meyerhold was director of Komissarzhevskaya's theatre for little more than a year (his first production, Ibsen's *Hedda Gabler*, opened on November 10, 1906, his last, Sologub's *The Triumph of Death*, on November 6, 1907). The partnership was an uneasy one and the break, when it came, bitter. If Meyerhold and Komissarzhevskaya were both explorers, their explorations were conducted in different regions: "She did not need the external contrivances of new acting techniques, but the possibility of expressing her soul"—what drew her to Symbolism was the movement's mystical and transcendental aspect; Meyerhold, on the other hand, was a scholar and a technician, fascinated by the stylization of past theatrical epochs and "theatre for theatre's sake." In a way, actress and director represented the division within Russian Symbolism itself.

The art of the Symbolist period was marked by a heightened awareness of developments in the west, a self-conscious return to the community of European culture. This internationalism of outlook was characteristic of the theatre on Ofitserskaya Street, which opened its doors with a defiantly anti-naturalistic production of a play by the Art Theatre's beloved Ibsen—*Hedda Gabler*, in which the heroine, attired in a gown that suggested some scaly creature of the deep, moved against the deep blue and orange of Sapunov's extravagant art nouveau set, a martyr to the aesthetic protest. Nevertheless, though foreign plays were preponderant in the repertoire, the year of the Meyerhold-Komissarzhevskaya collaboration saw the premieres of such plays as Blok's *Puppet Show*, Andreyev's *Life of Man* and Sologub's *Triumph of Death*; the first of these was the occasion of a great theatrical battle of the order of the first night of *Hernani* or *The Rite of Spring* and marked a turning point in the history of the Russian theatre. After Meyerhold's departure, Komissarzhevskaya, with the aid of such brilliant directors as her brother, Fyodor Komissarzhevsky, and Nikolai Evreinov, continued her policy of staging Symbolist plays until the banning of Wilde's *Salome* in the autumn of 1908 forced her to close her theatre the following year. Russian dramas premiered during this period included Remizov's *Devil's Comedy*, Andreyev's *Black Maskers* and Sologub's *Vanka the Steward and the Page Jehan*. With the closing of Komissarzhevskaya's theatre, the Symbolist drama was left without a theatre of its own. There was nothing to do but retreat to the little theatres and theatre-cabarets that were such a feature of the artistic life of St. Petersburg in the prerevolutionary years. This intimate atmosphere was well suited to such a master of chamber drama and *divertissement* as Kuzmin, and it also gave Meyerhold—since 1908 director of the Imperial Alexandrinsky Theatre—a chance to experiment with *commedia dell'arte* techniques in the guise of "Doctor Dapertutto." By 1912, when Leonid Andreyev in the first of his two "Letters about the Theatre," regretfully announced the demise of Symbolism in the theatre, Symbolism itself was fast on the wane as a movement. The only two native Symbolist dramas staged by Meyerhold at the Alexandrinsky—Sologub's *Hostages of Life* (1912) and Zinaida Gippius's *The Green Ring* (1915)—both represent a compromise with traditional realistic theatre. The most considerable late Symbolist drama, Blok's *The Rose and The Cross* (the carefully researched historical setting of which also, in a sense, represented a compromise), was never given the staging it deserved.

Such is the "external" history of the Symbolist theatre in Russia. It has seemed worth summarizing here, since all the dramatists included in the present volume, with the exception of the lonely figure of Annensky, were closely connected with it. Which is is to say that the plays of the Symbolists were not, at their best, works intended, like the dramatic poems of the Romantics, for the study rather than the stage: they were highly theatrical creations in a new style that demanded a new style of production. Was it, then, a matter of a new theatre in search of a drama, or a new drama in search of a theatre? Meyerhold gave the primacy to literature: "The *New Theatre*," he wrote in "Literary Intimations of the New Theatre" (1906), "has its roots *in literature*. Literature has always taken the initiative in breaking up dramatic forms. Chekhov wrote *The Seagull* before the Art Theatre came forward to stage it. Van Lerberghe and Maeterlinck existed before the theatre that staged them." Meyerhold added that by literature he meant not only "playwrights who create a new form demanding a different kind of technique," but also "critics who reject old forms." In both these capacities the Russian Symbolists helped Meyerhold to formulate the principles of his theatrical revolution. Briusov's rejection of stage naturalism in favor of stylization and Ivanov's demand for the abolition of the barrier between actor and spectator remained central to Meyerhold's thinking, while it would be difficult to overemphasize the key position that *The Puppet Show* occupied in his development. Meyerhold himself credited Blok's play with providing "the first impetus in finding the paths of my art," for it was here that he broke away from Maeterlinck's "static theatre" to create his own "grotesque theatre" of movement and surprise.

"The basis of the grotesque," wrote Meyerhold, "is the constant striving on the artist's part to thrust the spectator from a plane he has only just succeeded in comprehending to another for which he is utterly unprepared." Mystification, unease, ambiguity, a sense of the illusory and transient nature of things, a constant question of "reality," are at the very heart of the Symbolist drama. They spring inevitably from the dualism of the Symbolist vision, with its unresolved tension between transcendental and everyday reality. It is characteristic of Symbolist drama that its action proceeds on two or more intersecting but mutually uncomprehending planes, and that the transitions between these planes are abrupt, creating just that sense of dislocation envisaged by grotesque (in Meyerhold's sense) theatre. The method is most brilliantly deployed in Blok's *Puppet Show*, where the action attains a complex ambiguity far beyond the simpler binary opposition underlying most Symbolist drama. In Annensky's *Thamyris Kitharodos*, for example, the Apollonian world of high art represented by the ascetic protagonist co-exists with the Dionysian world of the Satyrs and Maenads. The lonely passion of Judas in Remizov's tragedy is counterpointed with the bizarre antics of Zif, Orif and the Monkey King. In the plays of Sologub, such as *The Triumph of Death* and *Vanka the Steward and the Page Jehan*, dualism is so all-pervasive as to assume the function of a constructive principle. Kuzmin's Count Stello in *The Venetian Madcaps* dwells in a world of pure aesthetic delight inaccessible to the play's *commedia dell'arte* characters. Misty Brittany, with its songs and legends, remains infinitely remote from the feudal realities of Languedoc in Blok's *The Rose and the Cross.*

These worlds co-exist rather than conflict, for there is no common ground between them on which conflict might take place. We might well say of these plays what Martin Esslin has said of the plays of the Theatre of the Absurd: that they reflect "one poet's most intimate and personal intuition of the human situation, his own *sense of being*, his individual vision of the world"; that each play "is a complex poetic image made of a complicated pattern of subsidiary images and themes, which are interwoven, like the themes of a musical composition, not, as in most well-made plays, to present a line of development, but to make in the spectator's mind a total, complex impression of a basic, and static, situation." This lack of dramatic conflict in the conventional sense is reflected in such terms as "Lyrical Drama" (as Blok designated his three playlets of 1906) or Sologub's "Theatre of the Single Will." Yet while Sologub announced with unmixed satisfaction that all *dramatis personae* were but masks, transparent to a greater or lesser extent, behind which the face of their creator might be glimpsed, Blok (like Yeats and

Hofmannsthal) came to distrust the lyrical, subjective element that was engulfing the stage, warning that "the subtle poisons of lyricism have eaten away the strong, simple chains that support the drama and hold it together." Condemning Maeterlinck, and with him Chekhov, "who has taken away from the Russian drama what Maeterlinck has taken away from the European drama," Blok proclaimed Ibsen to have been the last of the great European dramatists. Ironically, though, Blok's earliest and most purely lyrical plays remain his most convincing work for the theatre; even *The Rose and the Cross*, with all its beauties, has a slightly labored air beside the freshness of *The Puppet Show* and *The Stranger.*

Russian Symbolism not only anticipated the constructive principles of Absurdist drama, it was also capable of astonishingly prophetic insights into the function of the theatre in man's increasingly mechanized existence. "The Theatre of the Absurd," writes Martin Esslin, "forms part of the unceasing endeavor of the true artists of our time to breach this dead wall of complacency and automatism and to re-establish an awareness of man's situation when confronted with the ultimate reality of his condition"; it seeks "to instill in him again the lost sense of cosmic wonder and primeval anguish, to shock him out of an existence that has become trite, mechanical, complacent." In a letter to Meyerhold, written in 1906 under the immediate impression of a dress rehearsal of *The Puppet Show*, Blok used similar imagery to express virtually the same thought: "*Every* piece of buffoonery, including my own, seeks to become a *battering ram* to smash through all the deadness." The poet-buffoon, said Blok, may pretend to embrace the "crass and torpid" world of matter, but only in order to fool it; "at this point *the hour of mystery must strike*: matter has been fooled, disarmed and subdued; in this sense, I '*accept the world*'—the whole world with its stupidity, inertia and dead, dry colors—only in order to trick this bony old witch and make her young again. In the embrace of the Fool and the Buffoon the old world puts on youth and beauty, and its eyes become translucent, unfathomable."

The concept of the *Gesamtkunstwerk* haunted the synesthetic imagination of the Symbolists, and it is natural that the theatre, the meeting place of the arts, should have occupied a central place in their thinking. Rarely in the history of the arts have music, painting, poetry and dance entered into so fruitful a partnership as they did in Russia in these prerevolutionary years. The dominant art of the period was undoubtedly music—the condition to which, in Pater's well-known phrase, all art aspired. Andrei Bely, the leading theoretician of symbolism, had said that "music is the soul of all the arts," and that "music is the ideal expression of the symbol." If music could not occupy in the theatre of the word the supremacy it enjoyed in the ballet (which must be admitted the quintessential art form of these years), it is nevertheless a subtly pervasive element in the Symbolist drama, with its tendency toward the rhythmically organized language of verse and the dissolving of the action in song, mime and dance. Ivanov, Sologub and Annensky all envisaged a theatre in which there would be a place for the dance, while Meyerhold wished to "subordinate acting to the rhythm of speech and the rhythm of plastic movement" in anticipation of a "rebirth of the dance."

In the Symbolist theatre the painter's role assumed an importance it had not had since the days of the great baroque decorators, such as Viviani and Gonzago, who had worked in Russia. Jettisoning with relief the laboriously constructed three-dimensional stage models demanded by the Moscow Art Theatre, the artists of the Symbolist theatre once again made scene painting a "music for the eyes" that merged with the rhythm of the production. Though far less well known, the decorative achievement of the Symbolist theatre bears comparison with that of Diaghilev's Ballets Russes, which indeed, it anticipated. In an article entitled "The Artist in V. F. Komissarzhevskaya's Theatre," Evreinov wrote: "It seems a ridiculous thing to say, but it is the truth: in the field of painting, backward Russia suddenly overtook all other countries in theatre design." The ambience of the *World of Art*, with its emphasis on technique, its cult of the theatre and its taste for the grand style in architecture, be it of St. Petersburg or Versailles, fostered a number of artists who were not only skilled decorators, but whose entire oeuvre is permeated by the spirit of the theatre. If Bakst and Benois devoted their talent mainly to the ballet at this period, there were others hardly less gifted—Dobuzhinsky, Roerich, Golovin, Sapunov, Sudeikin—to provide the atmospheric and brilliantly stylized settings demanded by the Symbolist theatre. This new kind of decorator, who united in himself the creative artist and the man of the theatre, assumed a position of power next only to that of the director himself, with whom he worked in the closest collaboration Meyerhold spoke with reverence of Sapunov and Golovin—"those together with whom I joyously set out on a journey of exploration (. . .), before whom a secret door into Wonderland opened, as it did to me." Blok, as we shall see, was as suspicious of this new breed of decorator as he was of the dictator-director, seeing in him another pretender to the author's rightful primacy of place.

The Symbolist theatre was close to the *World of Art* in another respect—its intense preoccupation with the styles and conventions of the past. The retrospectivism that marked Russian art at the turn of the century was not mere nostalgia or escapism; it was the result of a profound feeling that the way to the future lay through a recovery of the past. Diaghilev, the organizing force behind the *World of Art*, gave prophetic expression to this feeling in 1905, when, summing up what the movement had accomplished, he spoke of "a culture that has risen through us but will sweep us aside." The scholar-artist and the scholar-poet, versed in a variety of cultures and with a protean ability to recreate them in their own work, were typical of the age. "Stylization"—a word that Briusov had put forward with some caution in 1902—soon became something of a catchword in cultivated drawing rooms.

In an attempt to break with the "untheatrical" realism of the immediate past, the theatre turned to what Meyerhold called "the truly theatrical epochs." We read in Meyerhold's theatre magazine *The Love of Three Oranges* of an attempt "to write a light comedy directly continuing the traditions of the eighteenth century and bypassing the line of development upon which Russian drama entered in the nineteenth century." In 1907 the "Ancient Theatre," founded by Evreinov and Baron Drizen with the aim of staging plays in the style of the period in which they were written, opened a season of medieval miracles and mysteries with Blok's translation of Rutebeuf's *Le Miracle de Théophile*; a second season in 1911 was devoted to the seventeenth century Spanish drama. What then were the "truly theatrical epochs" that the anti-realists sought to revive? Classical Greece, the Middle Ages, Elizabethan England, the France of Molière; but above all the lost golden age was located in late eighteenth century Venice, where Gozzi had brought about a miraculous rebirth of the *commedia dell'arte* with his fantastic, semi-improvisatory fairytale plays. Gozzi became the object of a cult: the title of his first great theatrical triumph was adopted by Meyerhold for a magazine largely devoted to making available in Russian the Italian dramatist's plays and memoirs. Small wonder, then, if the masks of the *commedia dell'arte* haunt the drama of these years.

So powerful was the retrospective spirit in the years immediately preceding the Revolution that in his article "Russian Dramatists" of 1911, Meyerhold says nothing of the individual qualities of the representatives of the "New Drama," but contents himself with an approving enumeration of their links with past theatrical traditions: Viacheslav Ivanov is reviving the ancient Greek *orchestra*; Blok is following the tradition of Italian popular comedy, while his outlook is close to that of such German Romantics as Novalis and Tieck; Remizov is laying the foundation for a modern mystery, modeled on the mystery plays of the Middle Ages; Kuzmin writes plays in the spirit of the medieval drama, and is also "reconstructing" the French comic theatre; Bely is trying to create an original modern mystery; Sologub is drawn to the classical Greek theatre *(The Gift of the Wise Bees)* or to the great age of Spanish drama *(The Triumph of Death)*. This is, of course, a one-sided view. Just as the figures in eighteenth century or eighteen thirties costume who move with slightly self-conscious theatricality in the shallow, stage-like picture-space of such *World of Art* affiliated artists as Somov, Sapunov and Sudeikin are clearly the artists' contemporaries playing at being aristocrats of the *ancien régime*, so the characters created by Symbolist playwrights reflect the sensibility of their own day. Count Stello in *The Venetian Madcaps is really* a St. Petersburg aesthete of the *fin de siècle*. Blok admitted that the men and women in his *The Rose and the Cross* were "modern people" and that "their tragedy is our tragedy." Annensky too conceded that, although he had "treated an ancient theme in an ancient form," his drama "very probably reflects the soul of modern man."

While Meyerhold looked to Gozzi and Tieck as the precursors of an absolute, self-sufficing theatre (though it is true that he also found links between Pushkin, Gogol, Lermontov and the great theatrical traditions of the past), it is possible to trace such an "anti-realistic" tradition—a minor one, to be sure—within the Russian theatre itself. Since Russian Symbolism was in many respects a return to the principles of Russian Romanticism, it is not surprising to find stirrings of discontent with the idea of verisimilitude as the basis of theatre in the writings of the Romantics. In a draft preface to *Boris Godunov*, Pushkin roundly declared that the very nature of drama excluded any such slavish copying of life: " . . . what kind of verisimilitude is there, for heaven's sake, in a room divided in two parts, one of which is occupied by two thousand people supposedly invisible to those on the stage?" Pushkin's friend, the Decembrist poet Küchelbecker, wrote a choric tragedy, *The Argives*, in which he attempted to return to the Greek theatre without the intermediacy of the French classicists. More startlingly, he recommended a revival of the mystery play, not on the model of Goethe's *Faust*, but in the style of "the artless allegorical popular spectacles of Hans Sachs, the *Frères de la Passion*, the English minstrels, the German mastersingers," and the *Sacramentales* of Calderon. He was attracted by the division of the medieval stage into two or three levels and also by the deliberate disruption of the theatrical illusion by direct appeals to the audience. All these features he attempted to incorporate into his own "Mystery," *Izhorsky* (1835).

Closer to the Theatre of the Absurd are the delightful nonsense plays of the comic team who wrote under the name of Kozma Prutkov. Not staged in their own day (with the exception of the first of them, *Fantasia*, which was banned after, or—as its "author" proudly pointed out—*during* its first performance in 1851, when an unamused Nicholas I stalked out in disgust), Prutkov's plays were later to enjoy something of a vogue in the little theatres and cabarets of St. Petersburg, where they were staged by such directors as Evreinov and Komissarzhevsky. It would, however, be unwise to place too heavy an ideological weight on these *jeux d'espirit*; Aleksei Tolstoi, the most distinguished member of the Prutkov team, was, *in propria persona*, the author of worthy blank verse historical dramas and an advocate of the well-made play who objected to the "pointlessness" of Ostrovsky's dialogue. Close in spirit to Prutkov's plays, and like them an ancestor of Blok's *Puppet Show*, is Vladimir Soloviov's skit, *The White Lily*. Blok himself pointed to Sukhovo-Kobylin's extraordinary black farce, *Tarelkin's Death* (1869) as a play in which "the ancient lineaments of the symbolical drama may be discerned."

If the Russian Symbolist drama was not entirely without ancestors on native soil, neither was it without progeny. The "trans-rational" drama of early Futurism, Mayakovsky's expressionistic tragedy *Vladimir Mayakovsky* (certainly the ultimate example of the "Drama of the Single Will") and his later satirical grotesques, the Pirandello-like plays of Evreinov (whose earlier stage works, such as the harlequinade, *A Merry Death*, must be regarded as part of the Symbolist theatre), the tragi-comic farces of Bulgakov and Erdman, the allegorical fairytales of Evgenii Schwarz—not to mention verse dramas, such as those of Gumiliov and Tsvetaeva, that follow the lyrical rather than the grotesque line of Symbolist drama—are all in some measure indebted to the Symbolists' short-lived theatrical revolution. It is hoped that, given the freedom to develop organically, the modern Soviet theatre will, like that of modern Poland, draw fruitfully upon the rich creative legacy of the Symbolist years.

VALERY BRIUSOV

Valery Briusov (1873-1924), poet, novelist, dramatist, critic and translator, was born in Moscow and came of a solid merchant family. Calculating and ambitious, he early saw "Decadence" as the literary movement of the future and resolved to become its leader. Between 1893 and 1895 he published several "anthologies" (actually written almost exclusively by himself under a variety of pseudonyms) entitled *Russian Symbolists*; though largely an exercise in youthful *épatage*, they did introduce the notion of Symbolism to a wide Russian public for the first time. Within a decade Briusov established himself as a formidable figure on the literary scene—the acknowledged "master" of the younger Symbolist poets and the editor of the influential Symbolist journal *The Scales*. With the decay of Symbolism as a movement after 1910 his influence began to wane. He was one of the few leading Symbolists to accept the October Revolution wholeheartedly and to attempt, not very successfully, to adapt his art to revolutionary themes. Because of this, his work has continued to be published, in highly selective editions, under the Soviets.

Briusov was essentially an aesthete and an eclectic. A tireless experimenter in poetic form, he also broadened the thematic range of Russian poetry with his urbanism and bold (if cold) eroticism. It may be, however, that his prose (which has yet to receive its due) has worn better than his verse. In contrast to most Symbolist prose, it exhibits a sobriety and restraint that can be traced back to Pushkin (of all the Symbolists, Briusov was the most devoted Pushkinian).

Briusov's interest in the theatre goes back to the beginning of his career. At the age of twenty, he wrote a comedy, *Country Passions*, which was banned by the censor because of its "sordid amorous intrigues"; the hero of this play (which has remained unpublished) was a "decadent" poet called Findesièclov. Briusov's best known dramatic work, the "Scenes from Future Times," *The Earth*, was published in 1905. Like his remarkable story "The Republic of the Southern Cross," it is a nightmarish vision of man living in a completely closed and controlled environment, shut off from nature and eventually destroyed by his own technological prowess. If the vision owes something to Wells, it also looks forward to Zamiatin's *We*. *The Earth* was never produced, and Briusov later included it in a collection of stories, maintaining that the play was written "more to be read than for performance." The poet returned to this "science fiction" theme in an unpublished play written in 1920, *The Dictator*; when read to an audience of writers, it aroused heated discussion by its temerity in suggesting that a socialist society, even in the distant future, might become a dictatorship.

Briusov's other published plays include *The Wayfarer* (1910), a "psychodrama" in one act, written perhaps under the influence of Evreinov's ideas about monodrama, in which there are only two characters and only one speaking role. His verse tragedy *Protesilaus Dead* (1912) is the third Russian Symbolist drama to treat the myth of Laodamia (the other two being Annensky's *Laodamia* and Sologub's *Gift of the Wise Bees*); Briusov's is certainly the most pedestrian of the three. Several more plays and film scenarios remain in the Briusov archives.

Active as a translator throughout his career, Briusov made Russian versions of a number of plays, including Racine's *Phaèdre*, Molière's *Amphitrion* (1913), Maeterlinck's *Pélleas et Mélisande* (1907) D'Annunzio's *Francesca da Rimini* (1908, in collaboration with Viacheslav Ivanov; these last two translations were intended for Komissarzhevskaya's theatre), Verhaeren's *Hélène de Sparte* (1909) and Oscar Wilde's *Duchess of Padua* (1911).

Briusov played a decisive role in encouraging the revolt against the naturalism of Stanislavsky's early Moscow Art Theatre productions. In Meyerhold's words, "Briusov was the first in Russia to speak of the futility of that 'truth' which our theatres have sought so strenuously to capture in recent years; he was also the first to point to other paths of dramatic presentation."

Valery Briusov

Against Naturalism in the Theatre[1] (from "Unnecessary Truth")

It is three years now that the Art Theatre has been with us in Moscow. Somehow it was an immediate success with everyone—the public, the press, the partisans of the new art and the defenders of the old. Not long ago, it was the custom to cite the Maly Theatre as the model of the Russian stage; these days people only laugh at its routine. And this same Maly Theatre and another Moscow theatre—Korsh's—have begun to adopt the new methods. For Muscovites the Art Theatre has become a kind of idol; they are proud of it, and it is the first thing they hasten to show off to the visitor. When the Art Theatre visited Petersburg, it performed here to packed houses, arousing universal interest. The Art Theatre ventured to stage plays that had failed in other theatres—Chekhov's *Seagull*, for example—and was successful. Most surprising of all, it was the Art Theatre's experimental spirit, its innovations in decor and acting, its daring choice of plays, that won the sympathy of the crowd.

What is the Art Theatre, then? Is it really the theatre of the future, as some have called it? Has it made a step toward the spiritualization of art, toward the overcoming of the fatal contradictions between the essence and the surface of art? Simple probability says no. If the Art Theatre had set itself such tasks, it would hardly have won universal acclaim so quickly. Success attests that what the Art Theatre offers its audience is not the genuinely new, but the old refurbished, that it offers no threat to the deep-rooted habits of the theatregoer. It has only achieved with greater perfection what other theatres, including its rival the Maly, have aimed at. Together with the entire European theatre, with insignificant exceptions, it is on a false path.

Modern theatres aim at the utmost verisimilitude in their depiction of life. They think that if everything on the stage is as it is in reality, then they have worthily fulfilled their function. Actors endeavor to speak as they would in a drawing room, scene-painters copy views from nature, costume designers work in accordance with archaeological data. In spite of all this, however, there remains much that the theatre has not succeeded in counterfeiting. The Art Theatre has set itself the aim of reducing this "much." The actors there have begun to sit with their backs to the audience without constraint; they have begun to talk to each other instead of "out" to the audience. In place of the usual box set has appeared the room placed at an oblique angle: other rooms are visible through the open doors, so that an entire apartment is presented to the viewer's gaze. The furniture is arranged as it usually is in people's homes. If a forest or a garden is to be represented, several trees are placed on the forestage. If the play requires rain to fall, the audience is made to listen to the sound of water. If the play is set in winter, snow can be seen falling outside the windows. If it is windy, curtains flutter, and so on.

First of all, one has to say that these innovations are very timid. They are concerned with secondary matters and leave the essential traditions of the theatre undisturbed. And until these traditions, which comprise the essence of any stage production, are changed, no alteration of detail will bring the theatre closer to reality. All theatres, including the Art Theatre, try to make everything on stage visible and audible. Stages are lit by footlights and strip lights, but in real life light either falls from the sky, or pours in through windows, or is cast by a lamp or a candle. If there is a night scene, the Art Theatre has ventured to leave the stage in greater darkness than is customary, although it has not dared to extinguish all the lights in the theatre; however, if it were really night on stage, the audience would obviously be unable to see anything. Similarly, the Art Theatre is at pains to ensure that all stage conversation is audible to the auditorium. Even if a large gathering is represented, only one actor speaks at a time. When a new group begins to speak, the previous one "moves upstage" and begins gesticulating energetically—and this a quarter of a century after Villiers de l'Isle Adam in his drama *Le nouveau monde* bracketed two pages of dialogue with the direction "Everybody speaks at once!"

But even if the Art Theatre were more daring, it would still fall short of its purpose. To reproduce life faithfully on the stage is impossible. The stage is conventional by its very nature. One set of conventions may be replaced by another, that is all. In Shakespeare's day a board would be set up with the inscription "forest." Not so long ago we used to be content with a backdrop of a forest with side wings depicting trees with branches incomprehensibly intertwined against the sky. In time to come, forests will be constructed from artificial three-dimensional trees with foliage and rounded trunks, or even from living trees with roots hidden in tubs under the stage . . . And all this, the last word in stage technique, will, like the Shakespearean inscription, be for the audience no more than a reminder, no more than a symbol of a forest. The modern theatregoer is not in the least taken in by a painted tree—he knows that a particular piece of lathe and canvas is intended to stand for a tree. In much the same way, a signboard meant "forest" to an Elizabethan audience and a stage sapling will mean a tree growing naturally to the audience of the future. The set is no more than a pointer to the imagination. In the Greek theatre, an actor playing someone who had just returned from foreign parts would enter from the left. At the Art Theatre, the actor is admitted to a small vestibule where he divests himself of sheepskin and galoshes as a sign that he has come from afar. But who among the audience is likely to forget that he arrived from the wings? In what way is the convention by which an actor removes his sheepskin more subtle than the one by which it is understood that if he enters from the left he is coming from foreign parts?

Not only the art of the theatre, but art of any kind cannot avoid formal convention, cannot be transformed into a re-creation of reality. Never, in looking at a picture by one of the great realist painters, will we be deceived like the birds of Zeuxis into thinking that before us are fruits or an open window through which we may glimpse a distant horizon. By infinitesimal gradations of light and shade, by the most elusive signals, the eye is able to distinguish reality from representation. Never will we bow to the marble bust of an acquaintance. It is unheard of that someone, on reading a story in which the author recounts in the first person how he came to commit suicide, should order a mass to be sung for the repose of his soul. And if there do exist reproductions of people and things that deceive the eye, such, for example, as bridges in a painted panorama or wax figures so convincing that they frighten children, we have difficulty in recognizing these creations as works of art. Not a single one of the spectators sitting in the orchestra and paying three or four roubles for his seat is going to believe that he is really looking at Hamlet, Prince of Denmark, and that in the final scene the Prince lies dead.

Each new technical device in art, be it that of the theatre or another, only arouses curiosity and suspicion in the spectator. A certain contemporary artist has, it is said, painted a new series of pictures in which the effect of moonlight is strikingly conveyed. When we see them, our first thought will be: how did he manage to do that? And then we will captiously seek out every discrepancy with reality. Only when we have satisfied our curiosity will we start looking at the picture as a work of art. When an avalanche of wadding descends on the stage, the members of the audience ask each other: how was that done? If Rubek and Irene[2] simply walked off into the wings, the audience would believe more readily in their destruction than it does now, when before their eyes two straw-stuffed dummies and armfuls of wadding go rolling over the boards. "It faded on the crowing of the cock," someone says of the Ghost in *Hamlet*, and this is enough for the audience to imagine the crowing of the cock. But in *Uncle Vanya* the Art Theatre has a cricket chirping. No one in the audience will imagine that the cricket is real, and the more lifelike the sound, the less convincing the illusion. In time, audiences will become used to the devices they now find so novel and will cease to notice them. But this will not come about because the audience will take wadding for snow in real earnest, or the rope that tugs at the curtains for wind, but because these devices will simply be numbered among the usual theatrical conventions. Would it not then be better to abandon the fruitless battle against the invincible conventions of the theatre, which only spring up with renewed strength, and rather than seeking to eradicate them, attempt to subjugate, to tame, to harness, to saddle them?

There are two kinds of convention. One kind arises from the inability to create successfully. A bad poet says of a beautiful woman: "She is as fresh as a rose." It may be that the poet really understood the vernal freshness of the woman's soul, but he was unable to express his feelings, substituting cliché for genuine expression. In the same way, people want to speak on the stage as they do in life but are unable to, stressing words unnaturally, pronouncing endings too emphatically and so on. But there is another kind of convention—that which is deliberately applied. It is a convention that statues of marble and bronze are left unpainted. They could be painted—at one time they even were—but it is unnecessary, since sculpture is concerned with form, not color. An engraving in which leaves are black and the sky striped observes certain conventions, but it nevertheless affords pure aesthetic enjoyment. Wherever there is art, there is convention. To oppose this is as absurd as to demand that science would dispense with logic and explain phenomena other than by their causal relationship.

It is time that the theatre stopped counterfeiting reality. A cloud depicted in a painting is flat, it does not move or change its form or luminiscence—but there is something about it that gives us the same feeling as a real cloud. The stage must provide everything that can most effectively help the spectator to recreate the setting demanded by the play in his imagination. If a battle is to be represented, it is absurd to send on stage a couple of dozen—or even a thousand—extras waving wooden swords: perhaps the audience will be better served by a musical picture from the orchestra. If a wind is called for, there is no need to blow a whistle and tug at the curtain with a rope: the actors themselves must convey the storm by behaving as people do in a strong wind. There is no need to do away with the setting, but it must be deliberately conventionalized. The setting must be, as it were, stylized. Types of setting must be devised that will be comprehensible to everyone, as a received language is comprehensible, as white statues, flat paintings and black engravings are comprehensible. Simplicity of setting will not be equivalent to banality and monotony. The principle will be changed, and there will be ample scope in particulars for the imagination of Messrs. set designers and technicians.

Dramatists too must in some degree perfect their artistic method. They are sovereign artists only when their work is read; on the stage their plays are only forms into which the actors pour their own content. Dramatists must renounce all superfluous, unnecessary and ultimately futile copying of life. Everything external in their work must be reduced to a minimum because it has little to do with the conduct of the drama. The drama can convey the external only through an intermediary—through the souls of the *dramatis personae*. The sculptor cannot take soul and emotion in his hands; he has to give the spirit bodily incarnation. The dramatist, on the contrary, should make it possible for the actor to express the physical in the spiritual. Something has already been achieved in the creation of a new drama. The most interesting attempts of this kind are the plays of Maeterlinck and the latest dramas of Ibsen. It is noteworthy that it is in the staging of these plays that the modern theatre has shown itself to be particularly ineffectual.

The ancient theatre had a single permanent set—the palace. With slight alterations it was made to represent the interior of a house, a square, the seashore. Actors wore masks and buckskins, which forced them to put aside any thought of imitating everyday life. The chorus sang sacred hymns around the altar and also intervened in the action. Everything was at once thoroughly conventionalized and utterly alive; the audience devoted its attention to the action and not to the setting, "for tragedy," says Aristotle, "is the imitation not of men, but of action." In our day, such simplicity of setting has been preserved in the folk theatre. I chanced to see a performance of *Tsar Maximilian*[3] given by factory workers. The scenery and props consisted of two chairs, the tsar's paper crown and the paper chains of his rebellious son Adolph. Watching this performance, I understood what powerful resources the theatre has at its disposal and how misguided it is in seeking the aid of painters and technicians.

The creative urge is the only reality that exists on earth. Everything external is, in the poet's words, "only a dream, a fleeting dream." Grant that in the theatre we may be partakers of the highest truth, the profoundest reality. Grant the actor his rightful place, set him upon the pedestal of the stage that he may rule it as an artist. By his art he will give content to the dramatic performance. Let your setting aim not at truth, but at the suggestion of truth. I summon you away from the unnecessary truth of the modern stage to the deliberate conventionalization of the ancient theatre.

1902

ALEKSANDR BLOK

Aleksandr Blok (1880-1921), poet, dramatist and critic, came of a comfortable academic background: his father was professor of jurisprudence at Warsaw University, his mother a writer and translator and his maternal grandfather rector of St. Petersburg University. His parents separated early, and the boy grew up in the care of his adoring mother and aunt. In 1903 he married Liubov Dmitrievna Mendeleyeva, daughter of the famous chemist. As a young man, Blok was profoundly influenced by the mystical philosophy of Vladimir Soloviov, and, together with Andrei Bely and Sergei Soloviov, the philosopher's nephew, formed a coterie devoted to eschatological expectation and the cult of the eternal feminine. The painful triangular situation that developed between Blok, his wife and Bely is reflected in *The Puppet Show*, which also signals his break with coterie mysticism and artistic coming of age (though Blok never ceased to be, in a broad sense, a romantic and a mystic).

Blok began to publish his poetry in 1903. His development as a poet might be compared to that of Yeats—away from a dreamy, backward-looking romanticism toward a direct and painful involvement with the bitter and painful reality of modern life. Blok's writing is haunted by a sense of impending catastrophe: he is the lyric voice of the "terrible years" between the failed revolution of 1905 and the successful one of 1917. It is ironic, though consistent with the logic of his development, that Blok, an aristocrat of the spirit and a gentleman of the old school, should, in *The Twelve*, have created the great poem of the Bolshevik Revolution. Blok's acceptance of the new order cost him a heroic effort and seems to have left him creatively exhausted. During his last years he worked for various Soviet cultural organizations. Disillusioned with the Revolution, his health undermined by the privations of the civil-war years, Blok already seemed a relic of a past age to many of his contemporaries when he died in August, 1921.

Lyricism is all-pervasive in Blok's work: his poetry, his plays and even his criticism all merge in a single lyric stream. Yet Blok wished to overcome the purely subjective element in his writing and (again like Yeats) felt that the theatre offered a means of doing so. Nonetheless, the three short plays—*The Puppet Show, The Beautiful Stranger* and *The King in the Square*—which he wrote in 1906, were published two years later under the collective title *Lyrical Dramas*, and it is more than incidental that the first two (which are also the best) developed out of identically titled lyrics.

These early playlets of Blok's are very much *sui generis*. Certainly, in Russian literature one can find foreshadowings of them in the nonsense dramas of Kozma Prutkov and Vladimir Soloviov; certainly there is a parodistic element in *The Puppet Show*, notably of the death-haunted early dramas of Maeterlinck and, closer to home, of Bely's lugubriously eschatological "fragment of an unwritten mystery," *The Newcomer*; but to point this out is not to detract from their originality. *The Puppet Show*, stripping away illusion after illusion to reveal at last only a void, anticipates the theatre of the absurd.

The Puppet Show has been called "one of the turning points of the Russian theatre." Meyerhold, who gave the play three separate productions, in the first of which he also played the part of Pierrot, declared that it showed Blok to be "a true magician of the theatre." The first performance took place at Komissarzhevskaya's theatre on December 30, 1906; with sets by the brilliant young painter Sapunov and music by Kuzmin, the production was a triumph for the Symbolist theatre—and the occasion for a pitched battle between the friends and foes of the "New Drama." In the words of a contemporary critic: "Solid, respectable citizens were on the point of entering into hand-to-hand combat; whistles and roars of hatred were interrupted by piercing howls filled with youthful fervor, defiance, rage and desperation: 'Blok, Sapunov, Kuzmin, M-e-y-e-r-h-o-l-d'—the names were born upon the air like the howls of drowning, dying men who still refuse to yield."

Blok's next play, *The Song of Destiny* (1908), though an artistic failure, was an important work for the poet, who returned to it again and again, revising it for the last time as late as 1919. Blok attempted here to reconcile two irreconcilables—the heroic romantism of Wagner and Ibsen's concern with contemporary social problems (he profoundly admired both these masters of the stage). It is characteristic of Blok that themes, images and even lines from *The Song of Destiny* are to be found in other works dating from this period, including, in the present collection, the essay "On the Theatre."

The Rose and the Cross, Blok's last important work for the stage, was originally conceived as a ballet scenario; the proposed ballet then became an opera libretto; however, the character of Bertrand ("not the hero, but the mind and heart of the drama") began to seem "more dramatic than musical," and the play was completed in its present form in January 1913. *The Rose and the Cross* marks a return to the medieval decor of Blok's early poetry. Although he devoted painstaking research to the historical background of his play (much the most concretely located he ever wrote), Blok stressed that "*The Rose and the Cross* is not a historical drama (...) The drama's earliest outlines, belonging to the stage of creation when the artist gathers himself into a single ball of nerves and does not allow himself to dissipate his energies—all of that was, so to speak, extra-historical. History and period lent their aid only at the point where the artist allows himself to look about him, to remember, to observe—the point where he 'lets himself go.' " For Blok, as for Annensky in his "classical" tragedies, the characters of the play "are modern people and their tragedy is our tragedy." The triangle Bertrand-Isaure-Aliscan (poetic dreamer-capricious beauty-dashing vulgarian) represents a recurring pattern in Blok's work, prefigured by the Pierrot-Columbine-Harlequin triangle in *The Puppet Show* and grotesquely echoed by the Petka-Katka-Vanka triangle in *The Twelve*.

Completing work on *The Rose and the Cross*, Blok wrote in his diary: "I have versified the last scene to the melodies of Wagner." Wagner's influence makes itself felt in a number of ways: as well as prose and the iambic pentameter traditional in Russian verse drama since Pushkin, Blok makes extensive use of an irregular triple meter similar to that of Wagnerian music drama; Brittany and the world of Celtic legend suggest *Tristan*, as does the heroine's name ("Izora" in Russian); "Gladness-in-Suffering," the leitmotif of Blok's play, is clearly related to *Tristan's* "Love-in-Death."

There is an odd coincidence of theme between *The Rose and the Cross* and Edmond Rostand's *Cyrano de Bergerac*: in both plays, a man of noble nature whose physical ugliness is dwelt on by the author nurses a chivalrous and undeclared passion for a capricious beauty, whose favor he is instrumental in gaining for a handsome but spiritually inferior rival. Of course, the lyricism of Blok's play belongs to a different world from that of Rostand's romantic rodomontade; nevertheless, it is interesting that Rostand is mentioned twice (unflatteringly, it is true) in letters written by Blok from Brittany during the summer of 1911—the period of the play's gestation. In 1913 he recorded in his diary without comment Ivanov-Razumnik's observation that the scene in which Aliscan climbs onto Bertrand's shoulders might be taken as an imitation of Rostand. *Cyrano*, then, may perhaps be allotted a modest part in the genesis of Blok's drama.

The stage presentation of *The Rose and the Cross* was dogged by misfortune. Blok, who for personal as well as artistic reasons had cooled considerably toward Meyerhold, was desperately anxious that his play should be directed by Stanislavsky; Stanislavsky, however, remained lukewarm toward the work. By the time the Moscow Art Theatre, largely as a result of Leonid Andreyev's advocacy, did take up *The Rose and the Cross*, war was in progress and revolution on the horizon. Blok did not live to see his play staged.

In addition to his original drama, Blok translated two plays for avant-garde theatres of the day. Baron Drizen's Ancient Theatre opened its doors in December, 1907 with Blok's version of *Le Miracle de Théophile* by the thirteenth century trouvère Rutebeuf. For Komissarzhevskaya he translated Grillparzer's *Die Ahnfrau*, attracted by the Austrian dramatist's "heroic (perhaps even melodramatic) romanticism." Directed by Fiodor Komissarzhevsky, with sets by Benois and music by Kuzmin, the play received its first performance in January, 1909.

Blok's passionate concern with the stage is reflected in a number of writings and reviews, notably in two long programmatic articles, "On the Drama" (1907) and "On the Theatre" (1908), in which he surveys the theatrical scene, past and present, with considerable acuteness and independence of judgment.

Aleksandr Blok

The Dictatorship of the Director[4] (from "On the Theatre")

It seems that we are passing through an era in which authors feel an unprecedented disdain, whether open or covert, for the theatrical presentation of their work. The most convincing confirmation of these words of mine I find in the fact that the question of the *director* has become the vital one facing the theatre today—one which is even in fashion with the public. The director is the invisible *dramatis persona* who takes the author's play from him, directs him to the nearest backstage exit (there are always such exits "in case of fire") and thereupon proceeds to interpret the play to the actors in the light of his own understanding, with the result that when the author attends a performance in order to view his work, he is not infrequently so overcome with amazement that he is unable to utter a word. Perhaps, though, the distortion of plays has become so much a matter of custom that authors have lost their capacity for amazement. I gave, of course, an extreme example of theatrical unceremoniousness. Let us imagine a more usual occurrence: the dramatist of today arrives at the theatre, for the most part, with little liking for the theatre as such, being a complete ignoramus in theatrical matters; as he enters the unfamiliar ambience, with its heady mingled scent of earth, stables, rouge and scenery, he glances about him fearfully, like an unaccustomed visitor to the circus. He is confronted by a whole phalanx of actors and actresses with whom he is completely unacquainted and whom he has long secretly despised, in accordance with the tradition outlined above; they in their turn are doubly contemptuous of him—a bookish alien, a stranger to bohemia—with the open contempt of the straightforward thespian soul, a contempt which is of long standing, for they would all like to play Macbeths and Cleopatras, and in the kind of play you get these days anything resembling a Macbeth or a Cleopatra is rarely to be met with. And so—the author is at a loss and would have no choice but to beat a retreat, were the director not at hand. These days the director is often a well-read person of advanced views who, into the bargain, is well versed in the craft of the theatre. However many "discussions," "readings" and so on the modern author takes part in, he will always be a "fifth wheel," because in this sphere he is an ignoramus, because he speaks to the actors in an alien, abstract, bookish dialect, because he has neither the desire nor the ability to consider his own play from a technical standpoint, because he involuntarily jumps ahead and talks about what he would have liked to have done rather than about what he has done, thus frequently throwing the actors into utter confusion. Perhaps at the same time he understands all this, but his understanding serves only to put the finishing touch to his confusion and helplessness.

The director, however, speaks to the actors in the language of the theatre. He is supported by the painter, who of late has also become closely involved with the theatre—to his credit, he has not disdained theatrical technique but has learned to know and love it. And so these two utter mysterious words, the meaning of which is known to them alone, about first beam spots, parallels, demmer boards and grids, understanding each other perfectly, while the author sits there understanding nothing, as unnecessary as a passenger on board a large ship; when the ship is at sea, he is entirely dependent on the captain's will, and as he listens idly to the words of naval commands he stares at signal flags and lights with a puzzled expression.

Was it always like this? We know that the opposite is true: the Greek tragedians, the dramatists of the Middle Ages, Shakespeare and Molière staged their dramas themselves. The rise of the director has come about for reasons which are quite comprehensible, if entirely negative: first of all, the author has given up the theatre as a bad job, he no longer expects it to realize his ideas and has forgotten what he knew of theatrecraft; secondly, the actor has lost his living soul and become a false, heroic doll, endurable only when held on a golden chain by a knowledgeable and sober individual. "The renewal began in the hearts of the directors," says Anichkov in his article on the theatre, "and suddenly the director found himself in a more prominent position than he himself would have wished. The directorial renascence does not consider itself to be more than a temporary theatrical apprenticeship and, together with the best contemporary directors, we must look to the future for a renascence of the actor's art."

"The director is now the autocrat of the theatre," says Andrei Bely. "He comes between actor, audience and dramatist. He keeps them apart. By thus intervening in the creative act, he usurps the author's rights. It is therefore necessary that he be wiser than the dramatist: he must not only be acquainted with the dramatist's deepest emotions but he must also provide an appropriate frame for those emotions. In this frame he carries the author into the auditorium. To struggle with the actor, to rectify the author's mistakes by his production and to show the audience the way to a new life—and all this simultaneously—such is the task of the modern director; and of course the task is an impossible one. Thus the director has imposed upon him the duty of being the mystagogue of the multitudes."

Finally I shall cite a third author, who, in my opinion, throws merciless light on the question of the director's role. The light is all the more merciless since it is shed by Meyerhold, himself a gifted director. In his ingenious schema, Meyerhold distinguishes two directorial methods: the first is, in his opinion, undesirable because it deprives not only the actor but also the spectator of creative freedom, compelling the former to submit to the director in all things and the latter to assimilate everything through the director; the second is the "theatre of the straight line," that is, a relationship in which author, director and actor are disposed along a single straight line vis-a-vis the spectator: the author hands over his conception to the director, while the actor, who assimilates his conception *through the director* reveals his soul *freely* to the spectator. All very well, but it is only too clear that the director owes his prominence to the fact that the author knows nothing about acting and the actor knows nothing about writing. Meyerhold then adds a note in response to my objection: "A. Blok is afraid that in such a theatre the actors 'might set fire to the ship of the play,' but in my view 'discord' and disaster can occur only if the straight line becomes crooked. *The danger is avoidable if the director understands the author correctly, correctly conveys him to the actor and the actor correctly understands the director.*" So that's all he wants! The whole point is that even if the director has the wisdom of Solomon he more often than not misunderstands the author and transmits his misunderstanding to the actor, who in his turn misunderstands the director!

The question of the director, then, is an extremely fashionable one. A further complication is that a man of the theatre is needed for the staging of *old* plays; but here too it should be possible to find a means of dispensing with a single individual who always instructs the actors according to the same method. There is an incontrovertible psychological truth that speaks against a permanent director: *habit* has a corrupting effect in every area of life—and this is no less true of the life of the theatre. Anyone who seeks to inspire, and in particular to inspire the actor, who has the wayward psychology of the bohemian, must be fresh, must be undulled by custom. Once the actor becomes accustomed to him, the director's fascination vanishes and he inevitably becomes a kind of spiritual drinking companion to the troupe and consequently the enemy, declared or undeclared, of the writer—of the writer's ideas, demands and dreams.

1908

Aleksandr Blok
For a Theatre of Action
(from "On the Theatre")

More than any other art form, the *theatre* points to the blasphemous futility of the formula "art for art's sake." For the theatre is the very flesh of art, the exalted region where "the word becomes flesh." That is why almost everyone, no matter to what party he belongs, is agreed that the drama is the highest manifestation of art. It is here that things are put to the test, and the time is not far off when the assertions of our critics about the "death of events"—the feeble assertions of people intoxicated by the heady wine of contradictions and by the false wings that their airy insubstantiality lends them—will fail this test and fall like the petals of sickly drawing-room flowers. It is in the theatre more than anywhere else that art must meet head-on with life itself, life in all its immutable songfulness, richness and diversity. The more people talk of the "death of events," the more prolonged the fatal and universal "strike" against the flesh so characteristic of our day, the more deadly the fatal weariness, the base enfeeblement that afflict certain groups in contemporary society—the clearer will be the singing of the streams, the more clamorous the spring's commotion, the louder in the nocturnal fields soon to be freed of winter's snow the distant echo of the straying hero's unquiet horn. It may be that as in former days the hero, striding forward in his winged helmet, sword slung over shoulder,[5] will encounter when he steps upon the stage only pitiful and unreal witches, those "bubbles of earth," in Shakespeare's words, insubstantial, unreal, "as breath into the wind." May the spring breeze scatter them and may they not incite some new Thane of Glamis to new murder and treachery.

We are speaking of the imminence of a theatre of great passions and tremendous events. But hardly will the hero of such a theatre set foot on the boards than the modern theatre public will quit the auditorium: they are not amused, they are not entertained, they find it all unpleasantly loud; they are tired, what they want on the stage is some pathetic petty-bourgeois existence or characters who, however refined they may be, bear a surprising resemblance to themselves—will-less, feeble people driven by a trivial fate, doomed to a trivial death, tormented by trivial love. Take, say, the phantasmal personages of Maurice Maeterlinck, a writer whose literary talent has put its stamp on an entire era but who is, it seems to me, organically hostile to the theatre, who has *blasphemously* trespassed on a region inaccessible to him. On those cold and terrible heights he wishes to go for a stroll in a duster. On the snowy peaks he wishes to build a theatre "of peace and beauty without tears"—"*un théâtre de paix et de beauté sans larmes.*" But the avalanche that buried even Irene and Rubek beneath it will flatten his house of cards, will smash his cosy bourgeois edifice to smithereens.

You will say to me: but was it not you yourselves who created this cosy atmosphere in the theatre? Your dramatists stooped to our everyday existence, exchanging snow-capped mountains for our peaceful valleys; they lost the ability to arouse exalted feelings in us, grew cold toward stage action and became absorbed in interminable psychologizing; your actors have lost their temperaments and their voices, they have become dreary phonographs, devoid of feeling for the stage. And so, you see, your theatre has ceased to be a necessity for us, and we ask nothing of it but to be entertained.

I answer: there is truth in your words. The reproach which you level at dramatists is especially deserving of attention. As far as the actor is concerned, I am prepared to argue with you. The question for me is: is it not better for the actor to be transformed, at least for a time, into a pitiful phonograph than to commit the blasphemy of transforming *any and every* work *of literature* into acting material—to hack a *libretto* from a Shakespearean tragedy, as even the greatest actors of the recent past have done? Note that the more gifted the actor, the less attention he (and consequently we too) will pay to the work which he is performing, and more often than not the high point of *theatrical* tension will be a wordless scene which the author did not anticipate even by a stage direction (an example—Duse in *La Dame aux camélias*).

But if there is truth in what you say about the dramatist and the actor, there is still more truth in the assertion that you will be unable to endure the *heightened action* which we passionately desire and which, I venture to think, we will either attain or perish. For the spring breeze of a new beauty and a new morality will prove too strong for the tired, blasé people who demand either the super-ordinary or the super-subtle—people who hide behind screens of social, class and national convention. If the public of today yawns and fidgets through the plays of Ibsen, who, by his own admission, spoke only of "forbidden" things, who denied and destroyed, then in what panic will it leave the auditorium when words of affirmation resound—uncompromising words that speak of the *splendor of duty* and of life's new paths? Petty-bourgeois existence has become entrenched on the stage—and behind the scenes too. This is because we work in a vacuum, because we ourselves are initiators, performers and judges. The fresh air of blessing or curse will never be wafted from auditorium to stage. Thus it is that small events seem big to us, as always happens when you live in solitude: Maurice Maeterlinck seems to us a tragedian, Mr. Hofmannsthal the reviver of ancient tragedy, Mr. Wedekind the preacher of a new morality. It is both frightening and heartening to think how all this will be reassessed when the new intelligentsia who will fill the auditorium give us their answer.

There is much I would like to say about those not unfruitful seeds that have been sown and are already stirring, about the shoots of delicate green that are turning toward air and light with all the stubbornness and determination of nature. I would like to write a whole book about the harbingers of the storm which is coming to birth in the ominous stillness, about the great thoughts that slumber in the minds of all those active in the theatre. We are still inclined to take the harsh screams of the wheeling swallows for profundity; but there already exists another kind of profundity—the silent meditation that precedes the storm. The very heart of the theatre trembles as before some mighty deed.

I will not venture to say much about the "*popular theatre*," if only because this name is bound up with too many disappointments, too much sentimentality, too much outdated rubbish. For the same reason I use the term "*melodrama*" with much trepidation. Nevertheless, in the course that the *Russian popular theatre* has followed in the less than forty years of its existence I see the truest portent of the theatre of the immediate future; and in the development of the melodrama—a word that is now on the lips of members of the most divergent camps—I see the first step toward a new theatre of action and passion.

1908

Aleksandr Blok

Vera Fiodorovna Komissarzhevskaya[6]

Almost as soon as I learned from the newspapers of the death of Vera Fiodorovna Komissarzhevskaya I realized what she had meant to all of us, what we lose with her passing and what a mysterious and meaningful event her untimely and painful death between winter and spring was for all of us.

Why is it that the living always come so dimly, so pallidly to our minds? Why are we incapable of valuing them at their true worth even when their existence is as precious as that of the young life that has gone from us? Vera Fiodorovna was indeed the youth of these last demented, terrible but beautiful years.

We—Symbolists—lived, thought and suffered long years in silence, utterly alone, as though we were waiting for something. Yes, of course we were waiting. And then, in the pre-revolutionary year, tall doors opened before us, heavy red curtains rose, and in the doorway, set against a white theatre interior, appeared a small figure, indistinct as yet in the dusk (indistinct as *living* people always are at their first appearance) with the passion of expection and hope in her deep blue eyes and with the tremor of spring in her voice; everything about her expressed aspiration, a reaching beyond the blue boundaries of man's life *here*. We did not know then who stood before us; we were blinded by the surrounding lights, stifled by the flowers, deafened by the triumphant music of this great and ever melodious soul. Of course, without being aware of it ourselves, we were all in love with Vera Fiodorovna Komissarzhevskaya—in love not only with her but with what shimmered behind her restless shoulders, with what her sleepless eyes and ever thrilling voice summoned us to. "Excuse me, you have forgotten nothing. It's just that you feel a bit ashamed. People don't forget such things...Hand over my kingdom, Master Builder. Right here on the table!"

Never shall I forget the insistent, capricious and imperious tones in which Vera Fiodorovna pronounced those words in the role of Hilde (In Ibsen's *The Master Builder*). Yes, how can *that* ever be forgotten?

I remember her light, quick figure in the semi-darkness of theatre corridors, the greeting she tossed you hastily before going on stage, the clasp of her little hand in her brightly lit dressing room; her sad and laughing eyes with their deep blue rings, her searching, insistent, captivating talk. She was all revolt, all spring, all Hilde, and it really seemed as if she were no more than fifteen years old. She was younger—O how much younger— than many of us...

Vera Fiodorovna's death is both moving and disturbing; for all its dreadful unexpectedness and undeserved cruelty, it is a beautiful death. And of course it is not death, not ordinary death. It is another sacred behest to us to stand resolutely on guard, a fresh reminder, a distant voice of blue Eternity telling those who have not been swept away by the terrible tide of anguish and rapture to live in expectation of the new, the wonderful, the impossible.

Yes, truth is a thousandfold behind the mortal unease of those soarings and plummetings of which Vera Fiodorovna Komissarzhevskaya was the living embodiment. She was, therefore she is. She has not died, she is alive in all of us. And I entreat her radiant shade—her winged shade— to let me twine among her roses and laurels the flower of my grieving and reverent adoration.

February 11, 1910

ALEKSANDR BLOK
THE PUPPET SHOW[7]

To Vsevolod Emilievich Meyerhold

DRAMATIS PERSONAE

COLUMBINE
PIERROT
HARLEQUIN
MYSTICS, *of both sexes in frock-coats and fashionable gowns; later in masks and masquerade costumes*
CHAIRMAN OF THE CONCLAVE OF MYSTICS
THREE PAIRS OF LOVERS
CLOWN
AUTHOR

A room as it is usually represented on stage—three walls, a window and door. At a lighted table are seated Mystics of both sexes; they are dressed in frock coats and fashionable gowns and have an air of great concentration. By the window, somewhat apart from them, sits Pierrot in a loose white smock and pantaloons, dreamy, dejected, with the pale, smooth, eyebrowless face common to all Pierrots.

The Mystics sit for some time in silence.

FIRST MYSTIC. Are you listening?
SECOND MYSTIC. Yes.
THIRD MYSTIC. An event is ripening.
PIERROT. O endless horror, endless dark!
FIRST MYSTIC. Are you waiting?
SECOND MYSTIC. I am waiting.
THIRD MYSTIC. The coming is at hand: The wind at the window gave a sign to us.

PIERROT.
Where are you, faithless one? Endlessly
The streetlamps stretch down dreaming streets,
And lovers pair by pair go wandering,
Warmed by their glowing love alone.
Where are you? Where? Cannot the two of us
Follow the last pair into the fated ring?
Beneath your window, plaintively,
My guitar will twang as you whirl with friends.
I'll rouge my face that glimmers moonily,
Pencil eyebrows, stick a moustache on.
My poor heart—can you hear it, Columbine,
Sobbing out its melancholy song?

Absorbed in his daydreams, Pierrot cheers up. Suddenly the worried Author emerges from a curtain to the side.

AUTHOR. What is he saying? Most respected public! I hasten to assure you that this actor is making a cruel mockery of my authorial rights. The action takes place in St. Petersburg in winter. Where did he get windows and guitars from? I didn't write my play for a sideshow at a fair . . . I assure you . . .

Suddenly overcome with confusion at his unexpected sortie, he takes refuge behind the curtain again.

PIERROT. *(He pays no attention to the author, but sits there sighing dreamily)* Columbine!

FIRST MYSTIC. Are you listening?

SECOND MYSTIC. Yes.

THIRD MYSTIC. A maiden from a far-off land draws near.

FIRST MYSTIC. O her features are like marble!

SECOND MYSTIC. O her eyes hold vacancy!

THIRD MYSTIC. O how pure she is, how white!

FIRST MYSTIC. At her approach all voices will fall silent.

SECOND MYSTIC. Yes. A silence will descend.

THIRD MYSTIC. For long?

FIRST MYSTIC. Yes.

SECOND MYSTIC. She is white, as white as snow.

THIRD MYSTIC. At her back a scythe.[8]

FIRST MYSTIC. Who is she?

The Second Mystic bends over and whispers something in the First Mystic's ear.

SECOND MYSTIC. You won't give me away?

FIRST MYSTIC. *(with unfeigned horror)* Never!

Once again the Author emerges apprehensively, only to vanish abruptly, as if someone had dragged him back by the coat-tails.

PIERROT. *(dreamily, as before)* Columbine! Come to me!

FIRST MYSTIC. Shhh! Do you hear footsteps?

SECOND MYSTIC. I hear rustlings and sighs.

THIRD MYSTIC. O who is in our midst?

FIRST MYSTIC. Who is at the window?

SECOND MYSTIC. Who behind the door?

THIRD MYSTIC. Impenetrable darkness.

FIRST MYSTIC. Give us light. Has *she* not come at this hour?

The Second Mystic raises a candle.

Quite unexpectedly, as if from nowhere, there appears at the table a girl of rare beauty; her face is simple and calm and of a matt whiteness. She is dressed in white. Her tranquil gaze expresses indifference. A plaited braid lies along her back.

The girl stands motionless. Overcome, Pierrot sinks to his knees in an attitude of prayer. He is visibly choked by tears. All this, for him, is beyond words. Horrified, the Mystics shrink back in their chairs. The foot of one of them swings impotently back and forth. Another gestures oddly. A third goggles. At last they recover themselves and speak in loud whispers.

It is she!
How white are her garments!
Her eyes hold vacancy!
Her features are pale as marble!
A scythe is at her back!
Death has come!

Pierrot hears them. Getting up slowly, he goes over to the girl and, taking her by the hand, leads her to the center of the stage. He speaks in a ringing, joyful voice, like the first peal of a bell.

PIERROT. Ladies and gentlemen! You are mistaken! She is Columbine! She is my betrothed!

General consternation. Hands fly up. Coat-tails flap. The Chairman of the Conclave approaches Pierrot solemnly.

CHAIRMAN. You have taken leave of your senses. All evening we have been awaiting an event. And it has come to pass. She has come to us, the silent liberator. Death has visited us.

PIERROT. *(in a clear, child-like voice)* I don't listen to fairy tales. I'm a simple man. You can't fool me. She is Columbine. She is my betrothed!

CHAIRMAN. Ladies and gentlemen! Fear has deprived our unfortunate friend of his wits. He has not given so much as a thought to that for which we have been preparing all our lives. He has not plumbed the depths, has not prepared himself to greet submissively the Pale Lady at the last hour. Let us be generous and pardon the simple fellow. *(Turning to Pierrot)*. Friend, you cannot remain here. You disturb the tranquillity of our last supper. But, I beg of you, look at her carefully once more: you see how white her garments are; you see the pallor of her face. O she is as white as the snow on the mountain tops! Her eyes are vacant mirrors. Do you not see the scythe at her back? Do you not recognize Death?

PIERROT. *(a helpless smile passes over his pale face)* I'm going. Either you are right and I am a wretched madman. Or it is you who are out of your minds and I am a lonely and misunderstood adorer. Whirl me through the streets, O blizzard! O endless horror! Endless dark!

COLUMBINE. *(following Pierrot to the exit)* I will not abandon you.

Pierrot stops, at a loss. The Chairman clasps his hands in a gesture of entreaty.

CHAIRMAN. Airy vision! All our lives we have been waiting for you! Do not desert us!

A graceful youth in harlequin costume appears. He is hung all over with little bells that sing with silvery voices.

HARLEQUIN. *(going over to Columbine)*
At the crossroads I wait for you, dear one,
In the gray light of wintry dusk.
My blizzard is singing above you,
For you it is jingling its bells!

He puts a hand on Pierrot's shoulder. Pierrot falls flat on his face and lies motionless in his white smock. Harlequin takes Columbine by the hand and leads her off. She gives him a smile. A general slackening of tension. The Mystics slump lifelessly in their chairs. Their hands disappear into the sleeves of their frock-coats, so that they seem to have no hands at all. Their heads vanish into their collars. It is as if empty coats were lying across the chairs. Suddenly Pierrot leaps to his feet and runs off. At the same moment a dishevelled and agitated Author leaps out onto the forestage.

AUTHOR. Ladies and Gentlemen! I apologize to you most humbly, but I must disclaim all responsibility! They are making a laughing stock of me! I wrote a perfectly realistic play, the essentials of which I consider it my duty to lay before you in a few words: what we are concerned with is the mutual love of two young hearts! A third personage places obstacles in their path, but eventually these obstacles are overcome and the loving pair are joined forever in holy matrimony! I never dressed my characters up like buffoons! Without my permission, they are staging some kind of ancient legend or other! I refuse to tolerate legends, myths or any other vulgar nonsense! Neither will I tolerate allegorical word-play: it is indecent to refer to a woman's braid as the scythe of death! It is a slander on the fair sex! Ladies and . . .

A hand thrust out from behind the curtain grabs the Author by the collar. He disappears into the wings with a yell. The curtains part swiftly. A ball. Masked figures circle to the subdued strains of a dance. Among them stroll other maskers, knights, ladies, clowns. Pierrot, a melancholy figure, sits on the bench where Venus and Tannhäuser are wont to kiss.

PIERROT. Between two streetlamps I lingered
And listened to their sighs;
Wrapped in their cloaks they whispered,
Night gently kissed their eyes.

The silvery blizzard wove for them
A hymeneal ring.
I saw her smile in the darkness,
Smile sweetly up at him.

O then a sleigh came racing—
My love and he climbed in.
And through the freezing fog I trudged,
Following on behind.

O in his toils he'd entangled her,
With laughter and jingling bells.
Then he drew her wrap about her—
And flat on her face she fell!

He did my love no mischief,
But flat in the snow fell she!
She couldn't keep her balance,
I couldn't keep back my glee!

As the needles of frost went whirling
Round my cardboard love as she lay,
He leaped in the air, bells ajingling—
The two of us danced round the sleigh!

And we sang in the dreaming street
"O what a terrible blow!"
High in the sky a star gleamed green
On my cardboard love below.

All night through the streets we wandered,
Harlequin and Pierrot . . .
He pressed so tenderly to me—
His feather tickled my nose!

He whispered: "We shall not be parted,
Brother, for many a day . . .
We'll mourn your betrothed together,
Your cardboard fiancée!"

Pierrot goes out sadly.

A little while later a pair of lovers are discovered on the bench where Pierrot was seated. He is dressed in pale blue, she in pink; their masks match their dress. Imagining themselves to be in church, they gaze up into the domes.

SHE. Dear one, you whisper, "Bend your head . . ."
With head thrown back, I gaze into the dome.
HE. My gaze is lost in space ineffable—
Where the dome drinks in the evening glow.
SHE. How worn with age the gold is there,
How softly in those heights the icons gleam.
HE. Our dreamy tale is full of quietude.
If you have closed your eyes, it is no sin.

They kiss.

SHE. . . . Who is that dark someone by the pillar?
With what a knowing eye he winks at us!
I am afraid of you, enamored one.
O let me hide myself beneath your cloak!

A silence.

HE. Look at the candle flames—how still they are,
The domes are flooded with the sunset's tide.
SHE. Yes. Are not our meetings sweet indeed?
So be it, then, I yield myself to you.

She presses against him.

The first couple are hidden from the audience by a muted dance of maskers and clowns.

A second pair of lovers burst into the dance. She leads, dressed in a black mask and a whirling red cloak. He follows, lithe, black-garbed, with a red mask and a black cloak. Their movements are impetuous. He pursues, now drawing level with her, now overtaking. A whirlwind of cloaks.

HE. Enough of this torment! Let me be!
Too dark is the fate you prophesy!
Exult then in your victory!
Will you doff your mask or be swallowed by night?

SHE. Follow me, follow! Hunt me down!
Forget your troth in my passion and pain!
Clasp me about with your arm of steel!
Drain my dark cup to the very lees!

HE. My passion was pledged to another!
I was caught in your flashing glance,
Into dark byways you led me,
Of a deadly poison gave me to drink!

SHE. I did not beckon—like a whirlwind
My cloak streamed out, my fiery friend!
Into my enchanted ring
You stepped of your own free will.

HE. Enchantress, beware! I'll doff my mask!
You shall see the faceless thing I am!
You made me blank, you lured to the dark
Where my double knew me and nodded!

SHE. I am a free spirit! Victorious my path!
Follow me, follow, wherever I lead!
O you will walk in my fiery wake
And share with me delirium!

HE. I go, submissive to relentless fate—
O stream in the wind, my fiery guide!
But three shall walk the ill-omened way—
You and I and my dark double with us!

They vanish in a whirlwind of cloaks. A third figure seems to break from the crowd and follow them. He is identical to the lover—a sinuous tongue of black flame.

A third pair of lovers emerges from among the dancers. They sit in the center of the stage.

The Middle Ages. Leaning forward pensively, she follows his movements with her eyes. Large and thoughtful, he is all straight lines; on his head he wears a cardboard helmet; with an enormous wooden sword he is tracing a circle on the floor in front of his companion.

HE. Do you understand the play in which we are playing not the least important role?

SHE. *(like a faint but distinct echo)* Role.

HE. Do you realize that the maskers have made this meeting wonderful?

SHE. Wonderful.

HE. You trust me then? O today you are lovelier than ever.

SHE. Ever.

HE. All things, past and to come, are known to you. You have understood the meaning of this circle.

SHE. Circle.

HE. O how entrancingly you talk! You have guessed the riddle of my soul! Your words speak volumes to my heart!

SHE. Heart.

HE. O endless happiness! Eternal bliss!

SHE. Bliss.

HE. *(with a sigh of relief and triumph)* Day is at hand. Soon it will be gone, this baleful night.

SHE. Night

At this moment one of the clowns takes it into his head to play a prank. He runs up to the Lover and sticks out a long tongue at him. The Lover brings his heavy wooden sword down on the clown's head with all his might. The clown is doubled over the footlights, where he remains hanging. A stream of cranberry juice gushes from his head.

CLOWN. *(in a piercing yell)* Help! I'm bleeding cranberry juice!

Having dangled there for a while, he gets up and goes out. Uproar. Confusion. Gleeful shouts: "Torches! Torches! A torchlight procession!" *Members of the chorus appear, carrying torches. Maskers throng, laughing and leaping about.*

CHORUS.

Drop by drop in the gloom it drips,
The faintly crackling gum!
Faces that darkness enshrouded
Are lit by a fitful gleam!
Drop by drop and spark by spark!

A pure and resinous rain!
Appear, O glittering, O fleet,
O leader fierce with flame!

Harlequin steps from the chorus in the role of coryphaeus.

HARLEQUIN. Through streets deep in snow, deep in slumber,
I dragged the poor booby along!
The world to my rebel eyes opened,
Above me the snowy wind sang!
How I longed with lungs young and lusty
To breathe deep, to leap into life!
To build in that desolate landscape
My own blithe altar to spring!
Here no one has courage to fathom
That spring's under way in the heights!
Here men have no notion of loving,
Here life is a desolate dream!
Greetings, world! Again you are with me!
Long have our souls been close!
I go to breathe deep of your springtime,
To leap through your window of gold!

He leaps through the window. The distant prospect framed by the window turns out to be painted on paper. The paper splits. Harlequin goes flying head over heels into the void. Only the brightening sky is visible through the gaping hole. Night is on the wane, the bustle of morning is beginning. Outlined against the breaking dawn stands Death, her long white robes stirring faintly in the dawn wind; her tenderly feminine face is of a matt whiteness. Over her shoulder she carries a scythe; the blade gleams silver, like an inverted crescent moon, in the morning light.

Horrified, everyone rushes off in all directions. The knight trips over his wooden sword. The ladies drop flowers all over the stage. The maskers, pressed flat against the wall as if crucified, seem like dolls from a museum of ethnography. The ladies hide their faces in their lovers' cloaks. The profile of the pale blue masker is delicately outlined against the morning sky. Kneeling in terror at his feet, the pink masker presses her lips to his hand.

Pierrot, who appears as if from nowhere, walks slowly from one side of the stage to the other, stretching out his hands toward Death. As he approaches her, her face gradually comes to life. A flush mounts to the dead whiteness of her cheeks. The silver scythe is veiled by the morning mist. In the window recess, silhouetted against the dawn, stands a beautiful girl, her tranquil face lit by a gentle smile—Columbine.

At that moment, as Pierrot reaches her and is just about to touch her hand with his, the Author's head thrusts itself triumphantly between them.

AUTHOR. Ladies and gentlemen of the audience! My cause is not lost! My rights have been restored to me! As you see, all obstacles have been removed! The gentleman disappeared through the window! All that remains is for you to witness the joyful reunion of two loving hearts after prolonged separation! It has cost them a great deal of effort to overcome these obstacles, but now they are rewarded by being joined for eternity!

The Author goes to join the hands of Pierrot and Columbine. Suddenly the entire set flies up and disappears. The maskers scatter.

The Author is left bending over the solitary figure of Pierrot, who lies helplessly on the empty stage in his white smock with its red pompons.

Suddenly aware of his situation, the Author makes a headlong dash for the wings.

PIERROT. *(he speaks plaintively and dreamily, lifting himself on one elbow)*
Where have you led me? How can I guess?
You've given me over to treacherous fate.
Pierrot, poor fellow, enough lying down—
Get up, get going, get a wife for yourself.
(He falls silent for a moment)

O how she glowed, the girls that's gone
(My jingling companion carried her off).
Down she fell (she was cardboard, you see).
And I came along to have a good laugh.

Flat on her face she lay, all white.
And O what a merry dance we danced!
But she couldn't get up—just couldn't at all.
A cardboard fiancée—that's all she was.

And here I stand with my oatmeal face;
It's no laughing matter, I'd have you know.
What's to be done? She fell on her face . . .
I'm in the dumps. So you think it's a joke?

Pensively, Pierrot takes a pipe from his pocket and begins to play a song about his pale face, about his hard life and about his betrothed, Columbine.

ALEKSANDR BLOK

THE ROSE AND THE CROSS[9]

To ***[10]

DRAMATIS PERSONAE

COUNT ARCHAMBAUT, *lord of a castle in Languedoc*
CHAPLAIN
DOCTOR
COOK
FIRST KNIGHT
SECOND KNIGHT
ALISCAN, *a page*
BERTRAND, *known as Sir Hapless, warden of the castle*
GAETAN, *seigneur of Troménec, a trouvère*
ISAURE, *the Count's wife*
ALYSE, *her lady-in-waiting*
KNIGHTS, VASSALS, GUESTS, LADIES-IN-WAITING, SCULLIONS AND OTHER SERVANTS, PEASANT GIRLS, MINSTRELS AND JONGLEURS

The action takes place at the beginning of the thirteenth century. The first, third and fourth acts are set in Languedoc, the second in Brittany.

ACT ONE

SCENE ONE

The castle courtyard. Dusk.

BERTRAND. *(sings in a tuneless voice)*
"Loss and misfortune prevail,
What end can there be to your quest?
Then hoist to the mast your rough sail,
And your coat of invincible mail
Mark with a cross on the breast."

Strange, this song of the sea
And a cross that burns above tempests . . .
The wit of a simple knight
Cannot hope to fathom its meaning.
This cracked voice of mine is powerless
To capture its haunting lilt.
Wherever I go, failure dogs me!
The song that Isaure loves best
I have not the voice to sing . . .

O time-weathered apple tree bole,
Shaken by February storms!
How you yearn for the coming of spring . . .
A warm wind will blow, and these ramparts
Be mantled with tenderest green . . .
And what will you answer, old friend,
To the brooks and the birds in full song?
Two or three sickly sprays of pale blossom
You'll stretch to the rain-washed air,
O black and storm-battered bole!

A like fate is yours, wretched Bertrand,
The ill-favored butt of all jests!
Comes the time of feasting and jousting,
The horn of the huntsman will sound,
Once more will the troubadour stir her heart

With his baffling song of the sea . . .
And how will you answer the spring, old friend?
With the turmoil of hopeless love?
O love, no shield is as heavy as you!
Suffering is all that you bring,
There is no joy in you, none!
What did the strange song foretell?
"The law of the heart is unchanging—
Gladness-in-Suffering alone!"
But how can suffering be gladness?
"Gladness, O Gladness-in-Suffering,
The anguish of wounds endured long . . ."

ALYSE. *(at the window)* Who is that singing and muttering to himself?

BERTRAND. The castle warden.

ALYSE. Oh, it's you, Sir Hapless. Stand further from the window, if you don't mind. My lady is not well; your singing upsets her.

BERTRAND. I'll go.

SCENE TWO

A passage in the castle.

ALYSE. Reverend Father, what a fright you gave me!

CHAPLAIN. I didn't mean to frighten you, fair lady.

ALYSE. You're waiting for the Count, I suppose?

CHAPLAIN. No, not for the Count.

ALYSE. Or for the page, so that he may convey to the Countess . . .

CHAPLAIN. Neither Count, nor Countess, nor page . . . You're not very perceptive, my beauty . . .

ALYSE. Reverend Father, I'm completely at a loss . . .

CHAPLAIN. *(embracing her)* The matter is simpler than you think, dear Alyse.

ALYSE. But your holy office, your years . . .

CHAPLAIN. I know all about those, you minx . . . You won't refuse to accept a little gift . . .

ALYSE. Someone's coming . . . Let go of me or I'll scream!

CHAPLAIN. *(running off)* Saint James preserve us! Very well, you'll be sorry for this . . .

ALISCAN. Who is that whispering in the darkness?

ALYSE. It's me . . . My handsome page, I'm terrified . . . I fancied I saw someone . . .

ALISCAN. No doubt you did, Alyse. His Reverence just went scurrying through that door.

ALYSE. disgusting old man!

ALISCAN. What has he done to you?

ALYSE. He made an attempt on my honor . . . Oh Aliscan, I think I'm going to faint . . . I'm falling . . . Help me . . .

ALISCAN. What can I do about it? Complain to the Count.

ALYSE. You won't help me then, my handsome page?

ALISCAN. I don't know what you're talking about, lady-in-waiting. Take me to your mistress. She longs for the strains of my lute.

SCENE THREE

Isaure's chambers.

ISAURE. *(singing to herself)*

"Snow flees the blast . . .
In a moment an age hurtles past . . .
We dream of a blest shore at last . . .

I can't remember how it went on . . . A strange song! "Gladness-in- Suffering . . .The law of the heart is unchanging . . ." Help me remember it, Alyse!

ALYSE. How can I help you, my lady, if even the doctor can't?

DOCTOR. All remedies have been tried, but have brought the patient no relief. Nevertheless, I steadfastly maintain, in accordance with the teachings of Galen and Hippocrates, that the name of your sickness is melancholy . . .

ISAURE. Leave me, doctor—you'll never understand what it is.

The doctor goes out.

"The law of the heart is unchanging . . ."—to love and to wait. "Gladness-in-Suffering . . ." Yes, with one's beloved even suffering is gladness! . . . Isn't that true, Alyse?

ALYSE. *(stealing a glance at Aliscan)* Yes, my lady, I think it is true.

ISAURE. Boredom, Alyse, nothing but boredom! Bring the chessmen over here! Page—a song!

ALISCAN. Shall I sing for you a song they sing at the court of Arras?

ISAURE. Sing what you like.

ALISCAN. "Glad the day and blest the hour,
Amorous the spring.
Tapping at my lady's bower,
Hark—a fine gold ring.
O'er the fragrant valley floating,
Roses' heady scent.
Philomel upon thee doting
Brings thee sweet content . . .
Aäliz, O rose, surrender
To the nightingale . . .
All the Holy Land I'll tender,
So my suit prevail . . ."

ALYSE. Your move, my lady.

ISAURE. *(playing the queen)* Ah me!

ALYSE. Lost in your thoughts again?
Sweet are the strains of languorous song . . .

ISAURE. What song?

ALISCAN. If only I knew the cause of your sorrow . . .

ISAURE. I myself do not know it.

ALISCAN. There's no denying you've changed . . .
To a rose among roses, what's a plain nightingale? . . .

ISAURE. You put things so prettily!
Surely a fairy taught you
The art of declaring love!

ALISCAN. Again you make fun of me . . .
Have I known any fairy but you?

ISAURE. What do I care for flattering speeches?
Am I some bright-winged butterfly?
Bitter to me are your honeyed words!

ALYSE. Check and checkmate!

ISAURE. Heaven be praised!
Enough of this tedious game!
Tell me, my page of the dusky curls,
How can I ease your grief?

ALISCAN. Remember the games that we used to play!
Remember—only last spring,
With light-hearted dance

In a grassy glade
We sped the light hours on their way . . .

ISAURE. Page, you forgot that I am your lady!

ALYSE. She's not well, Aliscan.

ISAURE. *(sings to herself)*
"The law of the heart is unchanging . . .
Gladness-in-Suffering . . ."

ALISCAN. That song you're eternally singing
You heard from some posturing hireling.

ISAURE. What of it? It wasn't his own . . .

ALISCAN. Some wretch of a fisherman
From outlandish, rude Brittany
Made up this meaningless song . . .

ISAURE. Jealous, my page?
Have no fear . . . I don't know him . . .
Ah, who can tell? That time may return,
And in some grassy glade
We'll know the old joy . . .
But no! . . How stupid and stale it all is!
Such a life is not waking or sleeping!

She goes out.

ALISCAN. There's not doubt about it, her mind's giving way . . .

ALYSE. It's given way, if you ask me . . . To prefer someone else to you . . . Who can it be?

ALISCAN. A tedious winter is in store for us . . .

ALYSE. Are you sad, my handsome page?

ALISCAN. She won't be coming back?

ALYSE. No, this is her time for daydreaming . . . and seeing visions . . . No one will come here now.

She embraces Aliscan.

SCENE FOUR

The Count's chambers.

COUNT. By Saint James of Compostella, I swear they're driving me insane!

You know that Otto is at death's door!

CHAPLAIN. I can't see why your Grace should be so disturbed. Send out another detachment of knights, and that will be the end of these mutinous villains.

COUNT. Was it so long ago that they almost clubbed poor Clari to death?

CHAPLAIN. You have better vassals than Otto and Clari. Besides, there is word that Count Simon de Montfort is already on his way from Paris to help us subdue the heretics . . .

COUNT. If he ever gets here! . . .
Call Bertrand here this instant!

Bertrand enters.

COUNT. Well, what news?

BERTRAND. The news is bad, your lordship. Count Raymond
Has raised an army in Toulouse . . .

COUNT. That murderer!

CHAPLAIN. And a libertine to boot: five wives and not a single legitimate son . . .

BERTRAND. Montségur has joined them . . .

COUNT. My own neighbor!

BERTRAND. To their new bishop he has sworn allegiance,
Distributing his wealth among the poor . . .

COUNT. The scoundrel! Clari owes his wounds to him.

BERTRAND. I doubt it. Though our enemies, these men
Revere the holy Gospel: unknown knights
They would not kill by stealth.

COUNT. They're all one band!
The peasants with their clubs, the suzerains,
Forgetful of Pope and God Almighty,
Their vassals too—ragtag and bobtail . . .

BERTRAND. But . . .

COUNT. Silence! It seems you're of that stripe yourself—
You're all the same, you failures and poltroons,
Unseated in the opening joust . . .

BERTRAND. Your Grace,
I'm told de Montfort is at Lyons now . . .

COUNT. So we may take our ease—is that your thought?

BERTRAND. Your lordship knows my readiness to serve
My lady and yourself . . .

COUNT. Sir Hapless, so
Be it. On this occasion show yourself
No coward, but a worthy knight! You leave
When darkness falls; your mission—to report
The whereabouts of Simon's force!

BERTRAND. I obey.

COUNT. Make sure this time you bring us better news.
Not croakings of misfortune. Off with you!

Bertrand goes out.

CHAPLAIN. Never a truer word— he's not a knight but a raven in knight's feathers . . .

COUNT. Worthy confessor, my head is spinning . . .

CHAPLAIN. Oh, set your mind at rest, your Grace. We'll settle those weavers, devil's spawn that they are. You'd do better to turn your attention to what's going on in the castle . . .

COUNT. Treachery?

CHAPLAIN. No . . . But . . .

COUNT. Out with it!

CHAPLAIN. *Isora, coniunx vestra, aliquantulum male sobria est.*

COUNT. I don't understand a word. Talk like a human being!

CHAPLAIN. Your Lordship's spouse . . .

COUNT. My wife!

CHAPLAIN. On her bedside table lies the romance of Floire . . .

COUNT. What of it?

CHAPLAIN . . . and Blancheflor . . . instead of the prayerbook. Are you not aware that romances are written by the enemies of the Holy Church?

COUNT. Rebels!

CHAPLAIN. Exactly. The pretender pope is honored by the men who kill your knights. And men who kill knights are praised by the writers of romances . . .

COUNT. I said they were all one band!

CHAPLAIN. And it's your spouse's lady-in-waiting who is responsible for teaching her these things . . .

COUNT. Damnation! If only I had known about this earlier!

CHAPLAIN. Calm yourself, your Lordship. She's coming now. Question her, giving no sign that you know of anything.

Alyse enters.

ALYSE. Your Grace, my lady is ill . . .

COUNT. Is she indeed! Since when?

ALYSE. She hasn't touched any food since this morning . . .

CHAPLAIN. Did you hear that, your Lordship? . . .

COUNT. Did you call the doctor?

ALYSE. The doctor said that her sickness was caused by melancholy; and when there's an excess of melancholy, the body falls into a decline and the reason is easily lost . . .

COUNT. Saint James preserve us!

ALYSE. By day, my lady is sunk in gloom, and at night she tosses and turns, biting her pillow and saying the same name over and over again . . .

COUNT. Whose name?

ALYSE. I haven't been able to make it out . . . It sounds as if she's mumbling something like "Pilgrim."

COUNT. "Pilgrim?"

ALYSE. That's the name of the knight . . . the one who wrote the song . . .

CHAPLAIN. There you are, your Lordship—a romance begets a song, a song begets a knight, and a knight begets . . .

ALYSE. Ever since the jongleurs sang here, my lady hasn't been able to get that song out of her head.

COUNT. What is it about, this song?

CHAPLAIN. That I can tell you in advance—a nightingale and a rose.

ALYSE. No, there's not a word in it about roses or nightingales. I can't make any sense of it, though I've heard it from my lady more than once.

COUNT. In that case, maybe she has taken leave of her senses!

ALYSE. That has occurred to me too, your Grace.

COUNT. Traitors! Let the doctor be summoned!

The doctor enters.

What's the matter with my wife?

DOCTOR. *Melancholia regnat . . .*

COUNT. A thousand curses! Whenever it comes to my wife, they all speak in Latin!

DOCTOR. Your Lordship's spouse is afflicted with a cold, dry and bitter melancholy. Melancholy is in the ascendant between the ides of August and the ides of February . . .

COUNT. Saint James! But February is already upon us!

DOCTOR. There's nothing to be done, your Grace, we shall have to wait a bit longer. The blood will start to gather, and when a superfluity has accumulated, we shall bleed her through the nose, in accordance with the teachings of the ancient sages, Galen and Hippocrates . . .

CHAPLAIN. There's something behind all this . . .

COUNT. I'm beginning to lose my own reason, by St. James! Reverend Father, what shall we do now?

CHAPLAIN. Rely on me, your Grace, for sound advice . . .

DOCTOR. *Idem—melancholia regnat . . .*

COUNT. Doctor, you'll live to be hanged!

SCENE FIVE

Isaure's chambers.

ALYSE. For heaven's sake, be more careful, my lady. The Count is disturbed; I think he's got wind of something; we're being watched. Your illness is nothing but winter megrims.

ISAURE. No, for spring fills my heart.
Yet in this, my seventeenth spring,
My heart felt a chill wind blow,
As though that gaunt trunk at the casement
Breathed a dank mist on me . . .
See how its black, ancient branches
Hold a cross to the drizzling sky . . .
As the apple tree grieves, my heart grieves . . .
"Gladness-in-Suffering . . .
The law of the heart unchanging . . ."

ALYSE. All this comes from Sir Hapless's mutterings. Spring will restore you to health and joy, believe me . . .

ISAURE. Listen, Alyse!

Last night as I slept,
I dreamed a strange dream . . .
Caught in a moonbeam, I slumbered,
The lapping of waves filled my ears,
And the air all about me was heavy
With the scent of mysterious resins . . .
All at once, from the earth's very depths,
As though from the dark of the tomb,
A stranger, a knight, rose before me . . .
Brighter than flax, his hair
Fell in loose curls to his shoulders . . .
My heart, how it beat—how it beat . . .
In rapture I fell to my knees,
Crying out, "Mysterious visitor,
I beg you, reveal your name! . ."
To touch him I did not dare,
But to adore him was strange and sweet!
On his bright breast there burned
A black rose—blacker than blood . . .
"Pilgrim!" I cried out, "Pilgrim!"
I heard a strange ringing, saw a great light,
And then I awoke in tears . . .
That melody haunts me still,
But not as the minstrel sang it . . .
You saw how I bit my pillow
And tore my shift at the shoulder!
You can hear how my heart is hammering . . .
In my ears that eternal refrain:
"Gladness-in-Suffering . . ."
No, I cannot repeat it! . .

ALYSE. Not so loud, in the name of all the saints! There's someone there . . .

CHAPLAIN. *(opening the door)* So those are the kind of dreams you've been dreaming! I'll tell the Count everything! You'll have time enough in the Round Tower for reading romances! . .

He goes out.

ISAURE. What did he say?

ALYSE. He threatened to have us locked up . . .

ISAURE. Saint Vidian! What can we do now?

ALYSE. I don't know . . . Wait . . . Submit . . .

ISAURE. A curse on them all! I'll rend their hearts! My mother doesn't have Spanish blood for nothing!

ALYSE. No so loud, my lady . . . There's someone below . . .

ISAURE. *(looking out of the window)* Bertrand! Sir Knight, come here! But be careful!

BERTRAND. *(entering)* My lady, how can I be of service to you?

ISAURE. *(coaxingly)*

Might I entrust you, Sir Knight,
With an errand on my behalf?

BERTRAND. *(surprised)*

Whatever lies in my power, my lady . . .
Commands I await, not requests . . .
Time is my only concern—
The Count is sending me north . . .

ISAURE. Sending you north!

BERTRAND. Yes, I must leave this evening.

ISAURE. Sir Knight, do I have your devotion?

BERTRAND. A question that need not be asked . . .

ISAURE. We must not delay!
I am threatened with prison . . .

BERTRAND. Do not torture my heart
With cruel confessions . . .

ISAURE. You are the castle warden.
The Round Tower is known to you?

BERTRAND. This many a year.
"The Tower of the Grieving Widow,"
they call it . . .

ISAURE. Listen further!
Every moment is precious!
There's a knight . . . and a song . . .
A song that gives me no rest.

BERTRAND. My lady, I know that song!

ISAURE. You know it!—
Then find me the singer,
Though the journey should take you
Through the realms of the mist and the snow!
His name is "The Pilgrim . . ."

On his breast a black rose is blazoned . . .
I saw all this in a vision!

BERTRAND. This errand of yours, my lady,
Seems more like a tale fit for children . . .
But my life has been harsh not in vain:
I know that in childish dreams
Lies hidden more truth than men think!
What you ask, I'll perform or perish:
Your pilgrim shall stand here before you!

ISAURE. And now you must swear to keep secret
All that has passed between us!

BERTRAND. By what shall I swear? . .
What need we of oaths?
I would swear by the rose,
But your beauty excels it . . .

ISAURE. *(in surprise)*
What? You too have learned flattering speeches?
You must swear me a weightier oath!

BERTRAND. No weightier oath
May a poor knight venture . . .

ISAURE. *(relentlessly)*
Swear, I say, swear!

BERTRAND. I swear that without your knight
I will not return here alive! . .
By my truth to my Lady I swear it!

ISAURE. *(inquisitively)*
And who is your Lady, Sir Knight?

BERTRAND. I dare not utter her name . . .

ISAURE. I can, if I wish, command you . . .

BERTRAND. Give me leave to depart—my journey is long . . .

ISAURE. *(slyly)*
Not yet, not yet . . . Her name's all I ask . . .

Bertrand falls on one knee before her.

Bertrand, my true-hearted vassal, arise!
Now I know I can trust you.

Moving away from him.

O the might and the glory of love!
Even the like of him—
Insignificant, oafish and base—
It endows with knightly devotion . . .

BERTRAND. *(to himself)*
Well then, poor wretch, go your way,
Without expectation or hope,
To serve a love not your own.

The Count enters, jangling a bunch of rusty keys.

COUNT. Not a word, traitress! I know everything!

To Bertrand

What are you doing here?

ALYSE. He forced his way in, your Grace! . .

COUNT. Scoundrel! I'd kill you on the spot if you weren't such a sorry sight! Scarecrow! Cur! Fine taste for a lady-in-waiting! . .

ALYSE. Your Grace . . .

COUNT. Silence! Base creature! You're supposed to watch over her, and this is what you get up to! You shall share your mistress's fate!

To Isaure.

Or do you want to be sent packing to your Martres-Tolosanes?
For all my care, you pay me in Toulouse gold![11]

ISAURE. I shall obey you, my lord and master.

COUNT. You realize that it is useless to argue with me! To the Tower of the Grieving Widow with you, now—this very minute! And may Saint James of Compostella help you mend your ways! Be off with you!

Isaure and Alyse go out.

As for you, unhappy wretch, all you're good for is to croak like a raven and pester the ladies-in-waiting! Perhaps you've forgotten my instructions!

BERTRAND. I shall leave this very night, as you commanded.

COUNT. Find out everything! I'll give you a month—two months. If the news you bring this time is as bad as the last, your head shall be forfeit! But if you bring me good news of the Count de Montfort, Sir Hapless, I shall pardon you!

He goes out after Isaure.

BERTRAND. Beautiful deceiver!
Help her I must, although in death's despite.
Then set forth boldly—northward into night!

He goes out.

ACT TWO

SCENE ONE

At the ocean.

BERTRAND. *(on horseback)* Where is this? The snow blinds me, the wind whistles in my ears! Madman! No matter—onward, my weary steed!

He vanishes behind a rock.

GAETAN. *(sings)*
"Beware of love's delirium!
In the wake of joy comes suffering!
In the wake of joy comes suffering!"

FISHERMAN. *(sings)*
"Awake, Gradlon, shake off your sleep,
Your town lies buried fathoms deep!
Ker-Is lies drowned on the salt sea-bed—
A curse be on your daughter's head!"

GAETAN. "A curse be on your daughter's head!"
Hey there, fisherman!

FISHERMAN. The power of the cross protect us! I can't make out a thing in this snow! Just now there was a knight here—and now you! I thought it was my own voice echoing among the rocks. Or are you a ghost?

GAETAN. You shout at me—but you sing my song, all the same.

FISHERMAN. What do you mean, your song? That song is sung in Plougasnou, in Plouézec and here in Plouguerneau as well.

GAETAN. And where was the city of Ker-Is?

FISHERMAN. Not far from here, they say. You see that pile of rocks on the shore?

GAETAN. Yes. A lion in front, then a horse . . .

FISHERMAN. There isn't any horse—just rocks. And in the middle of those rocks there's a backwater. That's where you'll find the fattest crabs in summer. And they say that Saint Gwénnolé walks there on Christmas eve. So where do you come from then?

GAETAN. I'm from Troménec.

FISHERMAN. Troménec? Never heard of it.

GAETAN. Aber-Grac'h isn't far from here, is it?

FISHERMAN. The monastery, you mean? . .

GAETAN. You have to go past the monastery gardens toward the well, then from the well you go uphill as far as the first houses of Landéda . . .

FISHERMAN. Who doesn't know Landéda! We all go there on holidays . . .

GAETAN. Turn left before you get to the church, by way of the fields, and you'll soon come to Troménec.

FISHERMAN. That castle's called Troménec then?

GAETAN. To be sure.

FISHERMAN. So that's Troménec . . . And the seigneur there must be an odd sort of fellow!

GAETAN. Why do you think that?

FISHERMAN. It's not just me—everyone thinks so; they say he pastures his own flock—if you can call three roosters a flock. A beggarly life he leads—must be a miser. Other knights feast and lay into each other at tourneys, but this one, they say, wanders about telling tales . . . And what do you do there?

GAETAN. To tell you the truth, fisherman, I am that very seigneur of Troménec.

FISHERMAN. The power of the cross protect us! Don't think that I spoke in mockery, seigneur—we get all sorts in these parts . . .

GAETAN. That is true, fisherman. There's a cross on my chest, and a cross is not given to be trifled with . . .

FISHERMAN. Yes, there is a cross on your chest—I couldn't make it out at first . . . Of course, my lord, the law wasn't made for the rich . . .

BERTRAND. *(returning)* Again the same rock! Who's that? Ho there, vagabond!

GAETAN. Don't shout at people for no reason. Who are you anyway?

BERTRAND. A knight.

GAETAN. And I am a seigneur.

BERTRAND. You don't look like one to me.

GAETAN. I'll prove that I'm telling the truth! Draw your sword!

They fight.

FISHERMAN. *(running away)* Lord save us! These knights are forever fighting!

BERTRAND. You're not much of a fighter, seigneur. Cry quarter or I'll cut off your head!

GAETAN. *(taking off his helmet)* Quarter. I'm old, as you can see.

BERTRAND. It wasn't worth dulling my sword on you, old man! Promise to perform anything that I ask of you.

GAETAN. I like you and will do as you bid. I hope you won't refuse to rest awhile at Troménec.

BERTRAND. Thank you. I'm not tired, but my horse is weary from the long journey.

SCENE TWO

The castle of Troménec.

GAETAN. . . . And so the old king fell asleep . . .
Then his treacherous daughter,
Having slyly stolen his keys,
Opened the door to her lover . . .
But the door was cut into the dike,
And the surging ocean rushed in . . .
So the town of Ker-Is was drowned,
So perished its ancient king . . .

BERTRAND. But where was this city, Ker-Is?

GAETAN. Over there, among those black rocks . . .
Hear me further: a curse on her head!
Saint Gwénnolé for her evil deed

Turned her into a sprite of the sea . . .
And now, when the ocean's in tumult,
The evil Morgana with dripping comb
Smooths the pale gold of her tresses.
She sings as she combs, but her voice
Is sad as the lapping of waves . . .

BERTRAND. A strange man you are indeed!
Much have you told me
Of sirens and kings
And sea-drowned cities,
But of yourself you say nothing.
I little thought when we battled
That your helmet hid silvery locks.
It's true you're not strong,
But you fight like a hothead;
It's true you're white-haired,
But your voice rings clear as a hunter's horn;
Your eyes shine bright as a stripling's.

GAETAN. I too never thought that your hair
Would be so besprent with gray!
Has life used you harshly?
Though your voice be hollow and sad, dear guest,
The look of you pleases me well!

BERTRAND. For your kindness, I thank you!
It is true, want and woe
Have been my life's lot.
But the warmth of your words
Has touched my sad heart.
Bertrand's my name, my birthplace Toulouse.
A name so obscure
Will not stir your memory.
But you have doubtless known riches and rank—
By your bearing and speech,
You must be a knight . . .
Did you fight for the Holy Sepulchre?
The cross on your breast is faded . . .

GAETAN. I too am a knight unknown to fame.
I never set sail for the Holy Land,
Although I've the look of a pilgrim . . .
Why do you stare at me, friend?

BERTRAND. Tell me your name.

GAETAN. I am called Gaétan.
My birthplace is lovely Armorica . . .
My domain you see all about you:
At dawn in my own Troménec
The earliest cocks begin crowing . . .
Then others beyond the hills take it up,
And more, and yet more . . . and the last to crow
Is the monastery cock . . .
I hear, as I wake with their crowing,
Through the mists of my homeland
The cool rain sifting
And the call of the restless ocean . . .
Again your brow quivers! . .

BERTRAND. The wonderful words that you utter
Recall my mission to mind . . .
Very well then, seigneur of Troménec,
Let each of us tell of his life . . .
An alliance forged in the clashing of swords
We'll make yet stronger with words!

GAETAN. Would I might be to you
More than a friend—
A brother! Tell your story first.

BERTRAND. Gaétan, my tale is a sad one.
From Toulouse, the son of a simple weaver,
I was early bound in service.
For the long years I served at the castle,
The Count conferred knighthood upon me . . .
It chanced one day at a tourney
That a dastardly stroke unhorsed me . . .
The clumsy giant—his shield bore a dolphin—
Planted a foot on my chest . . .
But a wave of my lady's kerchief
Secured my reprieve . . .
O how I burned with anger and shame!
How I begged them to run my heart through!
But the wretches left me to live . . .

GAETAN. A base time we live in!
The best of our knights are not honored!

BERTRAND. Since that day, my life has been torment—
Everyone laughs in my face.
And behind her high casement
I know she laughs too . . .
But pity, or the shadow of pity,
I have seen in her eyes alone . . .
From her I'm remote as grassblade from rose . . .
And how should the wit of a simple knight
Fathom the mystery of woman's soul?

GAETAN. Yours is a sad tale, brother . . .
What scoundrels and fools are these!
Why, I still feel the smart
Of your ardor in battle!
Tell me, what brought you among us? . .

BERTRAND. I came on a twofold mission:
First, to gain news of de Montfort—
He must help us put down the revolt . . .

GAETAN. Here too there is talk of de Montfort.
But I could not follow that banner,
No, not if they called me to arms . . .

BERTRAND. Brother, then you believe
That there flows in our veins one blood—
The holy blood of fair France?
The sword that cut down the infidel
Savage de Montfort now turns on his brothers . . .
Whose banner then will you fight under?

GAETAN. I owe no banner allegiance.
Alone I shall stand.

BERTRAND. For you, that's easy to say,
But I'm sworn to service . . .
An opulent castle's unhappy custodian!
For myself, I will take no part
In the hunting of destitute peasants . . .

GAETAN. Take your leave of that land!

BERTRAND. Take my leave! You have not understood me!
Like you, I lack faith in this new crusade,
God's hand does not guide de Montfort's sword . . .
But can I betray
What I've served all my life?

Betrayal remains betrayal,
Although of an unjust cause!
Where my heart is, there will I die!
Well did they name me "Sir Hapless."

GAETAN. You're bound then in service, poor friend?
Terrestrial chains
Must weight heavy indeed . . .
I've never worn them . . .
Is your second mission as hard?

BERTRAND. Call it a whim that drew me
Into your mists from the Toulouse road.
A knight's sacred duty it is
To cherish his Lady's secret.
I will not answer your question.

GAETAN. Your words leave me baffled . . .

BERTRAND. I burn with impatience
To hear out your tale!
Your glance and the sound of your voice
Stir a strange feeling within me!
I put little faith in omens,
But it comes to me now
That you have been sent
To reward my arduous journey!

GAETAN. Then listen! I am old
And my life is lonely,
But I tell you that life is thrice blessed!

BERTRAND. Say rather, thrice treacherous!

GAETAN. On a blue lake's shore,
In the mist of late evening,
My careless young mother
Left my cradle unguarded . . .
A fairy carried me off
To her palace under the water,
There to raise me in misty captivity . . .
A garland of roses she laid on my curls . . .

BERTRAND. Again you are telling me tales . . .

GAETAN. And cannot a tale have truth?

BERTRAND. Sometimes it can, indeed . . .

Pardon my slowness of wit . . .
It may be there lurks in your words
A meaning beyond my ken . . .
I beg you, continue . . .

GAETAN. Listen further!
I yearned to become a knight . . .
Long did the fairy clasp me fast,
And long she wept as her hair fell about me . . .
Of what she divined as she sat at her distaff
I have no knowledge . . .
At last she said, "Go now,
Into the world of rain,
Into the world of mist . . .
For there the Fate-spun thread leads . . ."

BERTRAND. The Fate-spun thread leads?

GAETAN. And further she spoke:
"An infinite joy in the world
I shall set in the depths of your heart!
Give ear to the songs of the ocean,
Feast your eyes on the crimson of sunsets!
Your summons shall stir men obscurely.
Though you may chance to move
The heart of an earthly maiden,
No one shall move
Your heart . . .
It lies in my power forever . . .
In the world you shall wander, a pilgrim!
In this lies your destiny,
Your Gladness-in-Suffering!"

BERTRAND. "Gladness-in-Suffering!"
What does that mean?

GAETAN. "The law of the heart unchanging"—
Those were her very words,
And then through her tears she repeated
"A wanderer's life lies before you.
What end can there be to your quest?
Your coat of invincible mail
Mark with a cross on the breast!"
So I blazoned my breast with a cross

And entered the world of mist . . .

BERTRAND. Enough!
I never gave credence
To fairytales!
This story of yours brings a song to mind!

GAETAN. You still do not trust me, Bertrand!
Wherever you go, you will hear my songs
On the lips of jongleurs and fishermen—
The songs that tell of my life . . .

BERTRAND. Wonder of wonders!
Am I waking or dreaming?
A radiant joy
Floods all of my heart . . .
You made this song then?

GAETAN. And many another!

BERTRAND. Then you are the Pilgrim?

GAETAN. The fairy so named me . . .

BERTRAND. You are dearer to me
Than all the world's riches!
Dearer than life, my brother!
It was you, none but you,
That I sought in the snow-laden mists!
Unhappy Bertrand, awake!
This is some shimmering dream—
The harsh truth of life will destroy it! . .

GAETAN. If you are happy,
Then why do you weep,
Most cherished of guests?

BERTRAND. Forgive me, my friend, O forgive me!
So often has life brought me low
That I greet even joy with tears! . .
The first of my joys is to meet you,
Whom never I thought to find in this world!
The second—and pardon me for it—
Is to see you advanced in years:
Isaure will listen the better
Untroubled by base manly beauty,
Enthralled by the song alone!

SCENE THREE

At the ocean. Gaétan and Bertrand on horseback.

GAETAN. The sunken city lies not far from here.
You hear the ringing of its bells?

BERTRAND. I hear
The sea's tumultuous song.

GAETAN. You do not see
Saint Gwénnolé's gray vestments streaming there,
Above the waves?

BERTRAND. I see the grayish mist dissolving.

GAETAN. Now look—do you not see
A rosy glow upon the water?

BERTRAND. Yes. The sun is rising through the mist.

GAETAN. Not so! You see the evil siren's scales! . . .
Morgana's skimming through the waves.
Look now: Saint Gwénnolé is lifting up his cross!

BERTRAND. Again the mist has thickened.

GAETAN. Moans—you hear them?

BERTRAND. I hear the waves' lamenting voice alone.
No lingering, friend! Into the mist—ride on!

ACT THREE

SCENE ONE

The Count's chambers.

COUNT. You saw with your own eyes, you say, the force
Raised by His Holiness?

BERTRAND. I did, your Grace.

COUNT. You saw de Montfort's glorious oriflamme?

BERTRAND. An argent lion upon a field of gules,
A tail with fourfold tufts, all four caught up

In a single knot.

COUNT. Saint James be praised!

BERTRAND. And now
They're putting Béziers to fire and sword.
"Spare none!" the legate said, "The Lord will
Know His own."

COUNT. It serves them right! Well done, my lads!
De Montfort cannot be far off.

BERTRAND. His way,
Your Grace, lies by Toulouse.

COUNT. So be it then.
Ably have you carried out your mission!
I grant you pardon. Ask for your reward.

BERTRAND. May I entreat your favor for another?

COUNT. Ask what you will.

BERTRAND. Your Grace, tomorrow is
The first of May. The custom far and wide
Has been to welcome in the spring with song.
I beg you, then: observe this holy day . . .

COUNT. Why all this bother? Such was my intent!

BERTRAND. A troubador rode back with me, your Grace,
Who brings with him new songs for our delight . . .

COUNT. To cheer our hearts—is that what you propose?
Let's hear him then—a good song's what I like!

BERTRAND. And set at liberty the young Countess,
Who long has languished in her tower . . .

COUNT. What's this?
You dare to raise the subject of my wife?

BERTRAND. You gave your word . . .

COUNT. I did, and will not fail
To honor it. What put it in your head
To ask this thing?

BERTRAND. Your Grace knows well, the day
That ushers in the spring begins the year.
Then let it dawn unshadowed, blithe and clear.

SCENE TWO

The castle kitchen. The scullions are playing pranks.

COOK. They say he even takes the key of the tower to bed with him. And ever since that day no one dares open his mouth.

DOCTOR. And did you see what he has on his head? Just like the devil in the picture. It's two months since he had his hair cut. When he smiles, he bares his teeth like a dog. Doesn't trust a soul except for his Reverence. But between ourselves, the good Father . . .

COOK. Sssh, here even walls have ears. Will you be quiet, you scamps! All right, it's ready now. What else?

DOCTOR. Just add a pinch of willow bark . . .

CHAPLAIN. *(entering)* Saints in heaven, what a pie! Who is it for?

COOK. For her Grace, the Countess Isaure.

CHAPLAIN. Wait a moment . . . What are you doing here, doctor?

DOCTOR. A pinch of *salix alba* . . . against melancholy . . .

CHAPLAIN. What's that—poison?

DOCTOR. A simple purgative, your Reverence . . .

CHAPLAIN. Let me taste it.

ALISCAN. *(entering)* Your Reverence, I've been looking for you everywhere.

CHAPLAIN. *(munching)* What can I do for you, young man?

ALISCAN. Tonight I'm on guard . . .

He slips the cook a note.

Put this in the pie and you'll get a ducat.

CHAPLAIN. Have you taken the purifying bath?

ALISCAN. I have, your Reverence.

CHAPLAIN. And how long have you fasted?

ALISCAN. Two months, your Reverence.

CHAPLAIN. Go to the chapel, young man: tomorrow at mass we shall dub you a knight.

ALISCAN. I'm ready.

COOK. Ready, your Reverence.

DOCTOR. Did you add the bark?

CHAPLAIN. Cover the dish and follow me.

SCENE THREE

The Tower of the Grieving Widow.

ISAURE. Merciful God! Better to be slave to an Armenian, better to drag stones and logs! Alyse! Come here!

ALYSE. What is it, my lady?

ISAURE. I'm dying of boredom, Alyse.

ALYSE. Be patient. Meekness turneth away the dragon's wrath.

ISAURE. I know all your words of comfort by heart. You'd do better to play some game with me.

ALYSE. Chess or checkers?

ISAURE. No . . . Let's play at make-believe; I'm at mass, and he's disguised himself as a cleric. It's dark in the church . . . The rascal follows me . . . Then he comes toward me with a prayerbook . . . Here, give me a book!

ALYSE. Here's the romance of Floire.

ISAURE. Come toward me as if you were he . . . That's right. What will he whisper as I kiss the prayerbook?

ALYSE. He'll heave a sigh to begin with, naturally . . .

ISAURE. Now I kiss the prayerbook . . . and he says, "Ah me." What should I answer?

ALYSE. You have to answer cautiously at first—"What's the matter, Sir Knight?" for instance.

ISAURE. Very well then . . . "What's the matter, Sir Knight?" Then what does he say?

ALYSE. He says, "I am dying."

ISAURE. *(entering into her role)* "Of what?"

ALYSE. "Of love."

ISAURE. "You're in love? . . With whom? . ."

ALYSE. "You."

ISAURE. *(lowering her eyes)* "What can I do?"

ALYSE. "Heal me."

ISAURE. "How?"

ALYSE. "With cunning."

ISAURE. "I rely on you."

ALYSE. "I'm ready."

ISAURE. "For what?"

ALYSE. "I shall come . . ."

ISAURE. "Where?"

ALYSE. "To the Tower of the Grieving Widow . . ."

ISAURE. "How?"

ALYSE. "By a secret passage."

ISAURE. "When?"

A knock at the door.

ALYSE. The Count!

ISAURE. *(carried away)* "When? When?" My God, he heard everything!

She runs off. The Count and the Chaplain enter.

COUNT. Give me the pie!

He takes off the lid.

Where's the crust?

CHAPLAIN. I ate it, out of concern for your honor . . .

COUNT. Traitor! What has my honor to do with it?

CHAPLAIN. In the first place, pies may contain poison. In the second place, food may serve as a means of transmitting messages.

COUNT. Reverend Father! Your forethought is greater than mine. Forgive me for insulting you! Where is my wife?

ALYSE. She is at vespers.

COUNT. Let her pray awhile—and may Saint James help her.

ALYSE. Your Grace, just look at yourself! What a change in two months!

COUNT. I know what I'm about! . . Better to keep a young wife hidden in a safe place than to waste time and trouble . . . How is she feeling?

ALYSE. She eats less and sleeps less from day to day.

COUNT. I dare say she's been having dreams again?

ALYSE. Only yesterday . . . a knight . . .

COUNT. Again!

ALYSE. Beautiful as Saint Hubert . . .

COUNT. Damnation!

ALYSE. What's more, his features brought yours to mind . . .

COUNT. Mine? That's good. Clearly things are on the mend if she's beginning to have that kind of dream.

ALYSE. My lady has one humble wish, but dares not make it known to you . . .

COUNT. Speak and have no fear! Archambaut is generous!

ALYSE. The Reverend Father's admonitions have helped her . . . She would like to pray in church . . . We were just talking about it . . .

COUNT. Are you pleased, Reverend Father?

CHAPLAIN. If my humble prayers have helped an erring child . . .

ISAURE. *(entering)*
My master and my lord . . .

COUNT. Now by Saint James,
What tresses have we here! A sterner spouse
Would long ago have shorn them!
There, don't cry . . . My little joke . . .

ISAURE. What injury have I done you
That I must languish in this wretched cage?

COUNT. Can you deny you read romances?
Can you deny you dreamed of gallant knights?

ISAURE. For my sins I have atoned a hundredfold . . .
I feel so weak . . . I think I'm going to die . . .

COUNT. I'm told you wish to go to church?

ISAURE. To church?

Alyse makes her a sign.

Ah yes . . . to kiss the holy book of prayer . . .

COUNT. A wish that meets with my approval.

ISAURE. *(weeping)*
I have been cruelly defamed!

COUNT. Tomorrow's May—

You know, the day that ushers in the spring
Begins the year.

ISAURE. What's May to me?

COUNT. Just wait—
I'll find a way to raise your spirits.
Meanwhile, your supper waits! This pie, I swear,
Is a baker's masterpiece; it cannot fail
To put you in a better frame of mind.

He goes out with the Chaplain.

ISAURE. Loathsome man! Another trick—I know it!

ALYSE. He seems to be relenting, all the same . . .

ISAURE. *(gazing at the rose at the casement)*
A flower such as this
He wore on his breast!
The pale bud of yesterday
Is black now as blood!
Tomorrow it fades,
And with it my life . . .

ALYSE. Pluck the rose for your hair . . .

ISAURE. What do I need of adornment?
Deceived and betrayed by all—
Even that wretch so enamored of me!
With as sorry an envoy as mine,
What use to me is a secret passage?

ALYSE. Perhaps he will soon return . . .

ISAURE. It's hopeless!

ALYSE. *(cutting the pie)* Oh!

ISAURE. What's the matter? What's that you're hiding?

ALYSE. Nothing, nothing at all . . .

ISAURE. *(snatching the note from her)* Give it to me! At last he has come!

ALYSE. My lady . . .

ISAURE. *(reading)* "Lady, you whose lips are redder than the rose, whose voice is sweeter than the nightingale's song, vouchsafe me a sign. I shall await the rising of the moon . . ." O how sweet is the language of his love! But what is this sign he awaits?

ALYSE. Come to your senses . . . It isn't meant for you . . .

ISAURE. Is this a dream, or is it happiness? . . Honest Bertrand! Or is it all a dream? . . Alyse, you shall have silks and jewels . . . and the handsomest of pages . . . Saint Vidian! What can it be, this sign?

SCENE FOUR

A rose thicket.

BERTRAND. Rest here among these roses till the day breaks.
No one will harm you here.
GAETAN. Tomorrow then
I sing before the king?
BERTRAND. Before the Count,
You mean?
GAETAN. But is she not the daughter
Of old King Gradlon?
BERTRAND. Those are fairytales!
Her father was no king, her mother
A simple seamstress from Martres de Toulouse.
GAETAN. The daughter of a seamstress! All the same,
She brought down ruin on an old man's head!
BERTRAND. Not so. It was he who wished her ill. He shut
Her in a lofty tower.
GAETAN. I understand!
Some gold-tressed damsel languishes in bondage,
And I must set her free!
BERTRAND. Her skin is dark,
Her braids as black as night.
GAETAN. At least her name's
Morgana, is it not? Tell me the truth!
BERTRAND. Little does it signify to whom
Your song brings liberty. Have trust in me.
GAETAN. I trust you, brother.
BERTRAND. Many the wondrous tales
You've told and many the songs you've sung me . . .
Pardon my simple wit . . . I cannot tell
With you where fancy ends and truth begins . . .

And so a fairy reared you?

GAETAN. Yes. You see
This cross she gave to me.

BERTRAND. And did you learn
Your songs from her?

GAETAN. From her, and from the sea.

BERTRAND. But what does this song mean? Explain to me
How suffering may be transformed to joy.

GAETAN. You know the song. What more is there to say?

BERTRAND. A meaning glimmers in my mind, which, rude,
Untutored, cannot plumb those radiant depths . . .
Tomorrow you shall sing. At break of day
I'll bring fine clothes for you to wear.
And now farewell. The castle's in my care.

SCENE FIVE

The Tower of the Grieving Widow. In the distance sentries can be heard calling to each other.

ALYSE. Midnight has come and gone, my lady. I'll push this useless slab back in place. The Count might come in and see it . . .

ISAURE. Do as you please. There's nothing left for me to hope for.

ALYSE. Didn't I say the note wasn't meant for you? . .

ISAURE. But who would dare write messages to another?

ALYSE. My lady . . . the page sent it to me.

ISAURE. Don't lie! Nothing you can say will comfort me . . .

ALYSE. I'll put back the slab . . .

ISAURE. By the angels, the archangels and all the heavenly powers, I conjure you, come to me! Saint Vidian, take pity on me!

ALYSE. My lady . . . you're not well . . . Lie down . . .

ISAURE. Go away, leave me alone!

Alyse goes out.

O how my heart is beating!
Beat, my wild heart, and sear my breast!

Holy Saint Vidian, I'm all on fire!
The roses are rustling—hark!
By the saints I beseech you! At last!

She falls to her knees. A vision of Gaétan appears in a moonbeam above the slab.

You! You at last! Or are you a dream?
O Pilgrim! Where is your rose?
A cross burns fierce on your breast! . .
O threaten me not with your gloomy cross!
I was taught by my mother to pray,
But your song is not of that . . .
Why are you silent,
Heavenly messenger?
It is sweet to adore you! . .
Louder, sing louder,
O nightingale voice!
In my poor native land
No nightingale sang
With tenderer voice!
To love . . . yes, to love . . . is gladness . . .
To know not of love . . . is suffering!
Again you fall silent,
And I hear my heart pounding . . .
That same well-loved face!
Curls that are brighter than flax,
And the pale blue flame of those eyes . . .
Threaten me not with your cross—
O let me reach out and touch you! . .

ALYSE. *(at the door)*
My lady, my lady . . .

ISAURE. *(plucking the rose at the casement)*
Here, take this rose!
My blood is as black as its petals!
Stay with me, stay—or I shall go mad!
Closer, I beg you, come closer!
Let me hide your grim cross
With a rose, a black rose! . .

She falls down in a swoon. The door opens. The vision disappears. Alyse and the Count enter.

COUNT. What's the matter with her?

ALYSE. Did you hear a cry? She's gone out of her mind! This is what prison has brought her to!

COUNT. Water! Revive her! More water! She's coming to! She's free—tell her she's free! Tomorrow is Mayday! Bertrand has brought back a minstrel with him! We're going to make her happy! Only revive her!

SCENE SIX

The castle courtyard.

BERTRAND. The night is troubled and the air is tense,
As though it quivered with an arrow's flight . . .
Or are these the delusions of a mind
Made weary by this long, unsleeping night?
The casement's black—yet from
That casement once she summoned me.
She summons me no more.
And you, old friend, do you rejoice at spring?
You stretch your branches, bare of blossom now,
Toward that empty space . . . The dawn, at last . . .
Grant her, O God, an undisturbed repose . . .
O bring her passionate young heart release
From misty visions and tormenting dreams . . .

ACT FOUR

SCENE ONE

A flowery meadow. Dawn.

ALISCAN. *(with a flower in his hand)*
A burdensome duty, this night watch!
In the chapel's blue dusk

I have stood all night long, open-eyed . . .
O May, you caress my languishing heart!
How transparent the morning air!
How sweetly the nightingales sing!

Perhaps that silly lady imagines I can't do without her! She must have received my note . . . and yet . . . I've waited all night . . . and there's been no sign from her! Very well, she'll be sorry! And anyway, I'm sick to death of her importunities . . .

How sweetly the nightingales sing! . .
The roses have stolen the breath of Isaure . . .
Should fingers as slender as these
Encircle a lance's rough shaft?
No, I was born for other things!
In fortunate Arras, they say,
Men are more gracious and manners more elegant!
In roses and violets
Their tables are smothered!
Fragrant their claret,
Unceasing its flow!
Their ladies are skilled in courtly love!
In Arras, no jealous old fool
Would dampen the courtiers' mirth.
"Jealousy is outmoded now"—
I read that once in a Latin book
My father brought me from Rome . . .

He gazes at his reflection in the pool.

These lips' tender curve
Is like Cupid's bow
Or the scarlet lips of Isaure . . .
Must I hide them under a mask of iron?
Shall the rude iron of a sword's rough hilt
Be permitted to mar this rosy nail?
No! For me, other men, other manners—
Then many a nightingale-haunted night
Would I pass with Isaure amid roses! . .

SCENE TWO

A rose thicket.

BERTRAND. *(carrying a minstrel's costume)*
O spring, how you quicken the blood!
O love, no shield weighs as heavy as you!
The pilgrim is sleeping . . .
He is deaf to the nightingale's song . . .
But what black shape
Hides the cross on his breast?
A rose! A black rose!

GAETAN. *(in his sleep)*
Morgana! Leave me! Don't stifle me!

BERTRAND. Awake, Gaétan!

GAETAN. *(awakening)*
Spare your old father, daughter! . .
Brother, it's you . . .
I was dreaming . . . The treacherous daughter
Had opened the sluice-gates . . .

BERTRAND. The scent of roses was stifling you, friend.
What is it that lies on your breast?

GAETAN. Well, bless me, a rose
Has dropped from the bush
On my breast as I slept . . .

BERTRAND. The roses above you
Are red, every one . . .
How came this black bloom
To lie on your heart?

GAETAN. Where else could it fall from?

BERTRAND. You have not forgotten
The promise you made
When I might have killed you?

GAETAN. I have not forgotten. Ask what you will . . .

BERTRAND. Give me the rose!

GAETAN. An easy request!
Take it—it's yours!

Are flowers hard to find?

BERTRAND. *(concealing the rose beneath his coat of mail)*
You gray-headed child, little you know
The service you've done me!
My thanks! Now here's finery for you:
Thus clad, you shall step forth a minstrel
Today in the flowering meadow!

SCENE THREE

A flowering meadow.

GIRLS. *(they carry in the maytree, singing)*
Welcome, May, happy May,
Welcome, happy May!
Wife, in God's name we implore,
Do not drive us from your door,
Let a fat purse be our pay!
Not a sup and not a bite
Till we set a candle bright
In the Holy Virgin's sight!

Welcome May, happy May!
Welcome, happy May!

In our fields stands wheat aplenty,
Christ returns for one gift twenty—
For your vines and for your grain,
Sure salvation be your gain!
God the Father, God the Son,
May Thy holy will be done—
Lead us to eternal day!

Welcome May, happy May,
Welcome, happy May!

During the singing, all those taking part in the festivities assemble as they come from mass: the Count with his courtiers, vassals, guests and knights, Isaure with her ladies. Trumpets.

BERTRAND. *(emerging from the crowd)* Your Grace, one word!

COUNT. You've grown rather bold of late, Sir Hapless. I can tell by your face that you're going to say something unsuitable to the occasion. We're merry as it is—you're unlikely to make us any merrier!

BERTRAND. The Sire de Montfort is far off . . .

COUNT. You said yourself that he was on the road to Toulouse!

BERTRAND. The road to Toulouse is long . . . The people are restless . . .

COUNT. *(pointing to the girls)* These are our people!

BERTRAND. Albi, Carcassonne, Val d'Aran are caught up in the revolt . . .

COUNT. Enough! Jesters are merrier than you! I'll hear no more! Sound, trumpets! Let our faithful Aliscan draw near!

Bertrand disappears into the crowd. Aliscan kneels. The Count touches him lightly with the flat of his sword. Knights fasten on his golden spurs.

ALISCAN. My lady, will you permit me to be your knight?

Isaure absently extends her hand for him to kiss. Aliscan sits down at her feet.

COUNT. The tournament's tomorrow, and you will set a worthy example for all knights! And now let the singers delight our ears.

The first minstrel steps forth from the crowd.

ISAURE. *(to Alyse)* Is this the new minstrel?

ALYSE. No, another one.

ALISCAN. Last year's.

ISAURE. I didn't ask you to jest, Sir Knight.

MINSTREL. *(sings)*

I love the soft breath of the radiant spring,
The brilliance of leafage and flower;
I love the blent voices of birds on the wing
As I lie in some halcyon bower,
  All latticed with branches of green;
I love the white tents in their militant stance,
Where the sun strikes golden on helmet and lance,
  And neighing of horses rings keen;
Beneath heavy breastplates,
Crusaders' hearts dance—

Impatient for battle, they burn to advance.

I joy in the heralds of pitiless war—
The spirit within me is moved!
The terrified flock and its shepherd fly far;
Through the thunder of steeds, iron-hooved,
        The voice of the trumpet sounds plain!
On castle and keep they press the attack,
And towers tumble down, and sturdy walls crack.
        And lo, in the empty terrain
Lie row upon row the unvisited dead,
And over their graves the poppy burns red.

I joy to see vassals in mettlesome mood:
Locked in battle, they sweat and they strain.
Their helmets are shattered,
Their swords red with blood,
And over the limitless plain
        Their horses, abandoned, run wild!
A hero begotten, a hero shall die!
My eye takes delight, my spirit rides high!
        As broadsword rings bravely on shield,
Let the meadow be stained with the crimson dye,
Let no man surrender—the foe we defy!

COUNT. Your song is a little too warlike, minstrel! As it is, we are weary with the cares of war! Let's hear something more cheerful!

SECOND MINSTREL. *(sings)*
Through the leafy wood
In springtime's flood,
On an evening in May
I rode my bay
        From Douet to Arras!
        Dorenlo, to Arras!

A brace of fair maids
In flowers arrayed,
With garlands crowned,
Blithe may in their hands,
        I met on my way,

Dorenlo, on my way!

A tribute to spring
They merrily bring,
Blithe may in their hands,
They sing and they dance:
Dorenlo, love is sweet!
Dorenlo, love is sweet!

I leapt from my steed,
Made haste to their side.
"Permit me, I pray,
To journey your way!"
Dorenlo, love is sweet!
Dorenlo, love is sweet!

With frolic and jest
We walked on abreast,
Weaving garlands together . . .
Farewell, my Arras!
Farewell, my Arras!

I wove garlands gay
And tuned a sweet lay,
And we all sang together:
O how I love you!
O how I love you!

COUNT. For the singer of this sweet song, the best coat from my wardrobe! Sit with us at table and tell us stories all summer long!

ISAURE. But where is the new minstrel?

ALYSE. There he is, just stepping from the ring . . .

ISAURE. Which one?

ALYSE. Look how his garments glitter . . .

ISAURE. That little fellow all hung with bells?

ALISCAN. But he's a veritable giant . . .

ISAURE. Don't talk to me, Sir Knight! The graceful one with the fair curls?

ALYSE. That's gray hair gleaming in the sun . . .

ISAURE. *(sinking back indifferently against the bench)* An old man!

GAETAN. *(sings)*

Hurricanes blow,
The sea murmurs low,
Snow flees the blast,

In a moment an age hurtles past,
We dream of a blest shore at last!

Deep in the caverns of darkness,
A spindle hums early and late.
The eyes of the unseen spinner
Probe ours as she spins out our fate.

The fiery band of the sunset
Relentlessly probes the knight's gaze.
And over his fortune predestined
The star-crowded skies are ablaze.

To the heart of the singer is given
An endless delight in the earth.
The tumultuous ocean calls him
To his fated and purposeless path.

To the impossible vision surrender,
Fate will lay claim to its own.
The law of the heart is unchanging—
Gladness-in-Suffering alone!

A wanderer's life lies before you,
The ocean's tumultuous song.
Gladness, O Gladness-in-Suffering—
The anguish of wounds endured long!

Loss and misfortune prevail,
What end can there be to your quest?
Then hoist to the mast your rough sail,
And your coat of invincible mail
Mark with a cross on the breast.
Hurricanes blow,
The sea murmurs low,
Snow flees the blast,

In a moment an age hurtles past,
We dream of a blest shore at last!

During the song, Isaure in her excitement leans forward and, without being aware of it, leans on Aliscan's shoulder.

ALYSE. Help, she's going to faint!

ALISCAN. Help!

ISAURE. *(losing consciousness)* The voice I heard in my dream!

COUNT. Old man, have you forgotten that spring is in the air? Your song has a smell of sodden February, as do your gray hairs. Sir Hapless has certainly brought back a merry fellow to entertain us!

Gaétan disappears into the crowd.

ISAURE. *(recovering consciousness)* "Gladness-in-Suffering" . . . Suffering . . .

ALYSE. My lady is delirious!

ISAURE. No . . . I'm all right . . . Where's the old man?

ALISCAN. He's disappeared.

ISAURE. Page . . . Sir Knight! Help me!

COUNT. Trumpeters, sound your trumpets! Bring on the buffoons!

The jongleurs come running out.

FIRST JONGLEUR. Knights, barons and ladies fair! I shall tell you of glorious King Arthur . . .

SECOND JONGLEUR. Don't listen to him, noble knights! I can play the cithern and walk on my head! . .

ISAURE. Sir Knight, did you ever dream strange dreams?

ALISCAN. There's a cure for strange dreams, my lady:
The perfume of roses and violets,
The strains of a lute, a true knight at your feet . . .

COUNT. Livelier, buffoons! Come now, strain every nerve!

FIRST JONGLEUR. I shall sing of true lovers: of Hero and Leander! Of Helen and Paris!

SECOND JONGLEUR. But I can dance on a tightrope, jump through a hoop, juggle with knives!

ALISCAN. A love-sick Narcissus,

In your eyes I am mirrored . . .

ISAURE. You flatter me, Sir Knight . . .

FIRST JONGLEUR. And that's how Narcissus gazed into the water and drowned . . .

SECOND JONGLEUR. Have you need of helmets for hares? Bridles for cows? Gloves for dogs? And don't forget that I apply cupping glasses to bulls and let the blood of cats!

ALISCAN. What are the beauties of Arras
Before the light in your eyes?!

ISAURE. Stand round me, my ladies, hide me
From the gaze of vassal and guest . . .

ALISCAN. Why keep from the light
Such a marvel of beauty?

ISAURE. Oh, my shoe-lace has come undone.
Tie it for me, Sir Knight . . .

KNIGHT. Your Grace! The enemy! A cross on a field of gules!

COUNT. The banner of Toulouse! Raise the drawbridge!

VASSALS. To horse! To arms! The weavers! In the name of God and de Montfort.

BERTRAND. (*throwing himself into the fray*) For the Sacred Rose!

SCENE FOUR

A passage in the castle.

FIRST KNIGHT. An army—this? A ragged band of weavers
Herded by Count Raymond from all Toulouse!

SECOND KNIGHT. But there are knights among them—that I saw:
That giant with the dolphin on his shield.

FIRST KNIGHT. The one that Bertrand toppled to the ground?

SECOND KNIGHT. With my own eyes I saw it. Bertrand
And he were locked in combat, till at last

Bertrand unsaddled him with one great blow,
Planted a foot upon his chest and made
Him beg for his life . . . At that, a tremor ran
Through all of Raymond's host—
And then they fled!
We called him "Hapless" who outfought us all
And turned the battle's tide . . .

FIRST KNIGHT. He's wounded?

SECOND KNIGHT. Yes.
Our new-made knight and he are different breeds . . .

FIRST KNIGHT. True, Aliscan was absent from the field . . .

Enter the Count and his vassals.

COUNT. Good vassals, sheath your swords! The day is ours!
The way lies clear for brave de Montfort now!
The wretched weavers fled like frightened hares!

VASSALS. Long live de Montfort! Long live Archambaut!

SECOND KNIGHT. We owe this victory to Bertrand . . .

COUNT. To Bertrand? Yes, he fought most valiantly—
But, after all, is it so great a feat
To drive off bandits?

FIRST KNIGHT. Weavers from Toulouse,
Mere commoners, unskilled in swordsmanship . . .

SECOND KNIGHT. He's wounded, nonetheless . . .

COUNT. What of it? Wounds
Do honor to a knight! But let him rest
Today! From guard duty he stands excused!
And now, my men—to bed! Tomorrow
We'll resume our revels! First, the tourney;
When that's done—to feasting! So good night!

All disperse.

ALYSE. *(entering)* Reverend Father!

CHAPLAIN. What is it, my daughter?

ALYSE. My soul is sick . . .

CHAPLAIN. Tomorrow, tomorrow—it's late, no time for Confession . . .

ALYSE. But Father . . .

CHAPLAIN. However, I will be in the courtyard at about midnight . . .

ALYSE. I'll be there too, Reverend Father . . .

They go out in different directions.

BERTRAND. *(entering)*
How black the night. My eyes see nothing.

SECOND KNIGHT. Bertrand,
You're wounded?

BERTRAND. Just a scratch.

SECOND KNIGHT. Tonight the Count
Excuses you from guard.

BERTRAND. Sir Knight, I thank
The Count for his concern.

SECOND KNIGHT. You've earned your rest:
You saved us from the fury of Raymond . . .

BERTRAND. I thank you, friend. And now, good night.

The knight goes out.

Rest . . . Or is it rest eternal?
O this wound, it sears my heart!
Shrewdly was that blow directed,
Piercing rose and breast at once . . .

ISAURE. *(appearing at the top of the staircase)*
Bertrand, is that you? Are all asleep?

BERTRAND. Yes, asleep. The hour grows late.

ISAURE. Valiantly you fought today.

BERTRAND. You alone keep watch, my lady.

Can it be that evil dreams
Still disturb your quiet rest?

ISAURE. Spring it is that keeps me waking.
All my dreams have left me . . . Visions
Trouble me no more with terrors . . .
Tell me then—was he a dream?

BERTRAND. Only a dream. Your fantasy.

ISAURE. Only a dream . . . My fantasy . . .
Bertrand, what is that your fingers
Clasp so tightly to your breast?

BERTRAND. It is the rose of my devotion.

ISAURE. The rose of your devotion . . . Yes,
Your devotion saved us all!

BERTRAND. What I did was simple duty.

ISAURE. May the Lord reward you for it—
He who made you loyal of heart,
Me a breaker of my troth . . .
Tell me, knight, am I to blame
For the waywardness of May?

BERTRAND. No. In all things you are blameless.

ISAURE. Bertrand . . . You stand guard tonight?

BERTRAND. Yes, if you have need of me.

ISAURE. He will come . . . Please understand . . .
You alone . . . My foes surround me . . .
I rely on you for warning . . .
Strike your sword but once . . . O knight!
Beautiful is May!

BERTRAND. As you are.

ISAURE. Here, knight, you may kiss my hand . . .
More, I know, you will not ask . . .

BERTRAND. O my lady, every wish
Of yours is holy law to me.
Who am I that I should dare
Touch with mine your rose hand?

SCENE FIVE

The castle courtyard.

BERTRAND. This way—sssh, tread softly!
Step where the moon casts no light!
Do you see the apple tree bole?
Its branches
Reach up to the window.

ALISCAN. How am I to climb that naked trunk?

ISAURE. *(at the window)* Is it you, Aliscan?

ALISCAN. It is I.

ISAURE. Come to me! Come!

BERTRAND. Stand on my shoulders! Good!
Now you can mount with ease.

ISAURE. O my beloved! Your face streams with light!
You are spring, you are passion!
I behold you as though with new eyes.
Never before did your face
Burn with such radiant beauty!
O now I feel them,
Your warm earthly hands,
Your warm earthly lips!
You are no phantom, you are no dream!
Yes, this is happiness!
Who's that below?

ALISCAN. It's Sir Hapless. Bertrand, I thank you!

ISAURE. Is that you, Bertrand?

BERTRAND. Yes, my lady.

ISAURE. How lovely this night!

BERTRAND. Yes, my lady.

ISAURE. Sir Knight! You haven't forgotten?

BERTRAND. I will stand guard till dawn.
You shall hear the ring of my sword.

ISAURE. Thank you, my faithful servant . . .
But now . . . you must leave my window . . .

BERTRAND. I obey.

He moves into the shadow by the wall.

Be happy, Isaure!
A handsome lad
Is better than misty and terrible dreams!
May your storm-tossed heart
Find peace and delight!
How far from you now
Is the fairy's gift—
The dim, faded cross!
Blossom, O rose,
In your secret garden,
Scatter your fragrance while spring,
Holy spring, soars above!
May the soul in your breast
Remain ever young
In the black days before you.
I hear, O I hear
The surge of the billows,
The roar of the ocean.
A cross burns bright above tempests—
Into the snow-laden dark it calls you!
My wounds throb with pain . . .
My strength ebbs fast!
Bertrand, stand firm at your post!
Let your sword be your prop!
Your rose will not fade.

ISAURE. *(at the casement)*
My knight! You are with me! At last!
Hot is the blood
And fragrant the night!
I am happy once more!
Gone are those terrible dreams!
The dreams that I dreamed
Were only of you!
Be silent—I know . . .
What are dreams,
What are songs to us now? . .

She disappears from the casement.

BERTRAND. Bertrand, stand firm at your post!

A plague on these wounds
That ravage my heart!
Burn, rose, burn!
Hark! I hear trumpets! . .
Trumpets that rise
From the depths of the sea
Call ever more urgently!
A rosy light gleams
On the white foaming crests
Of the leaden night waves!
Ah, what torment!
What rapture in torment's wake!
My heart feels the breath
Of unearthly delight!
How lovely this night!

The Chaplain enters with Alyse.

CHAPLAIN. This time you won't refuse a gift, my beauty . . .

ALYSE. Oh what a beautiful ring!

CHAPLAIN. And a costly one too, you little minx . . .

ALYSE. Reverend Father, your office . . .

CHAPLAIN. In what way am I worse than a knight?

ALYSE. Ah, knights are such deceivers . . .

CHAPLAIN. Well, I won't deceive you . . . Ssh! Do you hear . . . whispering? And . . . it sounds like kissing . . .

ALYSE. Yes . . .

CHAPLAIN. Let's listen some more.

The moonlight falls on Bertrand.

ALYSE. Saints in heaven! . . It's the warden . . . There, by the wall . . .

CHAPLAIN. Yes . . . It's him.

ALYSE. Let's leave . . .

CHAPLAIN. What's he doing here?

ALYSE. Don't go near him, Reverend Father . . . I'm frightened . . . I don't know what of . . . He's not moving . . . His face is as white as a sheet . . . There's a black stain on his chest . . .

CHAPLAIN. Let's go . . . We'd better wake the Count . . .

They go out.

BERTRAND. How lovely this night!
But hark—now a rustling intrudes
On the solemn voice of the trumpets . . .
And again there is silence . . .
Absolute calm.
O God, Thy thunderous silence
Rings in the ears of Thy servant!
My wound has opened,
My strength is fast failing . . .
Burn, O rose!
Death, you make the heart wise . . .
At last, Isaure, I have understood:
"The law of the heart is unchanging—
Gladness-in-Suffering alone . . .
Gladness, O Gladness-in-suffering,
The anguish of wounds endured long! . ."

ISAURE. *(at the casement)*
Sweeter to me than the sweetness of life,
Brighter than morning
Are your kisses to me!
See how the night grows pale . . .

Bertrand lets fall his sword, which makes a ringing sound on the flagstones.

Did you hear it? The stroke of a sword . . .
Farewell! Till tomorrow . . . Make haste!

Aliscan quickly slides down the apple tree and runs off.

Sir Knight! Sir Knight!
Did you really hear something?

Voices are heard. Isaure disappears from the casement. Enter the Count, Chaplain, Alyse, Doctor, Knights.

COUNT. What has happened? Why did you wake me?

CHAPLAIN. Your Grace, I had a foreboding . . .

ALYSE. It looks suspicious . . . My lady's window . . .

COUNT. Bertrand! Sir Hapless! Warden! Are you asleep?

DOCTOR. He's dead, your Grace.

ISAURE. *(at the casement)* Why am I being awakened so early?

COUNT. Is that you? You're not asleep?

ISAURE. You can search my rooms if you don't trust me . . . What has happened?

COUNT. The warden has died here in the courtyard . . .

DOCTOR. And so much blood! So much blood!

COUNT. What a nuisance! Who is to keep watch over the castle now? Isaure, what's the matter? You're weeping?

ISAURE. I am sorry for him. Say what you will, he was a faithful servant.

1912

VIACHESLAV IVANOV

Viacheslav Ivanov (1866-1949), poet and scholar, was born in Moscow, the son of a government official who died when the future writer was four years old. Ivanov was brought up by his mother, to whose gentle piety may be attributed his abiding devotion to the Christian faith. In 1886 he went to study under Mommsen in Berlin, where in 1895 he defended his doctoral dissertation (*"De societibus vectigalium publicorum populi Romani"*) on the Roman tax-farming system. In the 1890s occurred two events that were to shape his life: he discovered Nietzsche and he fell in love with Lidia Zinovieva- Annibal (a descendant of that same Gannibal whose blood ran in Pushkin's veins). Nietzsche's *Birth of Tragedy* led Ivanov to the cult of Dionysos, to which, as a scholar, he was to devote his life's work; the intense and gifted Zinovieva-Annibal (herself a writer who was later to make a stir with her frankly lesbian novella "Thirty-three Freaks") wakened the poet in him. After divorcing their previous partners, the two were at last married in 1899.

In 1905 the Ivanovs settled in St. Petersburg after their years of wandering in Italy, Germany, France and England. Their top-floor apartment opposite the Tauride Palace, known as the "Tower," immediately became the meeting place of the capital's liveliest and most original minds. The *jours-fixes* at the "Tower"—the famous "Wednesdays"—became, in the words of the philosopher Nikolai Berdiaev, himself a regular frequenter, a "refined cultural laboratory" where people of the most diverse interests—"mystical anarchists and adherents of the Orthodox Church, decadents and professors, neo-Christians and social democrats, poets and scholars, artists and thinkers, actors and public figures"—could interact. It would probably be difficult to overestimate the contribution of the "Wednesdays" to the cultural ferment of those extraordinary years; some mention has been made in the Introduction of the key role they played in the crystallization of a Symbolist theatre in Russia. The "Wednesdays" were never quite the same after Zinovieva-Annibal's untimely death in 1907, although they continued for some years.

Ivanov remained in the Soviet Union for some years after the Revolution. A two month stay in a writers' sanatorium in 1920, during which he shared a room with the literary historian Mikhail Gershenzon, resulted in the well-known *Correspondence between Two Corners*, in which Ivanov defended "memory"—the continuity of culture—against his opponent's view of the Revolution as a liberation from the burden of the past. From 1920 until 1924 Ivanov was professor of classical philology at Baku University. In 1924 he left the Soviet Union for good and spent the rest of his long life in Italy, teaching and writing. Always a devout Christian (for him, unlike Nietzsche, the religion of Dionysos had always been the religion of the suffering god, not opposed to, but prefiguring Christianity), Ivanov was received into the Roman Catholic Church in 1926—a step he regarded as a consummation rather than a rejection of Orthodoxy. Ivanov died in Rome in 1949. A collection of his later poetry, *Westering Light*, was published posthumously at Oxford in 1962.

Ivanov's first collection of poetry, *Pilot Stars*, appeared in 1903, and, although he belonged to an older generation than Blok and Bely, he represented together with them the second, "mystical" wave of Russian Symbolism; like them, he had been profoundly influenced by the teachings of Vladimir Soloviov, and like them he viewed poetry as a religious apprehension of life rather than an aesthetic activity. Ivanov was a considerable, though never a popular poet; his poetry, which displays great formal mastery, is stately, erudite and full of sonorous archaisms, often bringing to mind his own description of St. Mark's Cathedral:

> Stooping you stand, a patriarch in rich
> And heavy robes of forged brocade.

Together with Bely, Ivanov was the leading theorist of Russian Symbolism, and perhaps came closest to erecting an ordered and coherent aesthetic. For Ivanov, the symbol was the kernel of a religious myth, or, to put it another way, "myth is the symbol in its dynamic aspect." The creation of myth was the business of art, and of the theatre in particular—hence the theatre's central place in Ivanov's thinking. He wished to create a theatre of mystery in which the spectators would be transformed into participants in a religious rite, achieving the mystic communion *(sobornost)* in which Ivanov saw the highest goal of art.

Following Nietzsche, Ivanov looked back to the origins of the theatre in Dionysian rite. The Symbolists, he said, should "look to those distant ages when myths were truly being created." Unlike his fellow classicist among the Symbolists, Annensky (of whose work he nevertheless wrote a sensitive appreciation), Ivanov was drawn not to the "modern" Euripides (detested by Nietzsche), but to the dramatist closest to the ecstatic and religious wellspring of Greek drama—Aeschylus. It is upon the first of the Greek tragedians that he modeled his own dreams of heroic god-defiers, *Tantalus* (1904) and *Prometheus* (1915), works that, like Shelley's *Prometheus Unbound* or the second part of *Faust*, must be regarded as dramatic poems rather than dramas.

The discrepancy between Ivanov's oratorio-like, virtually unstageable plays and his longing for a vital renewal of the theatre, a "great popular art," points to a certain unreality that vitiates Ivanov's theoretical writings on the theatre. Nevertheless, his ideas had some influence on the theatrical avant-garde, particularly on Meyerhold.

Viacheslav Ivanov
The Need for a Dionysian Theatre
(from "Presentiments and Portents"[12])

It cannot be doubted that as the art of the stage belongs formally to the dynamic type of the arts, inasmuch as drama unfolds before us in time, its inherent nature is actively energetic; not only does it seek to enrich our consciousness by implanting within it a new image of beauty as an object of passive contemplation, but it also seeks to become an active factor in our spiritual life, to produce some kind of inner event in that life. As far back as the ancient Greeks, the "purgation" ("catharsis") of the spectator's soul was spoken of as the aim pursued and attained by genuine tragedy.

Nevertheless, the world-wide historical development of the theatre reveals a significant deviation from this primal self-definition of the theatrical Muse in the direction of plastic immobility. The drama was born, in Nietzsche's words, "out of the spirit of music," or, in more precise historical terms, of the choric dithyramb. In this dithyramb all is dynamic: every member of the liturgical choric ring is an active molecule in the orgiastic life of the body of Dionysos—his religious community. Out of the ecstatic sacrificial rite arose the Dionysian art of the choric drama. The sacrifice—genuine at first, later fictive—is the protagonist, a hypostasis of the orgiastic god himself, acting out within our circle the suffering lot of the doomed hero. The choric ring was originally a community of those who offered sacrifice and participated in the sacrificial mystery.

The subsequent fate of the Dionysian art is a result of the modification of the elements that constituted the original whole. The dithyramb becomes isolated as an independent lyric form. In the drama, the deeds and passions of the hero-protagonist take on exclusive significance, entirely absorbing the attention of those present and transforming former participants in a sacred drama and performers of a rite into spectators of a festive show. The chorus, long since detached from the community, becomes separated from the hero as well: now it is no more than an element accompanying the central event, repeating the peripeteia of the hero's fate until finally it becomes unnecessary and even a nuisance. Thus the "theatre" (θέατρον), i.e. "spectacle" *(spectacle, Schauspiel)*, comes into being. The actor's "mask" thickens and the visage of the orgiastic god, the god whose hypostasis the tragic hero had once been, can no longer be glimpsed through it: "mask" has thickened into "character."

In the age of Shakespeare, everything is designed to body forth this "character." And the French theatre of the seventeenth century—is it not the apogee of the theatre's approach to the plastic arts? The age that locked up the flowing music of nature in the frozen architectural forms of the gardens of Versailles, did it not render the faces of Melpomene no less static? We delight in the creations of that period of the drama as plastic creations. Like a statue, the hero stands before us, a living mechanism of muscles, each of which by its tension reveals the structure and movement of the rest. The logic of the fate with which we are solely occupied is such that all is interrelated and the loss of a single link in the pragmatic chain would destroy the whole. The development of the drama becomes the demonstration of a mathematical theorem, the stage an arena where the gladiators of passion and fate do battle. The crowd disperses, satisfied by the spectacle of the struggle, sated with killing, but uncleansed by sacrificial blood.

The new theatre gravitates toward the dynamic principle. Is this not true of the theatre of Ibsen, where, in an oppressive closeness, the electricity of unexpended energy accumulates and a few purgative thunderclaps break in demonic splendor, without, however, clearing the atmosphere of its ominous tension? Or the theatre of Maeterlinck, which leads us into a labyrinth of mystery in order to abandon us before an impenetrable door? Or the theatre of Verhaeren, where the crowd itself emerges as protagonist? Or Wagner's drama of Tristan and Isolde, where the faces of the lovers swim up, convulsed with tragic passion, from the waves of murky chaos, the universal Meon,[13] only to sink back and dissolve in it, paying as individuals by their death, in the words of ancient Aniximander, redemptive requital for their very coming into being, and leaving nothing before the mournful gaze of those who witness their fate but a boundless purple ocean of relentless universal Will and unassuaged universal Suffering?

The dynamic principle is perhaps most clearly manifested in the so-called realistic theatre, which aims deliberately to be *terre-à-terre* and thus expels the "hero," making "Life" itself as a fluid becoming and never-resolving process the central figure, as it were, of the drama. Those who go to contemplate these cinematographs of everyday life are aware beforehand that no new knot of living forces will be tied before their eyes and that they will see no "denouement," because "life" itself is the sole knot of that universal drama, an excerpt of which is about to be played before them, and reality has not yet provided the denouement. They will be satisfied if the dramatist brings to the fore a particular problem presented by "life," if he poses a question suitable for discussion in the open forum of public opinion. But the dynamic principle of drama here finds complete confirmation. The spectacle's aim is not so much aesthetic as psychological: the need to condense an inner experience common to all; to know horror on descrying and recognizing one's own double; to hurl a torch into the black abyss yawning at our feet in order that a fugitive beam might illuminate its bottomless immeasurability. But in this there is a thrill that approaches the Dionysian—"rapture at the grim abyss's brink."[14]

If, then, the new theatre is again to be a dynamic one, let it be so to the limit. Following the example of the Ancients, who treated frenzy with ecstatic music and the exciting rhythms of the dance, it behoves us to seek a musical heightening of effect as a means of bringing about a healing resolution. The theatre must reveal its dynamic essence to the full; it must therefore cease to be "theatre" in the sense of "spectacle" alone. Enough of spectacles—we have no need of *circenses*. We wish to gather together in order to create—"to make"—communally, and not merely to contemplate; *"zu schaffen, nicht zu schauen."* Enough of playacting—we want action. The spectator must become an actor—a participant in the ritual act. The crowd of spectators must unite in a choric body like the mystic community of the "orgies" and "mysteries" of old.

In the Dionysian orgies, the ancient cradle of the theatre, each participant had before him a twofold aim: to take part in the orgiastic drama and in the orgiastic purgation, to consecrate and to be consecrated, to summon the divine presence and to receive the blessed gift—a theurgic, active aim and a pathetic, passive aim.

The separation of the elements of the original drama led to an impoverishment of the community's inner experience: it was permitted only to "undergo" the enchantments of Dionysos; and the ancient theoretician of the drama, Aristotle, consequently speaks only of the spectator's passive emotions. It is not surprising that the action of the drama moves away from the *orchestra*[15] (the circular area set aside for the chorus and bounded by the horseshoe-shaped auditorium) to the proscenium, which rises ever higher above the level of the *orchestra*. And so is drawn the charmed line between spectator and actor that, in the guise of the footlights, to this day divides the theatre into two alien worlds, one exclusively active, the other exclusively contemplative—and there are no arteries to link these two divided bodies by the common bloodstream of creative energy.

The footlights have separated the community, no longer conscious of itself as such, from those who are conscious of themselves only as "players." The stage must step across the footlights and draw the community into itself, or the community must absorb the stage. This is an aim already acknowledged by some; but where is the means by which it is to be realized?

It would be useless to approach this aim by seeking to predetermine the content of the desired new drama. Whether the hoped-for theatre be a "theatre of youth and beauty" or the spectacle of "human happiness without tears" (as recently demanded by Maeterlinck the theoretician), a theatre of cherished memories or prophetic presentiments, of elusive fragrances or sacred awe, whether it be a didactic theatre seeking to inform or educate—a theatre-"platform" or a theatre-lectern—none of these programs provides the means to break the spell of the footlights. There are artifices whereby the intervention of the public may be facilitated; the audience can be provoked into shouting comments (such as are often heard at performances of Italian and French melodramas); if politics is involved, it is easy enough to transform the occasion into a public meeting; but of course none of this presents an aesthetic solution to the problem before us. Decorative innovations of a purely external nature are hardly more helpful: the modern theatre remains the same in spirit even when the open sky is blue above the audience's head or the volcanic contours of beautiful Lake Albano can be glimpsed beyond the stage.

It is fruitless to attempt to establish a link between the question of the footlights and the question of what the subject matter of the drama of the future ought to be. In the drama of the future there must be room for everything—for tragedy and comedy, mystery play and crude popular farce, myth and social problem. What matters is not the "what," but the "how"—"how" understood in both a musical and psychological sense and in the sense of the elaboration of forms capable of sustaining the dynamic energy of the future theatre. We see no means of fusing stage and auditorium other than by unleashing the hidden and fettered Dionysian element in the orchestral *symphony* and in the independent musical and plastic existence of the *chorus*.

At the present time the drama, on one hand, and the so-called "music drama" on the other lead independent lives; they flow in two separate channels, and the watershed between them seems impassable. A single flow of energy that feeds two parallel streams is diminished and enfeebled in each. Happily, there are signs that point to the temporary nature of the breach and to the inclination of the two streams to reach a point of confluence. Let us restrict ourselves to a single example. Is it not significant that Maeterlinck's drama *(Pelléas et Mélisande)* stands in need of musical interpretation and finds it in the music of Debussy? But what is Debussy's music to *Pelléas* if not a *reductio ad absurdum* of the Wagnerian principle of "endless melody" or, if you will, recitative determined at all costs to bar living speech and living drama from the charmed circle of music's domain? It remains only to take one more step and speech will triumph over the convention of song, now watered down to a dreary declamatory recitative.

It is clear that the music drama must become simply drama; music will maintain and strengthen its dominance in the symphony and in the chorus, with its massed outbursts and varied groupings, polyphonies, monodies and *soli*, on a special stage for dancing or in the *orchestra* of a unified synthetic drama, the individual roles of which will be performed on the stage by dramatic actors.

The drama, in fact, is drawn toward music, because only with music's aid is it able to express its dynamic nature, its Dionysian aspect, to the full; because music alone will lend the drama grandeur of style and make it the bearer of a genuinely national art—for the drama must not follow in the wake of the other arts but must lead them in the movement, ordained by the age, away from intimate and refined exclusiveness toward broad lines and commodious forms; from the miniature and the easel painting to the *al fresco*. Music must take into itself the drama of the word because alone it does not have the strength to solve the problem of synthetic theatre.

Only a cultural and historical conflict brought about by slowness in overcoming deep-rooted traditions can, it seems, explain the inner anomaly of Wagner's work, which excludes from its "ringdance of the arts"—in clear contradiction of the synthetic principle—not only the dramatic actor but also the chorus (in the proper sense of the word) with its singing and orchestics. It is true that, as far as the chorus is concerned, Wagner's formula rests upon some theoretical justification, criticism of which, however, is facilitated by none other than Wagner himself, inasmuch as he not only accepts the idea of the chorus in theory, but even views it as the true vehicle of the tragedy played out by the actors.

The chorus for Wagner is the very substance of the drama, the very Dionysian element, as we would express it, that brings it into being; but this chorus is hidden and without speech: it is the orchestral symphony, expressing the dynamic basis of existence. This symbolic, wordless chorus is dumb Will, whose unceasing surge casts up on the theatre's illusory island of Apollonian dreams human forms and voices of "endless melody." Those who gather at the *Festspiel* are envisioned as molecules of the orchestra's orgiastic being; they participate in the action, but only latently and symbolically. Wagner the hierophant does not grant the community choric voice and word. Why not? The community has the right to this voice because it is seen not as a crowd of spectators but as a gathering of participants in an orgiastic rite.

It might be objected that the orchestra represents a metaphysical chorus of universal Will; a human chorus, even as a mystical assembly, would be the voice of a consciousness no more than human. Such an objection fails because the singing of the chorus would not replace the symphony but simply become an integral part of it. The symbol of the choric word would worthily represent the Dionysian spirit of humanity caught up in the infinity of cosmic ecstasy, serving as that ecstasy's conscious and active vehicle, like the mythical Hippa, who received the new-born Bacchus into her snake-entwined cradle. Apart from this, some secret law of aesthetics demands that the artist be anthropomorphic in all things, avenging itself on those who trangress it by cursing them with amorphousness, dryness and monotony.

Wagner stopped in mid-course, leaving his final word unspoken. His synthesis of the arts is not harmonious and not complete. With a onesidedness at odds with his overall conception, he gives prominence to the solo singer and neglects the spoken word and the dance, mass vocalism and the symbolism of the multitude. In Wagner's music drama "as in the Ninth Symphony of Beethoven, wordless instruments strain to give utterance to the longed-for and ineffable. As in the Ninth Symphony, the human voice, and it alone, will speak the Word. The chorus must be resurrected completely, in the fullness of its ancient rights. Without it there is no communal drama and spectacle prevails" ("Wagner and the Dionysian Drama").

Thus, the formula for a synthetic drama which we have outlined demands first of all that the stage action should arise out of the orchestral symphony and be circumscribed by it, and that this same symphony should be the dynamic basis of the action that interrupts it with self-contained dramatic episodes—for out of the Dionysian sea of orgiastic emotions rises the Apollonian vision of the myth, to disappear again in those same ecstatic depths, having illuminated them by its miracle, when the circle of musical "catharsis" is completed; secondly, it demands that the chorus should become both part of the symphony and part of the action; thirdly, that the actors should speak and not sing from the stage.

A corollary to the second demand, a condition of its realization, is that the *orchestra* must be restored. The auditorium must be cleared for choric dance and choric action; it should resemble the flat bottom of a hollow surrounded by sloping hills, accessible from all sides and occupied in front by a stage, with banks for the spectators on the remaining sides. The musicians of the orchestra should either remain unseen in the cavity reserved for them in the Wagnerian theatre or they should be deployed elsewhere. The coryphaeus of the instrumentalists, dressed in a costume matching that of the chorus, with his magic wand and his rhythmic gestures of an all-powerful magician, does not offend our aesthetic sensibility: he may stand in full view of the entire community.

The chorus is most easily envisaged as a double one: a small chorus directly connected with the action as in the tragedies of Aeschylus and a chorus symbolic of the community as a whole and capable of being arbitrarily enlarged, a chorus, consequently, which is numerous and which intervenes in the action only at moments of the highest exaltation—an example is the dithyrambic chorus in Beethoven's Ninth Symphony. The first chorus, naturally, introduces more action and orchestics into the synthetic drama; the second is restricted to the more spirited rhythms, it forms grand ensembles (processions, *theorii*), making its effects by its massed might and by the collective authority of the community it represents. The autonomy of the chorus allows scope not only for a wide variety of musical forms but also for constant innovation in the devising of choric *intermezzi*, thus ensuring that the chorus will serve as reservoir of the creative power of the orgiastic communal consciousness.

Undoubtedly, a necessary precondition of these changes is that the theatre should renounce not only the realism of everyday life but also to a great extent the desire for theatrical "illusion." Neither of these sacrifices, however, is likely to frighten our contemporaries and is, of course, still less likely to frighten the popular masses of the future, with their immemorial prediliction for the ideal style. It seems that both everyday realism and stage illusionism have by now said all they have to say; the present age has completely exhausted their possibilities. At all events, in envisaging a new kind of theatre, we do not deny either the possibility of other kinds of theatre coexisting with it—both those we already know and utilize and others as yet undeveloped from obsolete or obsolescent forms.

There is no doubt that the theatre of the future, as we envisage it, would be an obedient instrument of the mythopoeia that, by force of inner necessity, will surely arise out of truly symbolic art if it ceases to be the property of isolated individuals and finds harmonious accord with the free development of the national spirit. For this reason, the most suitable forms for the synthetic drama would be a divine and heroic tragedy similar to that of the Ancients and a mystery more or less analogous to that of the Middle Ages.

These forms are more flexible than might appear at first glance. The political drama can be wholly fused with them, thus acquiring for the first time a choric, i.e. a symbolically nationwide resonance. Let us not forget that the mythopoeic tragedy of the Greeks was often at the same time a political drama, and that the community that celebrated in its theatre the festivals of the Great Dionysos was naturally tranformed into a village community meeting, casting its enthusiasm or its hatred into the civic scales of the popular assembly or the council of elders. A similar influence, though even greater in degree, was exerted on public opinion by high comedy—the comedy of Aristophanes.

Only in the choric forms of a musical drama will comedy, long chained to the mundane realities of everyday life, find the courage to take wing; these forms alone will enable it, without ceasing to make us laugh—on the contrary, by resurrecting the divine orgiastic feast of laughter—to transport the crowd to a world of the most grotesque and unbridled fantasy, while at the same time serving as an organ of free social development.

1906

Viacheslav Ivanov
Annensky as Dramatist
(from "The Poetry of Innokenty Annensky"[16])

Annensky, the humanist and translator of Euripides, himself became a dramatist—a pupil and imitator of the tragedian he loved, his continuator and perfectioner, as it were, in artistic invention and illusionistic convention. He chooses as his themes those treated by Euripides in tragedies that have not come down to us; in place of the lost *Ixion, Melanippe, Laodamia* and *Thamyris* he has created his own four identically titled dramas.

This was his caprice and no pretensions are implied in it: just as Annensky consciously and deliberately guards against all restrictive externally imposed canons of school and style, so he clearly and unmistakably prefers artistic license to any kind of archaizing or stylization. Truly, such was the way in which he worked, and such the conditions, that the poet's praise of the free dreamer, the gondolier-storyteller, can well be applied to him:

> He loves his song;[17] he sings to please himself,
> Taking no further thought, unknown to fame,
> To fear or hope . . .

Annensky wrote dramas on ancient themes not because he wished thereby to demonstrate some aesthetic thesis, but because ancient myth was close to him and seemed to him to have general validity and human—*no more* than human—significance, to be of sufficient flexibility to allow modernization and of sufficient scope to accommodate the most recent developments of Symbolism; and because he had grown accustomed to living among these dreams of Greece, or rather to beguiling himself with his own self-sufficient "reflections" of Greece; and because it was Euripides and none other who had served him as intermediary between the divided worlds of the modern personality and the classical spirit, and he imagined himself able to converse across the centuries with the first tragedian of the individual personality; and, finally, because his lyricism required a chorus, understood in an ultra-Euripidean sense infinitely remote from its original function, as musical accompaniment and "musical entr'acte," and no other dramatic form could offer this lyrical resource—more than that, the catharsis of a forlorn and isolated spirit. Neither was it possible to find in any other form of drama the element of the "touching," as he understood it, and the element of the contemplative: the opportunity to stand apart and gaze sympathetically on his hero without identifying with him, to be moved by and at the same time to weep for his *dramatis personae*, who always perform their tragic actions innocently and always under compulsion, never from excess of strength or in a spirit of defiance, always from the consciousness they feel of the constriction and poverty of their "incarnation"—not from "fullness," as Nietzsche demanded, but from insufficiency and "hunger."

Annensky thought he could understand Euripides' "new man" of long ago, perceiving in him the same disharmony and division he sensed in himself—a personality that, having freed consciousness and selfhood from the bonds of an outmoded social and religious collective, now found that it was locked up within itself, deprived of meaningful union with others, incapable of opening the door it had slammed shut on itself and of emerging from its cage to assert itself with might and majesty in rebellion or freely to submit like the god-fighters and submissive ones of Aeschylus or, finally, to fashion from itself one of the generalized and normative types of common humanity like the heroes of Sophocles . . . Oh, he was incapable of religious submission, to the secret of which the "new soul" was profoundly oblivious, but neither could he turn to brute force, even if only in his dreams, like Nietzsche—and he locked himself in his "underground," there quietly to "reflect" both the sunlit arrogance of the deafening world and the quiet suffering of wounded, unloved, earthbound souls.

Tragedy, in the strict sense, could not arise from this psychology; there did gape within the poet himself the abyss into which freedom—not compulsion—hurls the genuine tragic hero at the crossroads of his ultimate choice, like that Roman who leapt with his horse into the widening breach, freely offering himself as a sacrifice to the gods of the underworld for the redemption of the threatened city. However, Annensky was generally faithful to the Euripidean tragic formula, developing to their fullest extent the possibilities suggested by Euripides and, as it were, convincing us yet again that the aesthetic and psychological phenomenon known in modern Europe by the name of *décadence* is the revival of something we have inherited in entirety from the Ancients, a final inference drawn from something of which the characteristic features and formal traits had been apparent ever since Hellenic religion began to fall into decay.

Only a single outstanding feature, in essence, marks Annensky's dramas as unclassical in form, and here historical distance is seen to be more powerful than aesthetic and psychological closeness. What we have in mind is not the romantic spirit in the conception of the poet's first three dramas, something perfectly comprehensible to the ancient world, and not, of course, peculiarities of poetic tone and diction in these three dramas, not even the eclectic *barocco* of *Thamyris Kitharodos*. We have in mind the absence of the *mask*, with all the consequences its removal entails for the entire dramatic style.

For the mask compels the dialogue to be typical and rhetorical and concentrates the psychological interest in a few decisive moments of the drama's peripetaia, while the removal of the mask transforms the course of the dramatic action into a ceaseless ebb and flow of small, fleeting, half-conscious and mutually contradictory experiences. But then, Euripides himself is noticeably constricted by the static nature of the mask; it seems that he would have preferred the vividness and mobility of the uncovered face—did he not, after all, lower the buskin and make the chorus, once the vehicle of an unshakable objective norm, the voice of lyrical subjectivism?

One is tempted to define the tragic pathos of Annensky's dramas as a "pathos of distance" between earthly and human and the heavenly and divine and, springing from this, a pathos of resentment felt by mankind and for mankind; the idea that unites these works might be defined as that of the impossibility of love's realization on earth. The guilt of Annensky's guiltless heroes lies in the fact that they love too far above themselves; but true love—such is the poet's thought—does not arise, or at least cannot be realized, on the same plane for both lovers, the plane, that is, of earthly existence. Love selects for its object that which is truly worthy of love, the quintessentially real, either in the world beyond or in some temporary incarnation. In the first case, the soul striving to gain possession of the beloved is involuntarily guilty of pride and theomachy, like Ixion, who is easily absolved of his former crime but whose love for the divine Hera cannot be forgiven, or like the lyre-player Thamyris, the "unloving" lover of an Olympian Muse. Melanippe—the heroine of a beautiful and touching drama of a purely Euripidean cast—is condemned, like Thamyris, to blindness and to the long entombment of a soul that has renounced all earthly things in a body that pitilessly continues to live, as retribution for loving blue-curled Poseidon and for wedding a god, a thing forbidden to mortals. Love in *Laodamia*, the most exquisite and perfectly realized of the poet's three "Euripidean" dramas, is realized only through earthly separation and the liberating funeral pyre; to mortal understanding, it is realized in illusion and self-deception and is real only to the gods.

Suffering is the distinctive mark of genuine love, which is always in one way or another directed toward an unattainable object; it is its *titre de noblesse* and the criterion of its authenticity. This suffering is a mark of human dignity before the gods, even perhaps of human superiority over them. It is not in the nature of the gods to love: they are blessed.

—You think the gods can love? Was ever one
Unknown to suffering, unburned by doubt,
Given the power to love? A love devoid
Of thrill and mystery . . . The diadem
Of ice that crowns those distant heights, O Queen—
In sunlight it beguiles the eye, but nymphs
Love not its chilling irridescence.
—Can that be why great Zeus abandons us
And grows enamored of your maids? . .
(*Ixion*)

Yes, the gods become enamored of mortal maidens, as mortal heroes do of goddesses; and every time the divine element approaches the mortal, a human being is destroyed. Between gods and men a great gulf has been fixed. "How do you live, divine ones? With feasting and with love?" the leader of the chorus asks Hermes in *Laodamia*. Hermes replies:

O no! Feasting we find as dull as you—
The wise, at least, among you—and Eros' feast
Beguiles us rarely . . . Seated at the board,
We read our scrolls. The bright and busy world
Is interesting to us; it gives us notes
For music, colors to paint pictures with:
It holds the atoms of another being . . .

There is an Orphic verse:[18] "Olympus is the smile of the god; his tears are the race of man." This line could well serve as an epigraph to all Annensky's dramas. The relationship between the two worlds is such that disaster and torment on earth are equivalent to the blessing of the gods; what is bitter here is sweet there. An individual's assertion of his divine *I* ruptures his links with the earth and calls down inevitable retribution on his head; but there, on the divine plane . . . Beyond this point, however, our poet does not venture; here he finds himself too lacking in the strength of religion—or is it only a chaste reserve?—to make any kind of assertion. One thing he knows: on earth man has become profoundly forgetful of what he may once have known in heaven—he is forgetful of everything, of his very divinity, the memory of which reveals itself not in man's consciousness but in the virtue of the noblest, in the love of something that does not exist on earth and in "unlovingness" toward earthly things.

There is another thing we shall learn from the poet in answer to our questions and our doubts as to whether that divine reality exists and whether our tears—the smile of the gods—will restore to us that lost and forgotten divinity. In *Thamyris*, at the catastrophic moment that decides the hero's fate, we see gazing down from the heavens into the mirror of the world the ethereal countenance of the *smiling* Zeus. A striking image! Does the blessed father of the gods and of men know that all this pain and disaster below is the means by which man, transfigured by his sufferings, will return to his ancestral home, be he Herakles or the unchained Prometheus with the osier-wreath of peace upon his head and the iron ring of submission about his wrist? Or is it simply humor, the irony of the heaven-dwellers at the expense of man, that "long-legged cicada," in the words of Goethe's Mephistopheles? . . .*

It was here that the "underground" in the divided soul of our new Euripides took its inception, that "underground" he liked to exhibit as a mask of "cynical" scepticism, but to which he himself, in one of his most profound and revealing poems, gave a better name—"bewilderment."

1916

* Let us compare the following thought from Annensky's article "The Artistic Idealism of Gogol"—one of the few places in his work where he gave direct expression to his view of the world: "We are surrounded by, and probably compounded of two worlds: the world of things and the world of ideas. *These worlds are infinitely removed from each other, and in the whole of creation it is man alone who is their profoundly humorous—in a philosophical sense—and logically irreconcilable combination.*"

ANDREI BELY

Boris Bugaev (1880-1934), who was to publish poetry, novels and criticism under the pen name of Andrei Bely, was born in Moscow, the only child of a professor of mathematics at Moscow University and a society beauty with artistic inclinations; the union was not a happy one, and Bely was to trace the tragic dualism of his nature to the divided loyalties of his childhood. Throughout his life, scientist and artist lived within him in an uneasy, though often fruitful partnership.

While still a student, Bely came under the influence of the philosopher Vladimir Soloviov, and was the center of a small group of callow mystics who called themselves "Argonauts" and lived in expectation of the Second Coming. Bely's first collection of verse, *Gold in Azure*, appeared in 1904, and he was soon a leading contributor to Briusov's Symbolist journal *The Scales*. From this period dates the exalted beginning of his tormented friendship with Blok, which was to continue—broken off and again renewed—until the latter's death in 1921. In 1909 appeared Bely's first novel, *The Silver Dove*, which, together with its two successors, *Petersburg* (1913-14) and the autobiographical *Kotik Letaev* (1918), represents his greatest claim on the attention of posterity.

The outbreak of the First World War found Bely living in the anthroposophical colony centered about Rudolf Steiner at Dornach in Switzerland; Bely's devotion to Steiner ended, as his relationships and enthusiasms all too often did, in bitter disillusionment, although he never abandoned anthroposophy. Returning to Russia in 1916, Bely greeted the Revolution with the poem *Christ is Risen* and endured the trials of the civil war years. An unhappy interlude in Berlin (1921-23) ended with his permanent return to the Soviet Union.

Bely continued to be productive during his Soviet years, publishing novels (the two parts of *Moscow*), important critical and theoretical works (*Rhythm as Dialectic* and *The Mastery of Gogol*) and three brilliant books of memoirs in which, however, Bely's eagerness to erect a barrier between his Soviet and his Symbolist self leads him into distortion and caricature (though it must at the same time be admitted that distortion and caricature are central to his artistic vision).

If there is a frenetic quality about Bely's work that makes it wearying at times, one cannot deny its originality, range and influence. In his four early and experimental *Symphonies* (1903-1908) he attempted to organize large-scale prose works on musical principles. The "ornamental" prose of his novels, with its strong rhythmic and phonetic dominants (Bely claimed that the "content" of *Petersburg* was "derived" from a certain grouping of sounds) and its combination of the lyrically exalted and the grotesque, might be described as "neo-baroque." Equally original is Bely's work in the field of poetics, with its attempt to introduce strictly scientific methods; here he looks forward to the Formalists and even—for good or ill—to computer analysis techniques.

Bely's genius, so intimately bound up with the texture of language, was not suited to the theatre, and his two published plays, *The Newcomer* (1903) and *The Maw of Night* (1906) are immature works. However, in the context of the early Symbolist drama, these brief, fragmentary eschatological mysteries are not without interest. The two plays are clearly connected—probably parts of a large-scale uncompleted drama. Both are permeated with mystical expectation: in *The Newcomer* signs and portents tell of the imminence of the Second Coming; in *The Maw of Night* the sun has been extinguished and the last Christians await the end. In this last play the mysterious, threatening atmosphere and the cast of children, women and old men call Maeterlinck to mind, in particular *Les Aveugles* and *La Mort de Tintagiles*; indeed, Bely's plays might be described as an amalgam of Maeterlinck and Vladimir Soloviov. It is more than likely that the dialogue of the Mystics in Blok's *Puppet Show* was meant to parody such exchanges as the following:

> FIODOR. It is He . . . It is He . . .
> ILIA. He comes, and in his hands he bears a torch.
> FIODOR. His eyes are heavenly . . .
> ILIA. Above him burns the mark of mystery.
> FIODOR. He cometh. The Bridegroom cometh. The world hearkens unto him . . . He is the Light of the World.
> (*The Newcomer*)

Not only did Blok parody *The Newcomer*, but in his own drama of "last things," *The King in the Square*, some of the atmospherics of Bely's play—the ever-present tumult of the sea and the growing murmur of the mob—seem to have been borrowed.

In 1924 Bely made a stage adaptation of *Petersburg* under the title of *The Death of a Senator* (the bomb that explodes harmlessly in the novel kills Apollon Apollonovich in the play), and it was given its first performance the following year at the *Moscow* Art Theatre. A theatrical version of Moscow made in 1926 was never staged.

Under the influence of Viacheslav Ivanov, Bely experienced a brief "Dionysian" intoxication in 1904-1905, advocating a theatre of communal ecstasy and penning dithyrambs to the "whirling circle of separate experiences fused by music into a purple Dionysian flame, exalting those who take fire from it into the sapphirine grail of the heavens." The enthusiasm did not last, however, and Ivanov makes an appearance in the fourth *Symphony* (1907) as a "golden-haired mystic" who "tried to leap up into heaven, but plunged downwards and uttered beautiful lies." The excerpt from "The Theatre and Modern Drama" (1907) included here is, despite Bely's transparently disingenuous disclaimer, a savage attack on Ivanov's ideas.

Andrei Bely
The Cherry Orchard[19]

In attempting to reproduce reality, the realistic artist first of all sets to work on its most general features; next he becomes a photographer of reality. His perception develops. He is no longer content with a superficial depiction of a phenomenon. Having concentrated his attention on the distinct and the enduring, he now turns to the indistinct and transitory elements of which the distinct and the enduring are composed. He then weaves a fabric of moments. The isolated moment becomes the goal of the process of reproduction. Thus represented, life is a delicate, almost transparent lacework. If one absorbs oneself in it, a given moment of life becomes in itself a door to eternity. Being a loop in the lacework of life, it is not sufficient to itself: it frames an outlet to what lies beyond it. The experience is of an infinite intensity. The lacework of life, which is composed of separate loops, becomes a series of doors to parallel corridors that lead to another world. The realistic artist, even though he remains himself, cannot but portray not only the surface of life's fabric but also what is revealed in the depths of the parallel labyrinths of moments. In his portrayal, everything remains as it is, but permeated by *the other.* He himself does not suspect whence he is speaking. If you say to such an artist that he has penetrated into the *beyond*, he won't believe you. He approached it, after all, from the outside. He was studying reality. He will not believe that the reality he portrays is, in a sense, no longer reality.

The mechanism of life channels our feelings in a direction we do not desire, delivering us into the power of machines. Our dependence begins in general causes unknown to us and ends in horse-cars, telephones, elevators and railroad timetables. A closed, mechanical cycle, from which it is increasingly difficult to break out, is taking ever more definite shape among us. A wears himself out for B, B for C, but C too, for whom A and B sacrifice themselves, remaining zeros, instead of attaining a life organically unified by his emotional experiences, sacrifices himself for A, thus also being reduced to a zero. A machine is being created for the pointless destruction of souls.

The power of the moment is a natural protest against the mechanization of life. Having freed himself, man deepens the fortuitous moment of freedom by concentrating upon it all the powers of his soul. Under such conditions, man learns to perceive more and more in little things. Little things are increasingly the conductors of Eternity. Thus realism is imperceptibly transformed into symbolism.

Moments are panes of painted glass. We gaze through them into Eternity. We have to concentrate our attention on a single pane, otherwise we shall never gain a clear vision of what lies beyond the fortuitous. Familiarity dulls all things and we tire of gazing, no matter at what. But once we have experienced a certain moment with sufficient intensity, we wish it to be repeated. By repeating an experience, we penetrate more deeply into it. In doing so, we pass through various stages. A given moment becomes for us an unexpected outlet into mysticism: our inner path becomes clear and the wholeness of our spiritual life is restored. The mechanism of life is overcome from within, the isolated moment no longer has power over us. The lacework of life, spun from isolated moments, disappears when we find an outlet to what had previously glimmered beyond life. In reporting what we see, we arrange the material of reality according to our will.

Such is mystical symbolism, as opposed to realistic symbolism, which conveys the beyond in terms of the reality that surrounds us.

Chekhov is a realist. From which it does not follow that his work is lacking in symbols. Since the conditions of the reality in which we live have changed for modern man, he cannot but be a symbolist. As a result of the nervous refinement of the best among us, reality has become more transparent. Without abandoning the world, we move toward what is beyond the world. That is the true path of realism.

It was not very long ago that we stood upon solid ground. Now the earth itself has become transparent. We move as upon slippery transparent glass, and through the glass the eternal abyss watches us. And suddenly it seems to us that we are walking on air. It is fearful, this airy path. Can one speak today of the limits of realism? Under such conditions, can one oppose realism to symbolism? Today those who have turned away from life find themselves in the midst of life because life itself has changed. Today realists, in depicting the real world, become symbolic: where there was once a boundary line everything has become transparent, penetrable.

Such is Chekhov. His heroes are touched in from the outside, but we comprehend them from within. They walk about, drink, talk trivialities, but we see abysses of spirit glimmering through them. They talk like people locked up in a prison, but we have recognized in them something they have failed to notice in themselves. In the trivialities by which they live a kind of secret code is revealed to us—and the trivialities cease to be trivial. There is something that neutralizes the banality of their lives. At every moment a grandeur is revealed. Is this not to look through banality? And to look through *anything* is to be a symbolist. By *looking through* I unite the object with what is beyond it. Symbolism is the inevitable result of such an approach.

The manifestations of the spirit of music are extremely varied. It can permeate all the characters of a given play in equal measure. In that event each character is a note in a single chord. Chekhov's "plays of mood" are musical. Their symbolism guarantees that, for the symbol is always, in a general sense, musical. The symbolism of Chekhov differs substantially from the symbolism of Maeterlinck. Maeterlinck makes the heroes of his dramas the vessels of his own mysticism. Seeking to signal the approach of death, he makes his old man say: "Is there not someone else among us?" Too obvious a symbol. Is this not allegory? It is too general in its expression. Chekhov stumbles upon symbols in the process of refining reality. He is hardly aware of them. Nothing he puts into them is premeditated, for it is hardly likely that he has had any mystical experience. For this reason his symbols have an organic link with reality. The web-like fabric of phenomena is never torn. Thanks to this, he succeeds in disclosing in greater depth the symbols that reverberate at the back of trivial things.

A number of harassed people are sitting about, trying to forget the horrors of life, but *a stranger passes by . . . A bucket crashes in a distant mineshaft*. Clearly, this is horror. But perhaps it is all a dream? If we look at *The Cherry Orchard* from the viewpoint of unity of artistic effect, we will not find the perfection of *The Three Sisters*. In this respect, *The Cherry Orchard* is a less successful work. All the same, the psychological depth of certain moments is more perfectly conveyed here. If what we saw previously was a transparent lacework contemplated from a distance, the author has now, as it were, drawn closer to a few loops of that lace and seen more clearly what those loops frame. Other loops he has passed by. Because of this, the perspective has been disturbed and there is an unevenness about the play. Speaking relatively, Chekhov has taken a step backward. Absolutely, he has gone forward, refining his method still further. In places his realism is even more delicate, the symbols glimmer even more perceptibly.

How terrifying are the moments when fate creeps up soundlessly on its helpless victims. Everywhere is the disturbing leitmotif of the thunderstorm, everywhere a lowering cloud of horror. But, you might say, there's nothing to be horrified about: an estate is being sold off, that's all. But terrifying are the masks beneath which horror hides, peering through the eye-slits. How terrifying is the governess as she postures before the ruined family, or the footman Yasha, arguing about champagne, or the insolent post office clerk, or the passing stranger in the forest!

In the third act, Chekhov's method is somehow crystallized: in the front room a family drama is being enacted, while in the candle-lit back room masks of horror are frenziedly dancing: look at that post office functionary dancing with a little girl—perhaps he's really a scarecrow? Perhaps it's a stick with a mask tied on, or a uniform dangling from a clothes hanger. And the stationmaster? Where is he from, what is he doing here? They are all embodiments of fatal chaos. And now they are dancing and posturing in the presence of a family misfortune.

Trivial things take on a coloring hitherto unknown. Reality is split in two: a thing is itself and not itself; it is a mask for something else, and the people are dummies, phonographs of the depths—and it is fearful, fearful . . .

Chekhov, while remaining a realist, here parts the folds of life and what from a distance had seemed to be shadowy folds are revealed as an outlet to eternity.

1904

Andrei Bely
Against Reviving the Greek Theatre
(from "The Theatre and Modern Drama"[20])

The drama represents the dynamic principle of creative energy in art. The drama enshrines the synthetic principle. In the drama we touch the massive trunk, as it were, from which the manifold forms of art spring in all directions to form a luxuriant crown. When, however, the drama is seen exclusively as the common source of the various art forms, its vital significance is undermined. We often hear these days that the mystery play represents a synthesis of the arts, and that modern drama is drawing closer to the mystery. To my mind, this is symptomatic of the danger threatening modern drama. The drama will be crushed beneath a pyramid of idols. The musical principle will once again give way to eclecticism. All these seductive appeals from the mystery must be regarded with suspicion. They lull our resolution—a resolution we need, no less than we need hosts of heroes, for the fierce struggle that lies before us. It is in the struggle, and not in dreamy supplication, that we shall be transfigured. It is the drama that will reveal to us the maneuvers of the coming struggle with destiny. Dramatic culture *is* culture. Such was the view of Nietzsche, that great theoretician of the new drama. And he had a more correct understanding of it than Wagner or, say, Schuré.[21]

Nietzsche perceived in Wagner's music dramas a genuine struggle for the liberation of mankind. But even Nietzsche failed to reach a clear understanding of the fatal contradiction in modern drama. He sensed in it a summons to life, without distinguishing between the summons and the form in which it resounded. A return to life through what is new in the drama renders drama itself superfluous as an art form. Bowing before the drama's summons to life, Nietzsche canonized the form in which the summons was cast—the theatre. A monstrosity resulted: the summons to life from the stage was transformed into a summons to life on the stage. The products of Wagner's genius embody this unnatural summons. In the early period of his enthusiasm for Wagner, Nietzsche bowed before the drama as a form. The dramatic form became the slogan which he held up to art. He attributed the effect of the explosive charge to the outer casing of the bomb. He forgot that life itself and not the drama would provide the moment of explosion. Nietzsche bowed before music drama, the portent of an event, as before the event itself. He had created for himself an idol. And for that reason he tore Wagner's inspired music from his heart, just as he tore from it his own *Birth of Tragedy*—a deed to which his own declaration bears witness. Zarathustra—there is a real dramatic actor, intoxicated with mythopoeia, and not that beef-witted oaf Siegfried,[22] waving his cardboard sword about and tooting idiotically on his curved horn. *Zarathustra* was born on the stage and immediately set about playing to an audience. The stage represented the town of Bunte Kuh, and the virtuous Zarathustra walked about Bunte Kuh imparting wisdom. Then he gave it up as a bad job and left the stage for life. The third and fourth parts of Zarathustra are truly a drama of life. Here, in the innermost experiences of Zarathustra's life, and not in fine theories about some operatic Siegfried, is the real starting point of the explosion.

But the charge will explode only when mankind stands under a single tragic banner. The true visage of destiny will be revealed only when man rises above the class struggle, that obstacle to all genuine affirmation or denial of life. The fetishism of productivity is not, of course, destiny but rather the mask of destiny. And the struggle for liberation does not lie in the rejection or acceptance of forms of economic equality. It begins in new forms of social equality. When the masks of destiny fall, mankind will fight the final battle for life and happiness. Then from the shattered forms of art, as from the shattered forms of personal life, the holy fire of vital creation will burst forth. Then the explosive shell of the drama, loaded with the dynamite of the spirit, will burst. That is what Nietzsche failed to take into account. The concept of social drama was alien to him. At first he amused himself with the casing of the shell—the renascence of modern dramatic forms; then, in extracting the dynamite of vital creation from drama as an art form, he inadvertently smashed the shell. The bomb exploded not where it should have—outside the walls of our prison—but in the hands of its inventor. And for fifteen years Nietzsche—the inventor of explosives—sat on the balcony of a peaceful villa with his brain blown to pieces. The spot on the balcony where the mad Nietzsche used to sit by the hour is still pointed out to tourists.

Such was the fate that overtook the greatest theoretician of the modern drama.

The latest theoreticians of the drama take particular pleasure in analyzing Nietzsche's mistakes. They prescribe paths of their own for the drama, setting to rights the blunders of the mad genius. Instead of freeing the drama from the unhealthy growths of mystery mania that so infuriated Nietzsche, they are ready to affirm Nietzsche's mistakes, rejecting his healthy protests against the Wagnerian epidemic. You will remember how "the vilest of men" made his appearance in Zarathustra's cave and began singing hymns to dejection. Where the healthy song of the tragic actor Zarathustra once echoed, we now hear the vilest, the most cloyingly sweet songs.

The most recent theorists of the drama* establish, perhaps correctly, the link between the situation of today and the situation that gave rise to ancient drama (after Nietzsche, such a task is not hard to perform). They help us to resurrect the profound, sometimes forgotten significance of specific features of the drama; they point out that the drama developed from a sacrificial rite as a form of religious cult, and they attempt to revive ritual in modern drama. According to them, the theatre must become a temple. But why must the theatre become a temple when we already have temples as well as theatres? In these temples divine service is celebrated. Holy mysteries are wrought there. "Let holy mysteries be wrought in the theatre too"—that's what the latest theoreticians of the drama say. But what are we to understand by "holy mystery?" And what are we to understand by "divine service?"

Religions past and present give a positive and not a figurative answer to these questions. Whether or not we take this answer into consideration, we understand the sense of it. We also understand the link between the ancient Greek drama and the cult of Dionysos. In Greece, drama moved away from religion as it developed. Eventually the drama was emancipated from religion. We received as our heritage this emancipated drama.

The European theatre developed and fixed the forms in which this emancipation resulted. When we hear these days that theatre is ritual, the actor a priest and that by contemplating drama we are participating in a holy mystery, we understand the words "ritual," "priest," "mystery" in a vague, ambiguous, almost meaningless way. What is "ritual?" Is it

* I hasten to make a reservation: in analyzing the most recent views concerning the development of the drama, I do not have in mind the subtle and profound theory of V. I. Ivanov, with details of which I disagree while accepting its basic theses. I have no intention of analyzing this theory here, since space does not permit it. I do, however, strongly protest against vulgar interpretations of V. I. Ivanov's theory and against conclusions drawn too easily from its basic premises. It is with these too easily drawn conclusions that one has to deal among philosophizing modernists. While giving a serious thinker his due, I cannot but take account of the danger presented by the over-hasty popularization of his views.

some kind of religious act? But of *what* kind? Before whom is this ritual to be enacted? And to what god are wesupposed to pray? Whether or not we are being invited to return to those forms of religion out of which the drama developed remains veiled in mystery.

If we are to do so, then give us a goat for immolation! But what are we to do with a goat after Shakespeare? If some new ritual is implied, then let us know the name of the new god! Where is he? Who is he? Where, O expounders of the future theatre, did you find the new dramas dedicated to this new god? If you don't know the name of this god, if the religion of such a god does not exist, then all the partisan declarations about the future of the modern drama and the new theatre remain mere metaphors, changing nothing in the modern theatre. The "temple" remains the Mariinsky Theatre and rhetoric remains rhetoric.

But the matter is not so simple.

The astute propositions that the stage is an obstacle between actor and audience, between the mythic action and the contemplation of it, and that the spectator should enter into the sphere of the action as a member of the chorus compel us to pay attention to what modern dramatic theorists have to tell us. To the objection that we already have temples without the theatre they reply, not unpersuasively, that a temple is part of a religious cult; that throughout history religious cults, while enshrining a profound and important truth, have inevitably been strangled by scholasticism and dogmatism; that dogmatism paralyzes the free development of religion, but the theatre is a sanctuary that, housing the creative minds of past religions, will itself kindle with the fire of free creativity.

All this would be acceptable if the argument had some basis in reality. In fact, however, the argument runs counter to the work of modern dramatists. The dramatists of today have no thought of uniting stage and auditorium.

Where is the *orchestra* in Ibsen? Where is the *orchestra* in Maeterlinck? How is the dramatic action in Ibsen to be transformed into ritual? According to the prescriptions of the latest theories, should not the famous scene in *An Enemy of the People* (where Stockman makes his speech) be staged in such a way that the auditorium represents a public meeting? But then the choric role assumed by the audience would make a farce of Ibsen's drama. If anyone thought of reviving the ancient drama, it was surely Schiller and not Ibsen or Maeterlinck. However, in *The Bride of Messina* the choric principle is introduced in a formalized and therefore acceptable way.

Granted that the modern drama developed from the ancient, does that mean it will return to it? The rejoinder will be made that the ancient drama represents a thesis; modern drama developed the antithesis, and a synthesis is now being approached. Granted that the Greeks donned tragic masks and erected sacrificial altars, granted that elements of Greek culture have entered into our own—does that make Greeks of us? Does that mean we have to eat olives and prance round a goat? I'd like to see someone try to put that into practice. And so the latest interpreters of the drama remain without practical experience. They talk a great deal about what the drama ought to be. But where is it, this "ought-to-be" drama? It will come, they reply.

Better, though, if it never saw the light of day. And here is the reason why.

Let us suppose that we, the audience, have been transformed into a choric element. Further, that the choric element gives itself over to a dance of supplication. Only then will the remoteness of your supplicatory attitudes from a life unconverted into prayer be thrown into sharp relief. And the prayer will be crushed beneath the weight of life. We must not flee from life into the theatre to sing and dance about the dead goat of tragedy and then, finding ourselves back in the midst of life, feel astounded by our own odd behavior. What is this but a flight from destiny? And destiny will come bursting into the temple-theatre in pursuit, throwing our songs and dances into disarray. We must transform life itself into drama. Otherwise we shall enter the theatrical temple, array ourselves in white garments, crown ourselves with clusters of roses and act out the mystery (the theme of it is always the same—a godlike man locked in a struggle with fate); at the appropriate moment we shall clasp hands and begin to dance. Imagine yourself in such a role, reader, even for a moment. Are we really to whirl about the sacrificial altar, every one of us—the lady in the art nouveau dress, the stockbroker, the worker and the member of the State Council? I am certain that our prayers are unlikely to coincide. The lady in the art nouveau dress will pray to some poet or other in the image and likeness of Dionysos, the worker will pray for a shorter working day, and as for the state councilor—on what star will he fix his gaze? No, better to whirl in a waltz with a pretty young miss than to join hands in a ring dance with a privy councilor.

To this will come the reply that what we are concerned with is the democratic theatre of the future, that genuine community must be rooted in free communes where all is active creativity, that *orchestras* will be the generative focus of these communes. Then we shall be told that all our scepticism results from the fact that we represent a sheltered, secluded (in other words, bourgeois) way of life, that in the popular theatre unconstrained mythopoeia will be resurrected. But the popular theatre is the fairground sideshow where Churkin the bandit has long held sway, while the cinematograph is tending more and more to assume the role allotted to the future democratic theatre. Moreover, the cinematograph has its own mythopoeia: a man sneezes and bursts—an edifying victim of the fatal struggle . . . with the common cold. Further: if we are to speak of collective creation—it already exists. Why is the ringdance we can see in any village not an *orchestra*? Poor Russia, they are threatening to swamp her with *orchestra's* when she has long been swamped with them. Go for an evening stroll in the countryside and you will encounter both the choric element and collective creativity . . . of unprintable words. Such are the results of drawing conclusions from a theory that fails to take account of the concrete forms of life. They are preparing to swamp Russian with *orchestras* when the time has long been ripe to rid her of them.

As long as the class struggle exists, these appeals to aesthetic democratism have an odd ring. And how absurd, how infinitely absurd, is this democratic theatre-temple of communal mythopoeia (as yet, thank God, completely non-existent!). In the absence of such a theatre, they turn to the past. Aeschylus, Sophocles and Euripides are revived in the theatre. Sometimes the devices of Aeschylus are successfully imitated (V. Ivanov). But what democratism is there in this? Is it not an aristocratic satiety that compels us to seek aesthetic pleasure in the religious dramas of a people alien to us? If the sacrificial altar of Dionysos were to be solemnly raised in the new theatre, would it not become a symbol of supreme blasphemy against the theatre, against ourselves, against art and against the sacred beliefs of a noble people?

The emblematic invocations to Dionysos remain, thank God, the personal lyricism (a lyricism how beautiful and profound!), far removed from life, of the theorists of the new drama. But these invocations create no disturbance. The temple remains the Mariinsky Theatre.

The fatal contradiction in which the theorists of the new drama have become entangled is that in inviting us into the theatre as into a temple they have forgotten that a temple presupposes a cult, and a cult—the name of a god, i.e. a religion. As long as they do not have this name, their attempts at a new kind of religious creation have no basis. The bringing to birth of a new religion on the boards of the stage is an impossibility, as are the theatre as temple and the drama as ritual. Ritual devoid of form and purpose is nothing but the posturing of actors introduced into the sacred region of the spirit where burns the hope for the creation of life. If in the modern theatre—theatre pure and simple—the actor is no more than an actor, perhaps this limiting of his function allows him greater freedom in the creation of a particular role. The priestly diadem would have crushed the actor, had he not contrived to transform it into a jester's cap. At present the actor, by absorbing himself in his role, is able to make contact with those prototypes of vital creation which also obscurely agitated the dramatist. While to us he remains an actor, he is within himself the precursor of something different, something vital. But suppose we elevate him to be the tragic sacrifice; the very sacrificial element in his self-surrender to the prototypes of the life to come is made to ring false. The man is profaned in the actor.

The tragic dilemma of the theorists of the new drama lies in the fact that, while taking note of Nietzsche's error (he confused the inner fire of the drama with its form), they promise, remaining within the bounds of the theatre, to set off an explosion which will shatter the dead forms of life and creation by the transfiguration of form. What results is a mock explosion of bengal lights on the stage: life remains life, theatre theatre.

1908

FYODOR SOLOGUB

Fyodor Sologub (1863-1927), poet, novelist, dramatist and translator, was born in St. Petersburg of humble parentage. The aristocratic "Sologub" (Count Sollogub—with an extra "l"—was a popular writer of the mid-nineteenth century) was a pen name assumed on the advice of literary associates who found his real name, Teternikov, lacking in grace. In 1882 Sologub completed his studies at a teachers training college, after which he taught in the provinces until his removal to St. Petersburg in 1892. In 1899 he became a school inspector, and in 1907 growing literary success and a pension enabled him to devote himself exclusively to writing. Sologub's early years of struggle as a provincial schoolmaster in the gray, repressive 1880s are reflected in his novels *Bad Dreams* (1896) and *The Petty Demon* (1907); the second of these (which he successfully dramatized in 1909) was perhaps the last novel written in Russia to contribute a proverbial type to the national imagination in the figure of the odious Peredonov, who seems to concentrate in his person all the ignorance, malice, servility and paranoia of Russian minor officialdom.

With such a background, Sologub might have been expected to go the way of social protest, as the "plebeian" writers of the 1860s had done before him. Sologub's protest, however, was of a different kind: he became the most thoroughgoingly decadent of the Decadents (at least in his works), tirelessly reiterating the supremacy of art and the artist's creative will. A private mythology, strongly tinged with ninety-ish diabolism and Schopenhauerian pessimism, is pervasive in Sologub's work. His central myth is of the sun as a malevolent dragon who rules the world; thus life itself and all that draws us toward life are seen as an evil, darkness and death as a longed-for good. The potency of art is embodied in another favorite myth, drawn from *Don Quixote*: the figure of the simple peasant wench Aldonza metamorphosed by the Don's creative will into Dulcinea del Toboso, a vision of transcendental beauty. It may be objected that these "myths" of Sologub's are too deliberately invented, insufficiently steeped in the profoundest depths of the imagination; perhaps they are best regarded as something between a useful literary device and a strategy for survival.

Sologub's last years were tragic. Although he welcomed the end of tsarist rule, he was unsympathetic to the Bolsheviks. Plans to emigrate were abandoned after the suicide of his wife and literary collaborator

Anastasia Chebotariovskaya in 1921. Sologub published nothing after 1923, making a living by translation and occupying various posts in the Leningrad Writers' Union.

While Sologub's dramatic work does not quite reach the level of his best fiction and poetry (which Mirsky has called "the most refined and most delicate of all modern Russian poetry"), it exhibits at its best an impressive mastery of the theatre and a hard, ironic brilliance. The "Mystery" *A Liturgy for Myself* (1907), a hieratic ceremony of sacrifice and mystic communion that owes something to Viacheslav Ivanov, was Sologub's first attempt at dramatic form. His practical involvement with the theatre dates from his friendship with Meyerhold, "to whom," in his wife's words, "he more than once entrusted the production of his plays on the basis of their identity of outlook."

The Triumph of Death was Meyerhold's last production at Komissarzhevskaya's theatre (November, 1907). The play was interpreted by some as a parable of the failure of the 1905 Revolution: Algista, the beautiful daughter of the people, is broken by a petrified autocracy. The prologue, the most "Meyerholdian" part of the play, was in fact written after Meyerhold's production; its abrupt dislocation of planes bears unmistakable witness to the influence of Blok's *Puppet Show*. The decor demanded by the play, with its great sweeping staircases, offered considerable scenic possibilities; had Meyerhold been allowed to have his way and to bring the staircases down into the auditorium itself, *The Triumph of Death* would have formally broken the barrier between performers and audience, thus realizing a cherished dream of the Symbolist theatre.

The lyrical tragedy *The Gift of the Wise Bees* (1907) was the second of three dramas by Russian Symbolists to take as its subject the myth of Laodamia. Clearly, this parable of the supremacy of the creative imagination over death itself had a special fascination for the Symbolists. The play—one of the author's finest—was banned by the censor, possibly because Sologub had added some spice to his myth by providing the hero, Protesilaus, with a handsome young lover, the sculptor Lysippus, who is constrained to yield to Laodamia his wax figure of Protesilaus only by the intervention of Aphrodite. In general, the Symbolists were pioneers in treating sexually unorthodox themes; it was a natural consequence of their cult of individualism and self-fulfillment at all costs. In the original version of a short play written by Sologub at this time, *In the Name of Love*, a father and daughter confess their mutual passion and decide to confront the world; in the revised version, the daughter is revealed, at the last possible moment, to be adopted, but this *coup de théâtre* in no way alters the essence of the situation, since she has already declared: "It makes no difference to my heart whether you are my father or not."

Sologub's next play, *Vanka the Steward and the Page Jehan*, was given its first performance at Komissarzhevskaya's theatre in January 1909, under the direction of Evreinov, another kindred spirit, according to the author's wife. More rigorously than any other drama of the period, *Vanka* formalizes the duality of vision central to the Symbolist theatre by means of an ingenious constructive device: a simple tale of adultery is subjected to contrasting treatment in a series of alternating scenes; those set in ancient Russia strike a note of coarse lechery, while those set in medieval France breath an air of refined chivalry. Thus the spectator is constantly thrust from one plane to another, exactly in the manner prescibed by Meyerhold's "grotesque theatre." Curiously enough, only the play's "Russian" scenes were well received by contemporary audiences. For a later (1915) production, Sologub added a third, modern, variant of the adultery theme and gave the play a new title that might be rendered in English as *Hanky-Panky through the Ages* (this version has remained unpublished).

A kind of pendant to *Vanka*, and another playful excursion into *style russe*, was the parodistic fairytale play *Night Dances*, which bristles with facetious anachronisms and literary "in" jokes. Evreinov's 1909 production of this play was a lighthearted amateur affair that seems to have included in its cast half of literary and artistic St. Petersburg—among the writers, Voloshin, A. Tolstoi, Remizov and Gorodetsky, and among the painters, Bakst and Somov; the dances of the title were choreographed by Fokine.

Sologub's greatest theatrical success, if hardly his best play, was *Hostages of Life*, which Meyerhold staged at the Alexandrinsky Theatre in 1912 with elaborate art nouveau sets by Golovin and—a modish touch—some barefoot dancing à la Isadora Duncan (whom the author much admired). In *Hostages*, Sologub attempted, not altogether satisfactorily, to reconcile traditional realistic drama and the theatre of Symbolism by combining contemporary setting and types—some Chekhovian decaying gentry, a strong-willed "man of the future"—with characters whose function is almost purely symbolic, notably Lilith, "the first wife of Adam," who leaves the architect hero in order that her place may be taken by the more prosaic Katia. Lilith, we are given to understand, represents "The Dream" and Katia "Life," and the play concludes with the apotheosis of Lilith, "crowned with a golden diadem and her face lit by a solemn light," in which we recognize not only the tone, but also the familiar *Don Quixote* imagery of *The Triumph of Death*: "I am weary, mortally weary. Many centuries have passed over me—I summon man to me and, my noble task accomplished, I go my way. And still Dulcinea remains uncrowned." In his article "Aldonza Ascending," written at about this time for inclusion in a volume dedicated to the memory of Komissarzhevskaya, Sologub interpreted the great actress's career as the gradual transformation of Aldonza into Dulcinea.

Sologub's later plays reveal a catastrophic decline in his powers as a dramatist. *Love over the Abysses* (1914) is another attempt to write a symbolical drama of contemporary life, but this time it is entirely abstract, in the manner of Andreyev. The plot strongly recalls Andreyev's *To the Stars*, with its conflict between the contemplative and the active man—"He," who lives on a mountaintop and observes the stars, and "The Man of Earth," a Nietzschean entrepreneur of a type much in vogue during this period of industrial expansion. Even a final *Liebestod* fails to relieve the play's solemn banality.

"The Theatre of the Single Will" (1908), for all its perverse extremism and the arrogant solipsism of its tone, is perhaps Russian Symbolism's most ambitious attempt to formulate a coherent theatrical aesthetic—one which has much in common with Meyerhold's early "static" theatre. The term "single will" is borrowed from Sologub's favorite philosopher, Schopenhauer, whose method of argument—from subjective intuitions to sweeping generalizations—the Russian writer may also be said to have borrowed.

Fyodor Sologub
The Theatre of the Single Will[23]

> "Upon the vessel is a seal, upon the seal a name; what is concealed in the vessel is known only to him who affixed the seal and to the initiate."
>
> E. K. Vizener. *The Silence of the First Bride. A Novel.*[24]

> "You philosophize like a poet."
>
> Dostoevsky. *Letters.*

Of all things created by the genius of man, perhaps the most joyous on its visible surface and the most terrible in its depths, when fathomed, is the theatre. The fatal progression—play; spectacle; mystery . . . This is as true of light comedy and knockabout farce as it is of high tragedy.

Tragic horror and the laughter of the buffoon stir the fraying but still seductive veils of our world with equally irresistible force—the world that seemed so familiar to us, all at once, in the fluidity of play, becomes astonishing, dreadful, overwhelming or repulsive. Neither the tragic nor the comic mask will deceive the attentive spectator any more than, in enchanting him, they have deceived the participant in play, or will deceive, in admitting him to the sacrament, the participant in mystery.

Behind the mouldering vizards, behind the berouged mug of the fairground buffoon, behind the pale mask of the tragic actor, there glimmers a single Countenance. Terrible, summoning irresistibly . . . .

The fatal progression. We played when we were children—but now our hearts have become dead to carefree play, and, filled with curiosity, we have come to gaze at a spectacle; and the hour will strike when, transfigured in body and spirit, we shall find true union in liturgical drama, in sacramental rite . . . .

When we were children, when we were alive—

> "Children, only children live,
> We are dead, long dead"—[25]

we used to play. We allotted roles among ourselves and played them—until we were summoned to bed. Our theatre was partly that of everyday life—we were very observant and given to mimicry—partly symbolical, with strong leanings toward decadence, such was our fondness for fairytale, for the words of strange and ancient incantations, for the whole diverting and useless—from the practical point of view—ceremony of play. How delightful were the conventions, naiveties and absurdities of play. We knew very well that it wasn't real, that it was all make-believe. We made no great demands on the stage designer or the props man. We would harness a chair and agree among ourselves:

— Let that be a horse.

Or if we felt like running about more ourselves, then we would say:

— I'll be a horse.

Our play was not exclusive or one-sided in nature. There was the play meant for a big audience, for passages and halls, for gardens and fields, with crowds and hubbub and boisterousness—"half play, half brawl"—and there were intimate games played in secluded corners where grown-ups and strangers would never look. There we had been merry to the point of exhaustion, here it was creepy, but merry too, and our cheeks grew redder from this play than from boisterous chasing about, and in our eyes dim fires were kindled.

We played—and we did not know that our games were only cast-offs from the lives of the grown-ups. We played again what had been played before, as if it were new. And in this replaying of the games of others, we became infected with the potent poison of the dead.

However, it was not in the actual content of our play that its significance lay. The drops of burning poison dissolved in the external nectar of youth. The exuberance of life's novelty went to our heads like a light, sweet wine, swift running lent wings to our feet—in the bliss of bright self-forgetfulness, the oppressive burden of terrestrial time was consumed. And the sharp, swift moments were consumed, and from the ashes was fashioned a new world—our world. A world aflame with the ecstasy of youth . . . .

And even later did we desire anything more from play—from tragedy or comedy—which had now become no more than a spectacle to us? We love to go to the theatre—especially to first nights of famous plays—but what is it we want of the theatre? Is it that we wish to learn the art of life, to purge ourselves of dark emotions? To solve some moral, social, aesthetic or perhaps some other kind of problem? To gaze upon the "reed shaken by the wind? Upon a man arrayed in soft garments? Upon a prophet?"

Of course, all this and much else besides can be dragged into the theatre, not without reason and even not without profit—but in the true theatre all this must be consumed to ashes, as old clothes are burned on a bonfire. And however varied the external content of the drama, we always want of it—if any life from the carefree days of our childhood remains in us—the same thing that we wanted of our childish play: ardent delight to ravish the spirit from the constraining fetters of tedious and barren life. Enchantment and delight—these are what draw each of us to the theatre, these are the means by which the genius of tragedy involves us in its mysterious design. But of what does this design consist?

Either I have no idea why man needs the drama, or it exists in order to lead man unto Me; to transport him from the realm of the capricious Aisa,[26] from the strange and ridiculous world of chance, from the region of comedy, to the realm of the strict and consoling Ananka, the world of necessity and freedom, the region of high tragedy; to abolish life's temptations and to crown the eternal consolatrix—not the false one, but the one who will not deceive.

A theatrical spectacle to which we come to be amused and diverted will not remain simply a spectacle for long. Soon the spectator, wearied with a succession of scenes alien to him, will want to become a participant in mystery as he was once a participant in play. He who has been expelled from Eden will soon be knocking with a bold hand at the door behind which the bridegroom feasts with the wise virgins. He was a participant in innocent play when he was still alive, when he was still a dweller in paradise, in My beautiful garden between the two great rivers. And now his only path to resurrection is to become a participant in mystery, in liturgical rite to join his hand with the hand of his brother, with the hand of his sister, and to touch with lips ever parched the cup, the fullness whereof is a mystery, in which I "mingle blood with water"; to perform in a temple flooded with light and thronged with people that which is now performed only in the catacombs.

But the theatre of spectacle is an unavoidable transitional stage, and in our time, unfortunately, the theatre cannot yet be other than a mere spectacle, and frequently an empty one at that. Mere spectacle—that is, unless we are speaking of the intimate theatre that must be brought into being, but to speak of which—indeed, how can one speak of it? Would that not be a temptation for the uninitiate? . . . How can one speak of it but in hints and images?

It is spectacle that the modern theatre wishes above all to be. Everything is geared toward spectacle alone. Professional actors, footlights and curtain, skillfully painted sets aiming to give an illusion of reality, the ingenious contrivances of the realistic theatre, the profundities of the stylized theatre—all these exist for the sake of spectacle.

However, if the path along which the theatre must develop if it is to attain its high destiny has already become clear in our mind, then the task that confronts the man of the theatre—the dramatist, the director and the actor—is, in raising the theatrical spectacle to those heights that only spectacle can attain, to bring it closer to communal drama, to the mystery play, to liturgy.

It seems to me that the first obstacle to be overcome on this path is the performing actor. The actor claims too much of the spectator's attention, thus overshadowing both drama and author. The more talented the actor, the more intolerable to the author his tyranny, the more harmful to the tragedy. There are two ways of overthrowing this seductive but nevertheless harmful tyranny: either to move the center of the performance out to the spectator in the auditorium or to move it behind the scenes to the author.

The first thought that might logically follow upon the recognition of the theatre as an appropriate forum for the communal drama might be that it is necessary to abolish the footlights, to take away the curtain perhaps and to make the spectator a participant in, or even the creator of the performance. Instead of flat drops, to have four gaily painted walls or the open-air expanse of street or square or field; to transform spectacle into masquerade, which is in fact a combination of play and spectacle. But in that case what would be the point of gathering together? Simply in order than "the peoples should congregate," as a certain popular refrain has it? A harmless enough pastime, certainly—but where does it lead?

It is true that an element of the mysterious is admixed with play and spectacle in the masquerade—hints of it, secrets. But this is not the mystery itself. Just as the most terrible fears come at noontide, when, risen to his zenith and hidden behind his violet shields, the evil Dragon weaves his spells, so the deepest mystery is revealed only when the masks are removed.

All meridians meet at a single pole (or, if you like, two—but by the law of the identity of opposite poles, it is always sufficient to talk of a single pole), all earthly paths lead to a single eternal Rome—"always and in all things there is only I and no Other, there was not and shall not be"—every coming together of people is meaningful only insofar as it brings man to Me, from vain and delusive division to genuine union. The pathos of the mystery play is nourished by the transformation of the fortuitous many into a necessary unity. This pathos is a reminder that every individual earthly existence is only an instrument to serve Me, an instrument for exhausting in the infinity of earthly experiences the multitude of My potential existences, the totality of which creates laws while itself moving freely.

For this reason, then, there is in tragedy only one who acts and wills, which adds to the unities of action, place and time another unity—that of volitional impulse in the drama.

(Perhaps the thought transitions here will seem somewhat unexpected to some, but I am not conducting an argument, being incapable of doing so, but simply expounding my own thought. "I philosophize like a poet.").

There can never in tragedy be more than one who acts and wills, not in the sense that he is the leader of the choric action, but in that he expresses the inevitable, not in the person of the tragic hero, but by his fate.

The modern theatre presents a sad spectacle of divided will and, in consequence, fragmented action. "People are different from each other," thinks the simple-minded dramatist, "it takes all sorts to make a world." He goes all over the place, noting manners, customs, details of everyday living, he observes various people and depicts all of this in a very lifelike manner. Kozmodemiansky, Nalimov and Vaksel are able to recognize themselves and their neckties, and are delighted if the author, for friendship's sake, has flattered them, or they get angry if the author makes it clear that their appearance and behavior are not to his liking. The director is delighted to have the material to mount an entertaining production. The actor too is delighted to have the chance to demonstrate his skill in applying make-up, and proceeds to ape the quirks and appearance of the painter K, the poet U, the engineer A, the lawyer V . . . . The public is in raptures—it recognizes both those with whom it is acquainted and those with whom it is not—and is conscious of having one indisputable advantage: whatever commonplace peccadilloes are dragged onto the stage, every spectator, apart from a small number portrayed in the play, sees quite clearly that not he, but someone else, is under attack.

And none of this is needed. There is no everyday living, there are no customs—an eternal mystery is being played out, and that is all. There are no stories, no plots; all the expositions have long been exposed, all the revelations have long been revealed—there is only the eternal liturgy that is being accomplished. What are words and dialogues? There is only one eternal dialogue, and he who asks the question answers it himself and longs for an answer. And what are the themes? Only Love, only Death.

Different people do not exist—there is in the entire universe only a single being, a single I that wills, acts, suffers, burns with unquenchable fire and seeks refuge from the rage of life, with its horror and ugliness, in the comforting embraces of the eternal consoler—Death.

Many are the masks I don at will, but always and in all things I remain Myself—as a Chaliapine remains the same in all his roles. And beneath the terrible mask of the tragic hero, and beneath the ridiculous disguise of the jester, whom the comedy makes a jest of, and in the motley sewn together from rags of many colors worn by the clown whose grimaces amuse the gallery—beneath each of these camouflages the spectator must discover Me. The theatrical spectacle must present itself to his gaze like a problem containing a single unknown quantity.

It may be that the spectator has come to the theatre as the simple-minded come into the world, "to see the sun," but I, a poet, create drama in order to re-create the world according to my new conception. As My will alone is supreme in the great world, so in the smaller circle of the theatrical spectacle a single will—the poet's—must reign supreme.

The drama is the product of a single conception in the same way that the universe is the product of a single creative thought. The author alone is fate in tragedy, chance in comedy. Is his then the dominant will in everything? As he wills, so shall it be. At whim he can unite the lovers or bring about their sorrowful parting, raise up his protagonist or cast him down into the grim abyss of ruin and despair. He can, if he wishes, award the garland to beauty, youth, fidelity, courage, mad audacity, selflessness—but there is nothing to prevent him from exalting deformity and depravity and placing Judas the betrayer above all the apostles.

> "In reproach to the unjust day[28]
> I shall raise up detraction to rule the world,
> And tempting, shall not tempt in vain."

The actor is full of conceit. He has overshadowed the author by the irrelevancies of his interpretation, by his unsuitable and disjointed social and psychological observations; he has transformed the drama itself into a collection of roles for various *emplois*. Then the director comes along and appropriates the author's stage directions. At the director's command, the drama's nemesis, the hollow voice of imperious

Moira, is pent up in a prompter's box, and when rehearsals have been too few all the players stare at that single point, whence, to the vexation of the front rows, issues a voice. To make matters worse, the poet's words are mercilessly garbled.

But does anyone imagine that it is my wish that my voice should issue from a narrow subterranean cell? That the windows of my imagining should be transformed at the director's caprice into perfectly pointless pillars? That the words of my stage directions should be embodied in painted sets alone?

No, my word must ring out loud and clear. The theatre-goer must hear the poet rather than the actor.

This is how I envisage a theatrical performance: the author, or a reader standing in for him—and perhaps a reader would be better, not being agitated by authorial nervousness before an audience that will shout at him either in praise or blame (the one as unpleasant as the other), and who may even have brought keys with them to facilitate cheery whistling—the reader, then, will be seated close to the stage, somewhat to one side. In front of him will a desk, and on the desk the play that is to be presented. The reader will begin in due order, from the beginning:

He will read the title of the drama. The name of the author.

The epigraph, if there is one. Some interesting and instructive epigraphs are to be met with. For example, the epigraph to *The Inspector General*: "No use complaining about the mirror if your mug's crooked. Popular saying." A crude epigraph—such was this writer—but just, and an effective means of establishing the appropriate link between the audience and the stage action.

Then an enumeration of the *dramatis personae*.

The preface or author's remarks, if there are any.

The first act. The setting. The names of the characters on stage.

The entrances and exits of the actors, if they are indicated in the text of the drama.

All stage directions, not excluding the shortest, if only a single word.

As the reader proceeds, the curtain goes up, the setting indicated by the author is revealed and illuminated, the actors come on stage and do whatever they are prompted to by the author's stage directions and speak as directed by the text. If an actor forgets his lines—and when does he not forget them!—the reader reads them for him, as calmly and clearly as everything else.

The action unfolds before the audience as it unfolds before us in life itself: we walk about and talk, so it seems to us, by our own will; we do what we need to, or what comes into our head, and we try to realize what we suppose to be our own desires, insofar as the laws of nature or the desires of others do not hinder us; we see, hear, smell, touch, taste; we use all our senses and all our powers of intelligence to ascertain what exists in the world of reality, what has its own existence and its own laws, partly comprehensible to us, partly miraculous; we feel love toward one and hatred toward another, and we are moved by yet other passions, determining in accordance with them our relationship to people and to the world. Usually we are unaware that we have no independent will, that our every movement and every word are dictated to us and long ago anticipated, once and for all, in the daemonic creative plan of universal play. For us there can be neither choice nor freedom; even the charming interpolations of the actor are denied us, since they too are included in the text of the universal mystery play by some censor unknown; and the world we apprehend is nothing but a stage set, marvelous to the eye but hiding all the dirt and slovenliness of backstage. We play as best we can the role allotted to us, actors and spectators at once, alternately applauding and whistling each other, at once sacrificing and brought to the sacrifice.

Is the theatre able to offer us any spectacle except that of a world too wide for our powers and too narrow for our will? And indeed, should it? Act as you live, put life upon the stage—is this not exactly what the realistic theatre wants?

But what then will remain of the actor's art? The actor, it would seem, is to be transformed into a talking puppet, and this cannot but be displeasing to the actor, who loves "strong" roles, the undivided attention of the orchestra seats, the shrieks of the simple-minded gallery and the journalistic hubbub about his name. Such a theatre is unacceptable to the modern actor. He will say contemptuously:

That won't be a theatrical performance, but simply a literary reading with accompanying dialogue and movement. If that's what you want, you'd do better to go ahead and build a puppet theatre to amuse the children. Let painted dolls move, let one man behind the scenes speak in seven different voices—let him speak and pull the strings.

But why, after all, should the actor not be like a puppet? For a human being there is no insult in that. Such is the immutable law of universal play—that man should resemble a marvelously constructed puppet. And he cannot escape that; he cannot even forget it.

The hour appointed for all will strike; each of us, in the sight of his fellows, will turn into an inert, lifeless doll, no longer capable of performing any role . . . .

There on the sackcloth it lies, this discarded and useless doll, for the final ablution, its hands folded, its legs stretched out, its eyes closed—a pitiful puppet fit for tragic play alone! Back there, behind the scenes, someone used to jerk indifferently at your invisible string, some cruel being put you to the slow fire of suffering, some evil being terrified you with the pale horrors of loathsome existence, and in your death agony you turned your yearning gaze toward some being without pity. And here, in the orchestra seats, someone has been amused by your awkward movements as you responded to the jerking of the terrible string, by your incoherent words (so quietly did the hidden prompter whisper them), your useless tears and your laughter, no less pitiful than your tears. Enough; your lines have all been delivered after a fashion, all the stage directions have been followed faithfully enough; the string is wound up and in vain your parched lips attempt to utter a new word; they open, they shut mechanically—and are silent forever. They put a sheet over you, bury you, forget you . . . .

An actor, even the most gifted, is no more than a man. The role he plays, however powerful, is less than life and easier than life. Clearly it is better for him to be a talking puppet moving in obedience to the clear and unimpassioned voice of the reader than to make a desperate muddle of his part to the accompaniment of the hoarse whispering of the prompter hidden in his box.

The level and unimpassioned voice of the "man in black" alone directs the entire theatrical performance, and in conformity with this, everything on the stage must strive toward the unity essential if the spectator's precarious attention is to be held and not distracted in any way from the one important thing—the revelation through dramatic action of My countenance, ever one and unchanging beneath its manifold masks.

The performer is never alone on stage. Even when no other actors are visible, he who remains before the eyes of the audience is conducting an uninterrupted dialogue. The striving toward the one, toward Me, can proceed only from my polar opposite—from the many, the not-I. But all streams must mingle at last in a single sea and not be lost in the quicksands of the divided many. The one Countenance hidden beneath the masks must be revealed to the audience as the action proceeds; consequently there should be a single protagonist, a single personage upon whom the action rests, a single spot upon which the audience's attention should be fixed. All the rays of the stage action must meet in a single focal point; only then will the bright flame of rapture suddenly flare . . .

The other characters in the drama should be no more than necessary steps in the progression toward the one Countenance. Their dramatic significance will depend entirely on their closeness to the center of the drama's volitional impulse, as revealed in the protagonist. In their ordering on the descending steps of a single ladder of dramatic action lies the basis for their differentiation as individuals, for their distinctness as characters, which would not otherwise be of the slightest use to the drama. Desdemona is important in the tragic situation not because her role is a large and touching one, not because Othello loved her and destroyed her, but because she was the fatal one whose hand stripped him of his mask and at the same time revealed to him the fatally false and ambiguous nature of the world.

Given that the tragedy should have, in essence, a single actor, it follows that the theatre should free itself of acting as such. Acting, with all its variety of accurately observed and faithfully transmitted gestures and intonations, with everything that has passed into theatrical tradition, is acquired by assiduous study or invented anew by the imagination and intuition of the gifted actor—this familiar kind of acting, whether the product of inspiration or calculation, depicts the collision and the struggle between individuals who are quite separate from each other, who are sufficient unto themselves. But there are no such autonomous personalities on the face of the earth, and consequently there can be no struggles among them; there is only the appearance of struggle, a fatal dialectic expressed by the characters. Nor is it possible to conceive of a struggle with fate—there is only daemonic play, fate amusing itself with its puppets.

The better an actor plays the role of Man, the more pathetic his cry:

Let our shields ring, let our swords clash—the more ridiculously inappropriate his acting, the clearer his failure to understand his role. "Someone in Gray" has yet to accept a challenge to a duel. A little girl doesn't fight with her dolls—she rips them apart and breaks them, laughing or crying as the mood takes her.

We find acting that is too much in earnest ridiculous; splendid declamation, noble gesture, excessively painstaking reproduction of the particulars of everyday life—we feel a little uncomfortable in the presence of such wonders, much as we feel uncomfortable in polite society when someone suddenly begins talking loudly and agitatedly, waving his arms about. It isn't worth acting too much in earnest. Only the gallery is made to laugh and weep by what is being performed on the stage—the orchestra seats smile faintly, sometimes with a touch of sadness, sometimes almost gleefully, but always ironically. It's not worth acting for them.

Tragedy strips from the world its mask of enchantment, and where we thought we saw harmony, pre-established or created, it opens before us the eternal contradictoriness of the world, the eternal identity of good and evil and of other polar opposites. It confirms all contradictions, and to every one of life's pretensions, justified or otherwise, it returns an ironic *Yes!* Neither to good nor to evil will it return a lyrical *No!* Tragedy is always ironic, never lyric. And that is how it ought to be staged.

For this reason there must be no acting. Only a level word-by-word delivery. The calm enactment of situations, scene by scene. And the fewer there are of these scenes, the more slowly they succeed each other, the more clearly will the tragic idea emerge before the charmed spectator. Let not the tragic actor strain and strut—exaggerated gesture and pompous declamation should be left to buffoons and clowns. The actor must be cold and calm; his every word must be measured and grave, his every gesture deliberate and beautiful. A tragic presentation should not bring to mind the flickering scenes of a cinematograph. Without this flickering, which is both irritating and unnecessary, the attentive spectator must travel the long road to the understanding of tragedy.

Furthest of all from the spectator stands the tragic protagonist, the chief manifestation of My will—and the road to the understanding of him is the longest of all; to approach him, the spectator must climb steep steps, must surmount and vanquish many things both within him and without. The further from the protagonist, the closer to the spectator, the more comprehensible to him, until at last the personages of the drama become so close to the spectator that they emerge with him more or less completely. They become similar to the chorus in ancient tragedy, saying the things that any of those seated on the steps of the amphitheatre would say.

And so the peaceable, self-satisfied bourgeois comes to the theatre. How will he be able to accept exposition and denouement, what will he understand of the drama if all the speeches that resound from the stage are alien to his way of thought? As the tragedies of Shakespeare could not dispense with the clown, the modern drama cannot dispense with these banal tailor's dummies with their blank faces, their creaking mechanism somewhat in need of repair, their dim, commonplace words. And if the bourgeois himself should shudder at their intolerable banality, so much the better—it will be a comforting sign that he too is approaching an understanding of the one Countenance concealed beneath the various masks, profaned but not destroyed by the banality of terrestrial utterance.

Therein lies the true justification of light comedy, of farce—even of the buffoonery of the Punch and Judy show. And even of pornography.

There is yet another significance to this, since it is as yet the sole means available to the popular theatre—again I refrain from speaking of the intimate theatre, so close to our hearts but so difficult to speak of—the sole means of bringing the spectator into the action. The sole means—and in many cases perhaps an adequate one.

Even the mystery play itself, although a form of drama in the highest degree communal, nevertheless demands a single performer—both priest and sacrifice—for the sacrament of self-immolation. Not only the highest type of social activity, the mystery, but social achievement in general is at the same time utterly individual. Any common cause is carried through by the thought and planning of a single individual—any parliament will listen to an orator rather than sink into a cheerful hubbub of communion. "Upon the vessel is a seal, upon the seal a name; what is concealed in the vessel is known only to him who affixed the seal and to the initiate." The temple is open to all, but the name of the builder is incised upon the stone. He who approaches the altar must leave his anger at the threshold. Therefore the crowd—the audience—cannot participate in the tragedy unless their outworn and banal words be consumed by fire within them. Only in passivity. The dramatic performer is always alone.

How can it be in the interest of the stage to flood it with a multitude of players, each one of whom lays claim to a character of his own and an individual role in the drama? Their fleeting appearances can only be irritating to anyone with an understanding of the drama; it is hard to remember who they are supposed to be, and of little point to do so. For this reason drama is difficult to read—you have to keep glancing at the list of *dramatis personae*. No wonder drama is little favored by the bookseller.

Is it not a matter of indifference to me whether Shuisky or Vorotynsky[29] is bustling about on the stage if I know that the tragedy of imposture, so brilliantly conceived by the genius of Russian history (and so palely outlined by the genius of Russian literature), is being enacted before me? One man speaks, and after him another—but are these not your own words, simple-minded spectator? Mingled with the pure gold of poetry, are not these your own pennies—dull, worn, but nonetheless dear to your heart—rolling on the boards?

It is a naive calculation—but a wise and true one—that as the theatregoer greedily picks up his pennies, he will pick up My heavy gold with them and sell me in exchange his soul, which, though it be of little weight, is dear to me. All the same, the less of this small change rolling about the boards the better: a plea addressed to dramatists.

As there is in the drama but a single will, the author's, and a single performer, the actor, so there should also be a single spectator. The insane monarch who would attend a performance alone in his magnificent theatre, hidden behind a heavy curtain in the darkness and silence of the royal box, was right in this respect. In the tragic theatre, every spectator must feel himself to be this insane king, hidden from everybody. No one must see his face, and no one must be surprised if

> "With mystery he veiled[30]
> The play of his passions,
> Sometimes at graveside gay
> And gloomy at the feast."

And if he should lightly doze or even fall into a profound slumber, what is art but a golden sleep, and why should not the drama be a rhythmic dream? There will be no one to laugh at him, no one to be disturbed or shocked by an unexpected snore at the most pathetic moment.

The spectator himself should neither see nor hear anyone—neither those whose faces artlessly reflect all their feelings, moods, chagrins and sympathies, nor those who pretend to understanding and intelligence; neither the handkerchief raised to the reddened eye nor the glove nervously crumpled in the restless hand. He should remain impervious to those who blow their noses and snivel and to those who laugh, even if they laugh and weep in the right places. He who views the tragic show should sit in silence and darkness and solitude. Like the prompter in his narrow box. Like a theatre mouse.

With nothing extraneous to distract him, neither should the spectator be distracted by anything on stage that is not strictly necessary to the drama. Whether the decor consists of beautifully painted sets or simply drapes, the stage must be arranged in a single plane. The stage picture should be like a painting, and the spectator's gaze should not be drawn beyond the actor into the depths of a multidimensional stage, into the region of the hidden, when his attention should be concentrated on him who acts and wills and contemplates.

It is pleasant to have scenery—it immediately creates an appropriate mood, giving the spectator all the visual hints—what then should we have against it? In the great world outside also:

"At once all seemed to me
A flat backcloth—
The dawn stretched like painted paper,
A star sparkled like tinsel."

But he who is absorbed in the world of external decor has come to the theatre in order to find himself—in order to come unto Me.

His gaze should not be distracted by an oversumptuous diversity of scenery. For this reason, incidentally, it is better that one set should serve for the entire drama. At all events, at any given moment the spectator should know what he ought to be looking at, what it is that he should see and hear on stage. In this he will be assisted by the author's stage directions as clearly enunciated by the reader, and of course he will also be helped by all available mechanical devices. Everything in the stage picture must be significant, every detail of the setting must be carefully pondered, so that nothing superfluous, nothing apart from what is absolutely essential is presented to the spectator.

Toward the same end, care should be taken with lighting; perhaps the spectator should be shown only what he is supposed to be seeing at a given moment, while everything else should be swallowed in darkness—just as everything on which our present attention is not fixed slips beneath the threshold of consciousness. It exists, but at the same time it is as if it did not exist. Because there exists for me only that which is within Me and for Me—everything else, though it may possibly possess reality for someone, lies dormant in the world of the possible, no more than awaiting its turn to be.

Such, in outline, is the form the theatrical spectacle should take. And the content to be invested in this form—the tragic game Fate plays with its puppets, the spectacle of the fatal dissolution of all terrestrial masks—is the mystery of perfect self-affirmation. I play, my playthings being dolls and masks, and, as the world looks on, masks and veils fall away and My unique will rejoices in its triumph. It is my own fatal error that ties all the strands of the plot, and I must struggle in the ever-tightening toils of irresolvable earthly contradictions until the fatal knots are sundered by a sharp stiletto that pierces Me to the heart. My lighthearted play has brought worlds into being—I am sacrifice and I am priest. Burning love consoles and, burning, is consumed; the ultimate consoler is Death.

The theatre, it is clear, gravitates toward tragedy. It must become tragic.

In our time, any farce will become tragedy; to a sensitive ear, our laughter is more terrible than our weeping and our rapture follows on hysteria. In the old days it was the lighthearted and healthy who laughed. The victors laughed. The conquered wept. With us it is the sorrowful and the mad who laugh. Gogol laughs . . . The eyes of My madness are full of merriment.

Our comedy, to put it simply, is nothing but tragedy that makes us laugh. But then we find tragedy itself laughable.

The sufferings of young Werther? No—the sufferings of a self-aware schoolboy.[31] All very funny, but very serious too. He might have escaped with a birching, but he puts a bullet through his head. Young girls crowd about his freshly dug grave, roses are showered on his coffin—his parents weep and blow their noses. They wanted to give him a whipping, but they were too late. It wasn't their fault.

Fragile laughter hangs like music in the air about us. There is perhaps a rhythm to it. It calls for dancing. Who can say that only Death dances on fresh graves? We too can dance. We are a merry crowd indeed; we dance like a family of undertakers during a cholera epidemic . . .

Whatever may be the content of the tragedy of the future, it will not be able to dispense with the dance. Not for nothing do shrewd dramatists even now insert the cakewalk, the maxixe or similar tomfoolery into their plays.

I hope, though, that the dance will be choric in nature. It is to accommodate such dancing that footlights should be removed from theatres.

The modern theatregoer is able to participate in the theatrical spectacle only to the extent that he is able to recognize himself in the more or less crooked mirrors that the theatre places before him; the next stage in his participation in the tragic drama must be his participation in the tragic dance.

It is fortunate that we have Isadora Duncan to wing the dance with her naked feet . . .

"How sweet to know another life is with us!"[32]
(Valery Briusov)

Soon we shall all become infected with this "other life," and we shall stream onto the stage like Khlysts to whirl about in frenzied ritual.

The action of the tragedy will be accompanied by and interspersed with dance. Will the dance be merry? Perhaps. At all events, it will be frenzied to a greater or lesser degree. For the dance is nothing but the rhythmic frenzy of soul and body as they surrender themselves to the tragic element of music.

You are mistaken if you look at a dancer and think to yourself that he must be drenched with sweat as he whirls about, and that's the reason he loves to drench himself with the delicate fragrance of perfume. It is not he who whirls before your eyes, but the world that revolves about him ever faster, shimmering, dissolving, melting away in swift, untrammelled, airy motion. You have failed to perceive this universal gyration because you are timid and sensible, because you do not dare to surrender to the frenzied rhythm of the dance that will shatter the fetters of everyday existence. You see only the ridiculous—the red faces, the arm awkwardly obtrusive or ungracefully bent, the damp locks of hair, the droplets so repellent on a youthful skin. You do not know that it is the world's spinning that breathes sweet fire upon the frenzied body given up to the universal dance; that the dews of Eden mingled delicious coolness with delicious heat.

The black ringlet whips the white neck, the toe of a white shoe flashes beneath a white dress, a smile of delight gleams and is born away on scarlet lips, the train of a dress streams out, brushing against you. Draw on your gloves, invite any lady you like; don't be afraid—this is only a ball, you're not on the Brocken but in a ballroom at the mansion of Baroness Jour-fixe. The floor is polished with wax—"the gift of the wise bees"—but not at all dangerous. "Miss Snandulia dances only with those who would be a suitable match" (Wedekind: *Spring's Awakening*); she is a well-brought-up young lady, although "her dress is low-cut—to the waist at the back and in front to drive a man insane. She can't possibly be wearing a petticoat."

The ballroom dance is only a hint of what the tragic dance ought to be. True, the lady's corset, gloves and shoes correspond—to a very limited extent—to the mask of the tragic player of old. We know now, however, that we have no need of masks, however beautiful, made by the theatre property man. We always wear our own masks, and they fulfill their function so well that we often deceive not only others but even ourselves with their play of expression.

The whole world is nothing but a stage set behind which the creative spirit—My spirit—conceals itself. All earthly faces, all earthly bodies are only masks, only puppets for a single performance of the earthly tragicomedy—puppets wound up to speak, gesture, laugh and weep. And then comes tragedy, attenuating mask and decor until we glimpse through them the world transfigured by Me, the world of My spirit, the consummation of My unique will; through the masks and disguises we glimpse My unique face, My transfigured flesh. Flesh that is beautiful and liberated.

The rhythm of liberation is the rhythm of the dance. The pathos of liberation is the joy of the beautiful naked body.

The dancing spectators, male and female, will come to the theatre, leaving their ugly philistine clothes at the threshold. They will be caught up in the airy dance.

In this way the crowd that came to gaze will be transformed into a circle of dancers who have come to take part in the tragic drama.

1908

FYODOR SOLOGUB[33]

THE TRIUMPH OF DEATH

Tragedy in three acts, with a prologue

To my sister

FOREWORD

The author of this tragedy has exchanged his mask for a half-mask, but still does not reveal his face. He wishes to be recognized by the smile that coils at the corners of his lips.

But if he should not be recognized . . .

With all the words at his command, he speaks of one, unchanging thing. Untiringly he summons to one, unchanging thing.

But if he should not be heard . . .

Is his verse not beautiful? Is his prose not fragrant? Is he not a lord of language?

He smiles and passes on, drawing his cloak about him.

And she is with him, the serpent-eyed one.

THE SERPENT-EYED ONE IN THE PROUD CASTLE

PROLOGUE TO THE TRAGEDY THE TRIUMPH OF DEATH

DRAMATIS PERSONAE

KING
ALDONZA, *called Queen Ortruda*
DULCINEA, *called Aldonza*
DAGOBERT, *a page*
THE POET, *in a frock coat*
THE LADY, *in a silk dress*

An antechamber of the royal castle. The walls are of immense, rough-hewn stones. In the front of the wall is the great arch of the entrance, through which the hall is visible to the audience. In the foreground is a wide, gently slanting staircase leading down to the auditorium, which corresponds to the inner courtyard of the castle. Halfway up the staircase is a shallow landing from which two somewhat narrower staircases branch off left and right: they lead through the side-walls to the castle's outer courtyards. The antechamber is lined along sides and back with massive columns. Three short stairways ascend from the antechamber: the wide central one leads to the hall of banquets and ceremonial receptions; the two side stairways are narrow; the one on the right leads to the King's bedchamber. This last stairway is partly lit by the moon. The King is sitting on the steps. He gazes into the darkness of the unlit courtyard and speaks softly, as if to some unseen companion.

KING. Who summons me I do not know, and what I am summoned to I do not understand. Dark phantom, what do you want of me? Your voice is indistinct and your face is dark, as if masked in mist. I do not know why I have come here, to this gaping darkness filled with midnight terrors. The great-winged prophetic bird awakened me, and I stole from my bedchamber, leaving my dear wife sweetly slumbering. And now I am here and a multitude of unknown faces seem to float before me, as if all the courtyard of my ancestral castle were thronged and the pale shades of the long-dead were peering at me from all the windows, from the galleries, from the balconies—silently. They gaze at me—but they won't speak to me. O the wearisome apathy, the terrible indifference of these visitors!

Dulcinea ascends the side stairway. She appears in the guise of a poor peasant girl, known to everyone as Aldonza. Her clothes are ragged, poverty-stricken; her hair is falling out of curl; her arms and feet are bare. Over her shoulders she carries a yoke with two buckets.

DULCINEA. I'm tired, O God I'm tired. They make me go to the springs of living and dead water, and when I bring back my buckets filled, they tell me the water is undrinkable. They make me wash the floors with it and they beat me for bringing them water that's harsh and bitter. They don't know that the water I bring them in my buckets is sweet. I'm tired.

She sets down the buckets on the bottom step. She sits down on the stairs near the King, looks at him for a long time in silence, and at last says to him softly:

DULCINEA. Are you the king who lives in this proud castle and rules this land of darkness?

KING. Yes, serpent-eyed one, I am the king of this land—but mine is a land of light.

He looks closely at her and speaks.

KING. I recognize you. You are the peasant girl Aldonza, the one the urchins laugh at because a madman has called you by the sweet name of Dulcinea, the adorable enchantress, the loveliest of earthly maidens. You have learned to cast spells and to work enchantment, serpent-eyed one, but you have not found yourself a bridegroom.

DULCINEA. I am waiting for a king and for a poet who will crown me. They will crown beauty and overthrow ugliness. They will spurn the ordinary and strive after the impossible.

KING. Your buckets stand empty, those who sent you are waiting for their water and will beat you if you tarry along the way. Put your tawny young shoulder under the yoke, take up your buckets, fetch your water, serve him who has hired you for little pay.

DULCINEA. For little pay!

KING. Your lowly labor is not worthy of heavy, ringing gold. The rough embraces of the master's son in a dark hallway smelling of goat and dog—that's your proper reward. You have learned to work enchantment—but of what use are your conjurations?

DULCINEA. A poet is coming here—and you and he together must crown me, Dulcinea.

KING. Fetch your water.

DULCINEA. So that's your mercy, King! Weary though I am, you send me forth again. I shall do your will, I shall bring living water and I shall bring dead water. And now, King, accept from me this little gift.

She gives him an amulet and leaves with her yoke and buckets.

KING. What has she given me, the sorceress? Is there an evil charm in this amulet? Or does it portend well? I'll put it around my neck, anyway.

He puts on the amulet.

KING. How easy and relaxed everything about me is becoming. Life is easy, so easy! Death is easy, so easy! And all that lies ahead is becoming a sweet dream. A golden dream.

He sinks down on the steps. Dagobert the page enters.

DAGOBERT. The King is asleep on the steps, bewitched by the serpent-eyed gaze of Aldonza. Queen Ortruda is alone. Fate smiles upon me.

He makes his way stealthily to the King's chamber. The Poet and the Lady enter.

POET. We certainly found a good cabbie.

LADY. Yes, he drove very fast. The wind whistled in my ears and my heart almost stopped beating. But he was strange. He sat there like a dead man. Where has he brought us, Mr. Poet? Everything here is quiet and dark and still.

POET. It's an inn. All the same, I liked the coachman. In the poem I shall write about this journey, I shall call him Troika.

LADY. If I were you, Mr. Poet, I'd call him Automobile.

POET. No, dear lady, Troika is better. And I've found some wonderful rhymes for it too.

LADY. And what are they, Mr. Poet?

POET. "*Charodeika*"[34] and "*vodka*."

LADY. Those *are* good rhymes, Mr. Poet. But I only like the first one.

POET. But there aren't any good rhymes for the word "automobile."

LADY. Perhaps there are, all the same.

POET. For example?

A dispassionate voice is heard.
—Death.[35]

LADY. Did you hear that?

POET. Yes, I did. Someone is hiding and playing a joke on us.

LADY. There's someone sitting on the stairs.

POET. It's the porter.

LADY. You're nearsighted, Mr. Poet. Take a good look—it's the King.

POET. You're mistaken, dear lady: kings don't sit on stairs.

LADY. Perhaps you're right, Mr. Poet. But it's frightening here—and boring too.

POET. We'll have some wine and a bite to eat.

Turning to empty space—the auditorium—he calls.

POET. Waiter!

They wait, peering into the darkness.

LADY. How dark it is here!

POET. That's unavoidable. They'll switch on the electric light in a moment . . . Waiter!

Dulcinea emerges, bent beneath the burden of her yoke.

POET. My dear girl, are you the waitress here? Let's have the menu.

DULCINEA. I bring buckets filled with living water and dead water.[36]

POET. This inn has a language all its own. What we have here is red and white wine. Which will you have, dear lady?

LADY. I'll have the white.

POET. That's apparently called "dead water" here. Pour us some dead water, my dear girl.

Dulcinea approaches. She dips her ladle and serves the Poet, who draws back slightly.

POET. Do you mean to say the wine here is served in buckets? That it can only be drunk from a ladle?

LADY. I think that's original.

POET. I think it's repulsive.

LADY. You're right, Mr. Poet. Original, but repulsive. We won't drink this dirty water from these filthy buckets, out of this rusty ladle.

DULCINEA. You're mistaken, my dear. This is living and dead water, and you ought to drink some of it. You would see yourself in a magic mirror.

LADY. *(capriciously)* I don't want to.

DULCINEA. I have waited for you a long time, Mr. Poet. You have come here, to the depths of time . . .

POET. *(to the lady)* This inn is called "The Depths of Time."

DULCINEA. *(continuing)* . . . to sing in praise of me, the loveliest of earthly maidens, the enchantress Dulcinea, who here, in this dark land, is wrongly called Aldonza.

POET. That's not why I came here.

DULCINEA. Sing my praises, Mr. Poet, and then the King will crown me. Sing my praises, dear Poet, and then a handsome youth will fall in love with me. Sing my praises, dear and wonderful Poet, and then my real name will be revealed to all.

POET. You're an impostor. The real Dulcinea lives in a proud castle. She doesn't have to carry heavy buckets. On her feet are satin slippers embroidered with pearls.

DULCINEA. Look into my eyes, Mr. Poet, and write poetry for me.

POET. I'm afraid of your eyes, serpent-eyed one. I've published all my poems—I don't have any new ones.

DULCINEA. You shall not escape my enchantments, Mr. Poet, come what may. And this woman, who is a stranger to you, shall not help you. Sit down on these steps and watch what will be enacted here.

POET. I feel a strange weariness. Let's sit down here, dear lady; this odd girl has promised us a show.

DULCINEA. Whether it remains merely a show or becomes a mystery depends on you.

POET. She's talking about the intimate theatre. Let's watch.

The King continues to doze in the middle of the staircase. The Poet and his Lady sit down by a column to the right, snuggling up to each other, and gaze at the spectacle as if it were a golden dream.

DULCINEA. The King is fast asleep—and does not wish to crown me. The weary poet has sunk down on the castle steps, his shoulder pressed to that of his chance companion—he does not wish to sing my praises, he refuses to recognize Dulcinea. I shall summon the young and the beautiful, I shall exalt love's mysteries to the heights of bliss!

Turning toward the King's bedchamber, Dulcinea calls out her summons.

DULCINEA. Aldonza—she who is here called Queen Ortruda! And you, young page Dagobert! Come to me.

Queen Ortruda and the page Dagobert appear at the top of the stairs.

DAGOBERT. My dear lady Ortruda, why have you come out here? The King, bewitched by the serpent eyes of crazy Aldonza, would have dozed for a long time, and we would have been free to taste the sweet delights of our love.

ORTRUDA. Someone summoned me, and there was such authority in the summons.

DAGOBERT. She's here too, the serpent-eyed one!

DULCINEA. Dear Dagobert, surely you know who it is you love?

DAGOBERT. I love Queen Ortruda. And she loves me.

DULCINEA. Can't you see that it's Aldonza? Her eyes are lustreless, her voice too piercing. Love me, sweet stripling, love me—the beautiful Dulcinea. Reject the Queen, give her back to her husband.

ORTRUDA. She's mad. Don't listen to her, Dagobert.

DULCINEA. Be silent!

Without a word, the Queen sinks down on the steps next to the King and watches the spectacle with spellbound gaze.

DULCINEA. Love me, sweet Dagobert.

DAGOBERT. You're a beauty, darling Aldonza. And you know how to weave spells. There they sit on the steps, the ones you've bewitched. Will you bewitch me too, cunning Aldonza?

DULCINEA. Don't call me Aldonza. I am Dulcinea.

DAGOBERT. Everyone knows you're Aldonza. But it's all the same to me. I'll call you whatever you like. I'll be none the worse for it.

He embraces Dulcinea and tries to kiss her. Dulcinea frees herself. She speaks softly.

DULCINEA. Even you don't believe me. And the most terrible mockery of all is that you call me by the name that belongs to me without believing in it. I have no need of that kind of love. Return to your lady.

Dagobert sits down next to Ortruda, puts his arm round her and dozes off with his head on her shoulder.

DULCINEA. Again spectacle remains spectacle and does not become mystery. Again I remain uncrowned, again my praises are unsung, again love is denied the real beauty of this world—the enchantress Dulcinea in the guise of the serpent-eyed Aldonza. But I will not abandon my design. Undaunted, I shall strive for the crowning of beauty and the overthrow of ugliness. Never tiring, I shall appear to the poet, the lover and the king in many guises. Sing my praise—I shall say—love me, crown me. Come to me, follow me. Only I am alive in life and in death, only in me is there life, mine alone is the ultimate triumph. Now I shall assume the form of the bondwoman Malgista and I shall send forth my daughter Algista to accomplish a great deed, to fulfill my eternal design. With her virginal freshness I shall mingle my eternal enchantments. Whether life triumph, or death—the triumph shall be mine.

THE TRIUMPH OF DEATH

Tragedy
in three acts

DRAMATIS PERSONAE

KING CLODOVEG
BERTHA, *his wife*
ALGISTA, *her servant*
MALGISTA, *mother of Algista*
ETHELBERT, *brother of Bertha*
LINGARD, *a page*
KNIGHTS, LADIES, PAGES, SERVANTS AND SERVING-WOMEN

ACT ONE

The antechamber is dimly lit by torches inserted in the iron rings of the columns. From the doors of the banqueting hall come the loud voices of revellers, songs, laughter and the clink of goblets.

Song (from the hall).

The cup is filled with heady wine —
Bridegroom, kiss your bride!
Beneath her veil the queen sits calm,
Behind that mist keen-eyed.
To lift a corner of that veil
None but a king may dare.
To press your lips upon your bride's
Is sweet beyond compare!

Algista and Malgista stand near the entrance to the banqueting hall, hidden behind a column. Algista's face is covered by a gray veil. They speak softly.

MALGISTA. Algista, dearest daughter, you're not afraid?

ALGISTA. I'm not afraid.

MALGISTA. The time has come to carry out our great design—to crown beauty and to overthrow ugliness.

ALGISTA. Ugly and wicked, stupid and greedy, worthy daughter of generations of cruel and perfidious men, she rejoices, triumphant. She wishes to be queen—why?

MALGISTA. No, not Bertha the cripple, the daughter of the bloodthirsty king Coloman, but you, my beautiful Algista, deserve to be queen.

ALGISTA. I will be queen. And Algista shall be no more—the very name of Algista shall be forgotten. And I will be queen.

MALGISTA. Perhaps this is the last time I shall call you my daughter. Let me kiss once more the face of my Algista, the blooming roses of my dear daughter's lips. Tomorrow I shall bow down before you, like a slave before her mistress.

Algista quickly throws back her veil. Her mother gazes at her adoringly and kisses her lovely face. Algista covers her face again.

ALGISTA. For a long time I stood here alone, hidden in a dark corner behind the pillars. After the wedding ceremony, here, before my eyes, the knights who had escorted our Queen Bertha took their leave of the King. They left the castle and rode away, and now only the two of us are left to serve her. Then I watched while the King of this land entered the hall with Bertha and the wedding guests and they took their places at table. They sit and feast while I stand alone and watch. From where I stand I can see the King's face and Bertha next to him.

MALGISTA. Our lady Bertha, in accordance with ancient custom, sits covered with gold-embroidered Levantine cloth.

ALGISTA. What if Bertha be hidden by her veil of woven gold—I know and remember her face, pitted with smallpox; I know that one of my lady's legs is shorter than the other, and that she conceals it by means of cunningly fashioned golden heels.

MALGISTA. *(laughs softly and speaks in a whisper)* Our rulers have invented many splendid ceremonies in order to elevate themselves above us. Sometimes we can even turn their vanity to our advantage. King Clodoveg has not yet seen our lady's face.

ALGISTA. I know. They wanted to deceive the king of this land. He would have seen her for the first time tomorrow morning, but then it would have been too late. You can't drive out a woman who's shared you bed, no matter how repulsive she may be.

MALGISTA. No, we shall give him a wife who is beautiful and wise. He's fuddled with wine. He won't be able to see her face in the darkness of the bedchamber, and afterwards he won't understand who's deceived him and how.

ALGISTA. Deceit and perfidy are not our invention. The rulers of this world, the crowned and the mighty, have opened the way to perfidy and evil.

MALGISTA. The feast is drawing to an end. I'll go now. We mustn't be seen together.

Quickly she kisses Algista and goes out. The page Lingard appears from the banqueting hall.

LINGARD. I'm tired. I'm ready to sit down on the floor. It's no joke to be on your feet from morning to night.

He goes to the corner where Algista is hiding.

LINGARD. Why, there's someone here. Who are you?

ALGISTA. *(in a feigned hoarse voice)* I am Algista, a servant of Queen Bertha.

LINGARD. What are you doing here in the dark? You should be feasting with the other girls. They're all drunk. Or are you tired too? Let's sit together and rest awhile.

He embraces Algista and tries to kiss her.

ALGISTA. Get away from me or I'll scream.

LINGARD. Touch-me-not! Don't you find me attractive?

ALGISTA. You're handsome, but we have no time for kissing today. And besides, we mustn't. They'll be getting up from the feast any moment, and I'll have to undress our lady Bertha and put out the lights in the bedchamber so that the King won't get a look at what he shouldn't before the proper time.

LINGARD. And what shouldn't he look at?

ALGISTA. What shouldn't he look at? Things will go ill if the bridegroom sees the pockmarked face of his queen too soon. He'll probably drive her out, saying 'Go, while you're still a maid.'

She feigns laughter.

LINGARD. So Bertha, you say, is pockmarked.

ALGISTA. Like a cuckoo. And lame too.

LINGARD. *(laughs)* And so the King has been deceived.

ALGISTA. Yes. But keep quiet for the time being.

She moves away, pretending to limp.

LINGARD. And why do you keep your face hidden? And it looks like you've got a limp too. Like mistress, like maid!

ALGISTA. What are you talking about? I've never limped in my life!

She leans against the wall.

LINGARD. Let me take a look for myself. You' re not pockmarked too, by any chance?

He catches hold of her cloak. Algista lets out a piercing scream.

LINGARD. Stupid girl—the likes of you can put a noose around a man's neck.

He runs off. The King, knights, ladies, pages, menservants and serving-women enter from the banqueting hall.

KING. Someone here was calling for help. Who dares disturb our carefree and joyous feast? Find the insolent fellow and bring him before us.

Algista mingles with the King's serving-women. Pages and servants rush about the antechamber, making a fearful din. The knights stand in bellicose and slightly ludicrous attitudes, rolling their eyes threateningly; their faces are red with the wine they have drunk in abundance.

KING. Are you frightened, my dear wife Bertha? Are you trembling?

BERTHA. No, my lord, with you at my side I'm afraid of nothing.

KING. Someone raised a drunken outcry and then made off—frightened at his own impudence. We forgive the insolent one for our joy's sake. Leave your searching, our trusted servants. Women, conduct the queen to our bedchamber.

Bertha, ladies and serving-women disappear into the bedchamber; Algista goes with them.

KING. As for us, my friends—we'll go back to the board and drink a last cup.

The King, knights, pages and servants go into the banqueting hall. The ladies who conducted the Queen to the bedchamber return and then leave by the stairs on the left. The antechamber empties. From the banqueting hall come shouts, bawdy songs and drunken laughter. Malgista cautiously mounts the side staircase. She looks about her. She steals to the door of the bedchamber. She listens, then quickly conceals herself behind the columns. The serving-women emerge from the bedchamber. They are laughing. They speak in drunken voices.

SERVING-WOMEN. She's a modest one! Didn't want to undress in front of us. Wouldn't even uncover her face.

— She only kept her young maidservant with her.

— She's a strange one too — all wrapped up in her shawl and doesn't say a word.

— Old Malgista whispered to me on the sly that her daughter is pock-marked.

— And she's supposed to be lame too: they say she wears shoes with different heels — one high, one low.

— Anyway, we'll soon see — they can't hide beneath their long veils forever.

They descend the staircase. The stage is empty. Algista appears from the bedchamber; barefoot, she wears a shift and is wrapped in a big dark shawl. She draws a dagger across her breast, drawing blood. Then she moves into the shadows and, half-covering herself with her cloak, lies down.

The King comes out of the banqueting hall, accompanied by a noisy crowd. They escort him to his bedchamber.

KING. My friends! I thank you for sharing with me this feast of celebration, and for diverting the Queen and myself with merry songs and seemly jokes. Now you may go to your beds, except for those who are to stand guard here—and may God bless you all.

Knights, pages and servants respond with raucous shouts: God grant our King and Queen long life. May He send good fortune to our King, our Queen and our crown prince! And may he send us a crown prince! We wish Your Majesty a good night—and a successful one!

The King goes out. The knights quiet the noisy, giggling pages. They all go out. Two armed knights remain at the doors of the bedchamber. They talk in whispers, then fall into a doze, leaning upon their spears, their backs against the columns. Two or three of the torches go out. Rustlings and stirrings are heard in the darkness. Algista moans. The knights give a start.

FIRST. There's someone here.

SECOND. You remember how someone cried out when we were still at the feast?

FIRST. There's a woman lying here.

They both bend toward Algista.

ALGISTA. (*with a moan*) Help!

The knights hold their torches over her.

FIRST. A real beauty!

SECOND. Someone has slashed her breast with a knife.

FIRST. A feeble blow. Our beauty's frightened, but not seriously wounded. A poorly aimed blow—a child or a woman might have done it.

SECOND. Who are you, my beauty?

ALGISTA. Bertha.

SECOND. She's calling for Bertha.

ALGISTA. I *am* Bertha.

FIRST. The Queen?

ALGISTA. Yes.

FIRST. But the Queen is in the bedchamber with the King. You're delirious, my beauty.

SECOND. She's closed her eyes again.

FIRST. What shall we do with her?

SECOND. Let's call the seneschal.

FIRST. Will it be a good thing if everyone gets to know of this strange, dark tale?

SECOND. What should we do?

FIRST. Let's knock at the King's door. He'll praise us for our discretion. Who knows, perhaps this beauty—or maybe someone else—will have to be dispatched quietly so that no one finds out what happened here.

SECOND. You may well be right.

They leave Algista. She moans loudly. Malgista runs across the stage wailing.

MALGISTA. Where is my daughter Algista? Algista, Algista, where are you?

She runs off. Her wails can be heard backstage. Knights, women and pages come running in. The noise brings on the King. Exclamations, noise.

ALGISTA. Clodoveg, my lord—save me!

KING. Who is this woman?

FIRST KNIGHT. She was lying here, wounded, in a dark corner. We asked her who she was, and she said, Queen Bertha.

KING. What is she saying? The Queen lies in bed in my chamber.

ALGISTA. *(in a weak voice)* They undressed me and left. I was alone. Her face was covered. But I recognized her. She struck me with a dagger. Then she dragged me out here. My slave Algista plotted evil against me.

KING. What are you saying, unhappy woman! Can it be that I have been sharing my bed with a slave?

ALGISTA. Woe is me! I am dying, I, the daughter of a king, I, a king's bride, I, in the flower of my youth and beauty—and she, my slave, lame, pockmarked Algista, is to be queen! I lie here on stones while my slave lies in my bed!

KING. Go, women, to my chamber, dress the Queen and bring her here. In my presence the Queen shall unmask the impostor and truth shall shine brighter than the sun.

MALGISTA *(running in)* Good people, tell me, where is my daughter Algista?

KING. Look, is this not your daughter lying wounded here?

MALGISTA. Algista, my child, who has done you harm?

She rushes over to Algista. She looks at her closely. She leaps up with a loud cry. She backs away. She throws herself on her knees before Algista.

MALGISTA. My dear lady Bertha, what's the matter? Why are you lying here on the cold stones, half-naked? Why has your husband driven you from his bed?

ALGISTA. My faithful Malgista, what grief! What shame! While your daughter was undressing me, she struck me with a dagger. I fell at her feet as if dead. She dragged me out here, threw me into a dark corner and went herself to my bed.

MALGISTA. O woe is me! Algista, you madwoman, what have you done?

Bertha comes out of the bedchamber, the women with her.

MALGISTA. My wretched daughter, my mad Algista! What made you raise your hand against your mistress?

LINGARD. So that's why she was trying to make me believe the Queen was pockmarked and lame!

FIRST KNIGHT. When was that? What are you saying?

LINGARD. Wait, I'll tell the King everything.

BERTHA. Malgista, what are you saying? Or has grief darkened your reason? This is your daughter Algista lying here wounded.

MALGISTA. Falsehearted creature! *You* are Algista, *you* are my daughter, and our lady Bertha is lying here. You plotted to kill her, but she lives to unmask you, traitress!

KING. Who am I to believe?

BERTHA. I am Bertha, daughter of King Coloman.

ALGISTA. I am Queen Bertha.

BERTHA. I am your bride, King.

ALGISTA. I am your bride, Clodoveg.

BERTHA. I sat next to you at the feast.

ALGISTA. When we were sitting at the feast, I said to you: "My lord, kiss me on the shoulder."

BERTHA. I said those words.

ALGISTA. Aloud?

BERTHA. I whispered them in my lord's ear.

ALGISTA. Then how would I have heard them?

BERTHA. Malgista told you.

ALGISTA. No one told me anything—I wished my lord to caress me.

BERTHA. Bring back the knights who escorted me here—they'll tell you . . .

ALGISTA. King, naturally my father's emissaries told you that I was beautiful?

KING. Yes. Would I have married an ugly woman?

ALGISTA. See, King, how beautiful I am and how pockmarked she is.

BERTHA. Yes, but I am Queen, and you, my beautiful Algista, are my serving maid.

ALGISTA. Look, King—one of her legs is shorter than the other.

BERTHA. I am lame, but I am Queen.

ALGISTA. Surely, King, my father's emissaries did not tell you that Bertha was pockmarked and lame?

KING. No. I would not have taken a lame and pockmarked woman to wife, and I don't think that King Coloman would have deceived me.

Algista pretends to lose consciousness.

MALGISTA. *(bending over her)* My dear lady!

BERTHA. A web of deceit, a great web of deceit has been spun about me. Who will help me break the clinging threads of treachery? To whom shall I cry for help? I stand here defenseless, the victim of deceit.

KING. I can see which of these two is the deceiver. But tell me, barons and knights, what do you think—which one is the Queen?

KNIGHTS. This beautiful wounded lady.

KING. And the impostor?

KNIGHTS. That lame, pockmarked woman.

KING. What shall I do with her?

MALGISTA. King, pardon my daughter. The evil one clouded her reason. For my loyalty to the Queen, pardon my daughter.

KING. Take her deep into the forest and let it be as God wills. As for her mother . . .

ALGISTA. King, let this faithful woman remain with me. You saw how she unmasked her own daughter, the dear, devoted soul!

KING. It shall be as you wish, sweet Queen.

BERTHA. Poor King, you have been deceived.

Bertha is led away. Algista is raised up and carried to the bedchamber. The people leave. A dispassionate voice is heard:

— A night passes. A day. A night. A day. Nights and days. Years. In the murk of time the years slip quickly by. Ten years.

ACT TWO

The same antechamber. Algista enters precipitately through the center doors. She is splendidly arrayed, as befits a queen. She rushes distractedly about the antechamber. She is followed by Malgista. The last words of a song are heard.

So to a white-haired wizard
The trusting king gave ear,
And drove from throne and threshold
The wife who loved him dear.
The people, sore deluded,
To a witch swear fealty—
Together they rule the kingdom,
The sorcerer and she.
The queen—where is she now then?
The forest hides her wrong.
The queen-will she return then?
I'll sing of that ere long.

ALGISTA. Has the King noticed anything?

MALGISTA. No, my lady—everyone was listening spellbound to the wandering minstrel's songs.

ALGISTA. Did you recognize him?

Malgista makes no reply.

ALGISTA. What are we to do?

MALGISTA. He won't dare to say anything. He's not going to admit that King Coloman—Bertha's father and his—is a cheat.

ALGISTA. I'm terrified!

MALGISTA. Don't be afraid, my darling daughter.

ALGISTA. No, not terrified—tired. I was wrong. I believed that people wanted freedom and light. O with what persistence, what ingenuity—night after night, day after day—I kept drumming the same thing into the King's ears, always finding new ways to say it! He trusted me, and eventually he learned to think as I do. But he can do nothing except what his ancestors did before him: make war, pass judgment, reward. Nothing audacious. Rulers want to rule—that I understand. But the people—all these simple people, artisans and tillers of the soil—O how they want to be slaves! Slaves, and nothing more!

MALGISTA. Everyone says that under your influence the King has become merciful to the people, generous to his servants, just to all those who seek justice from him. The people bless your name, Bertha, our beloved queen.

ALGISTA. They glorify the name of Bertha! But if the truth is revealed, if the King finds out my true name, will he glorify the sweet name of Algista?

MALGISTA. The King won't find out.

ALGISTA. He will.

MALGISTA. Even if he does, he won't believe it.

ALGISTA. They're coming.

Malgista moves away from her and stands behind a column. Algista stands to the front of the antechamber, half turned away from the center doors so that her face is in shadow. The King, Prince Ethelbert in the garb of a wandering minstrel, knights, ladies and pages enter from the banqueting hall.

KING. Dearest Bertha, light of my eyes, why did you leave us? He sang two more songs, each better than the last.

ALGISTA. Great is the art of this wandering minstrel. What mere mortal could sing so sweetly and so insidiously. Is it not some evil demon that inspires his cunning melodies?

KING. To all appearances he is a godfearing man.

ALGISTA. The Evil One can wear a priest's robe. His devilish songs made my head spin.

KING. Forgive me, dear Bertha—I thought he would give you pleasure. Minstrel, take this gold and rest yourself. Your songs are beautiful, your art is great—but I fear that there may be the power of magic in it.

ETHELBERT. My sister sings better, and if my songs drove your gracious lady Bertha from the King's merry feast, perhaps my sister's singing will bring comfort to Her Majesty.

KING. Where is your sister?

ETHELBERT. Here, waiting in the courtyard. If you will permit me, King, I shall bring her to you.

KING. Do so.

ETHELBERT. *(passing Algista)* The serving wench Algista makes a fine queen.

ALGISTA. The deceiver's son comes with deceit against deceit.

ETHELBERT. Your lovely body shall be given to the scourge and the birch, and to a shameful death.

He goes out.

KING. What was that the wandering minstrel muttered?

ALGISTA. Incomprehensible words. He is possessed by an evil spirit; his mind is prey to cruel and monstrous visions. He is haunted by treachery, deceit, blood, torture and death. You should not have commanded him to bring his sister here. If she is like her brother, they will cast evil spells on you, dear my lord, and on me, your wretched queen.

KING. Very well, let them be forbidden to enter.

But hardly has the King begun to speak when Bertha and a little boy are seen mounting the central staircase; they are followed by Ethelbert.

KING. My good minstrel, your songs have been sweet to our ears. I don't doubt that your sister's singing would be still more skilled and delightful—but the Queen is weary and cannot listen to songs. And you, my songstress, do not be vexed that you waited your turn to sing in vain. Take this gold and go your way. Perhaps the Queen and I will send for you tomorrow.

BERTHA. I—Bertha, the Queen—am also weary. Driven out by you, my dear husband, because you trusted the deceitful Algista and not me, long have I roamed dense forests, steep mountains and broad valleys. The wild winds blew about me, the pouring rain drenched me, the fair sun scorched me, thorns rent my garments and tore my flesh, my feet bled from sand and stone. Under a haystack in a field, King, I gave birth to your son. An old beggar woman served me as midwife; I had him christened in a humble village church; I called him Charles; he will be a great king. Take him, dear King, and do not drive me from your bed.

ALGISTA. No one wanted to listen to you, my songbird, but you've sung your song all the same. Well then, let's hear you sing some more; you've sung about yourself—now sing about me.

BERTHA. You are my serving maid Algista. Your mother, Malgista, is hiding behind that column, pale with rage and fear.

EHTELBERT. Dear Bertha, don't lower yourself by arguing with a slave. Know, King, that I am Ethelbert, son of King Coloman, brother of your unfortunate wife Bertha, whom you drove out, deceived by the evil Algista.

ALGISTA. He is mad, and his sister no less so.

ETHELBERT. The knights who brought Bertha to you ten years ago are with me. You will recognize them and they will tell you the truth.

He blows a golden horn. Twelve knights mount the central staircase.

ETHELBERT. And here, King, is a letter from King Coloman.

He gives the King the letter. The King takes it.

KING. Chancellor, unseal this letter, and we shall read it, as it is fitting that royal missives should be read, standing in royal state. And now, wandering minstrel calling yourself by the name of Prince Ethelbert, will you assert once more that this woman, brought here by you, is indeed the beautiful Bertha, daughter of King Coloman?

ETHELBERT. Yes, this is Queen Bertha, your wife and the daughter of King Coloman.

ALGISTA. *(laughing)* Beautiful Bertha! A fine beauty! See, King, what a big mouth she has! How pockmarked she is! And one of her legs is longer than the other.

BERTHA. You remember all this very well, Algista—but then, how could you forget it? You it was who dressed and shod me.

ETHELBERT. My sister was beautiful, but as we were journeying here Algista marred her beauty with evil spells. See, King, how much my sister resembles me.

ALGISTA. Yes, another redheaded monstrosity.

ETHELBERT. Be that as it may, the girls of my homeland, and of other countries too, have found it hard to take their eyes off me, and any one of them . . .

ALGISTA. Jingle your gold and some strumpet will hang around your neck.

ETHELBERT. Question my companions, King. Perhaps their faces will be familiar to you.

KING. We shall return to our royal castle, read this letter, ponder the matter and resolve it according to our conscience. And terrible shall be our judgment on those who plotted treachery.

He goes out through the center door. All follow him, except for Algista and Malgista.

MALGISTA. *(approaching her daughter)* Dear lady, take your place beside the King. Fear nothing. Confess nothing. The King loves you and will believe none but you.

ALGISTA. I shall remain here. I am tired. And I have no wish to be Bertha.

MALGISTA. What are you saying, you insane creature? You ruin yourself—and me with you.

ALGISTA. Am I not beautiful? Have I not been true to him? Have I not born him a son? Did you see? They dragged in some sickly little runt with them, while my son, my son is strong and beautiful—O my son Chilperic!

MALGISTA. You see, everything is in your favor, my darling daughter. So have no fear: go in boldly and take your place—the King will believe none but you.

ALGISTA. The hour of my final ordeal has come. If he loves me, if long days and sweet nights have bound us forever, he will not reject me: he will crown Algista. I shall go, I shall reveal my name.

MALGISTA. You're mad! What you wish cannot be.

ALGISTA. I must go!

She walks toward the door leading to the hall. Malgista tries to hold her back. A brief struggle.

ALGISTA. *(crying out)* King, I am Algista!

Quickly she enters the hall. Malgista runs after her.
(offstage)

KING. Algista?

Uproar. Cries of amazement.

ALGISTA. I am Algista. I stand here before you, Clodoveg, judge me as you will; put me to death or pardon me, but remember, King, how I . . .

KING. Silence! An impostor, a slave has brought shame to my bed!

KNIGHTS AND LADIES. Impostor! Slave! Let her die!

ALGISTA. Clodoveg, my sweet King, I was a faithful wife to you.

KING. Silence. A shameful death . . .

ALGISTA. Clodoveg, my sweet husband Clodoveg . . .

KING. Silence her, women!

Algista gives a suppressed cry. Uproar, exclamations, above which a single voice is heard.

CHANCELLOR. Be silent! The King will pronounce his dread sentence.

KING. Divest the impostor of her queenly crown, her necklet and her robes. And you, dear Queen Bertha, assume your rightful place. The impostor shall die a terrible and shameful death before the people. Her naked body shall be given to the scourge and the birch; she shall be beaten to death and her body shall be cast into the moat for dogs to eat. The boy too shall be beaten and hanged. Let us go, my Queen: together we shall watch her torments and listen to her cries from a high balcony. Let the impostor be whipped!

Algista's muffled screams. The wailing of Malgista. Laughter. Uproar. Shouts. The noise grows gradually louder. Coarse guffaws are heard. Knights, ladies, pages, menservants and serving-women begin to emerge from the hall. Shouts come from the milling throng.

KNIGHTS, LADIES, MENSERVANTS, SERVING-WOMEN.

—The impostor has been unmasked!
— It's Algista, just a common wench.
—They ripped all her finery off and put it on the real Queen.
—Where's the sentence going to be carried out?
— Here in the courtyard, in front of this mob who have come to gaze at the spectacle.
— Look, they're undressing her.
—The impostor will be put to death this very day.
—A terrible and shameful death.
—They are going to flog her to death with birch switches and scourges of rawhide.
—And they're going to hang her brat.
— I spat right in her eye!
— She got a slap or two from me!
— She only has her shift on, but we'll soon rip that off her.
—They're bringing her out, they're bringing her out!

Algista is led through the door of the hall. Everyone crowds about her, laughing, mocking, shouting. She is led down the wide stairway into the pit, where the great door of the castle is. The antechamber is wrapped in darkness. Malgista is heard wailing.

MALGISTA. Good people, good people, save my daughter Algista!

ACT THREE

The same antechamber. The howling of dogs is heard. The full moon casts a bright strip of light on the upper stairs and the edge of the landing, leaving the rest in shadow. At first the antechamber is empty. Then Malgista slowly climbs the side stairway. On her shoulders she carries the body of Algista, half-naked, barely covered by its torn and bloody clothing. She lays Algista's body in the moonlight, kneels over her and weeps, keening softly.

MALGISTA. My daughter, my daughter! They beat you, they tortured you to death. Long did the blows of their merciless scourges rain upon you while boys and servants laughed. And my Algista died. They threw her in the castle moat for dogs to eat—but the dogs wouldn't touch her, howling mournfully over the body of their gentle mistress. The moon rose, the dogs howled, and my sorrow mounted to the heavens.

Her weeping rises to a howl. The howling of dogs is heard. Malgista gets up quietly and goes out keening.

MALGISTA. My sorrow mounts to the cold moon, to the bright heavens. The dogs howl, scenting the blood of their gentle mistress, and I too shall go and howl on the spot where the earth drank her blood as it gushed forth.

She goes out. Algista lifts herself up and cries out.

ALGISTA. Sleepers, arise!

All is quiet. Algista falls back. Malgista returns. She is carrying the child in her arms. She lays him at Algista's side. She kneels over them, weeping and keening.

MALGISTA. Even the innocent boy they did not spare. They beat him, they tortured him, they murdered him and threw his body by his mother's. O Algista, Algista, my daughter!

Algista lifts herself up and cries out.

ALGISTA. Sleepers, arise!

Malgista bends over her and asks softly.

MALGISTA. Daughter, dear one, are you alive?

ALGISTA. At this fearful hour only the dead are alive.

The shouted challenges and responses of the sentries can be heard outside. Someone comes up the side staircase and peers into the antechamber. Little by little the castle becomes filled with soft rustlings and noises, which grow ever louder.

MALGISTA. Tell me, my daughter—you didn't die? You're alive?

ALGISTA. The hour of the final ordeal is at hand.

MALGISTA. Or have you risen from the dead, awakened by the power of her who weaves her spells in the quiet heavens or by the secret whisper of her who wanders at night at the crossroads?

ALGISTA. See, there are two paths. He will choose one of them. Whether I be living or dead . . .

She gets up slowly and cries out.

ALGISTA. Whether you be living or dead, my son Chilperic, arise.

The boy gets up. The moonlight falls on the pale faces of Algista and the boy, and on their bloody garments. Algista turns toward the King's bedchamber and cries out in a loud and terrible voice that echoes through the building's immensity.

ALGISTA. Sleepers, arise!

Commotion, shouting, the clangor of arms are heard from the castle interior. Servants, pages, knights and women run across the antechamber, into which the common people now crowd. Exclamations are heard.

MENSERVANTS, SERVING-WOMEN, PAGES, KNIGHTS, LADIES.

— Who was shouting so loudly here?

— What has happened?

— Has there been an enemy attack?

— Or have the dead risen from their graves?

— Was it the archangel's trumpet we heard summoning us to the Last Judgement?

— I'm frightened!

— The blood that has been shed cries out to the heavens.

— It's dark.

— Where are the torches?

Someone brings in a torch, then another, then more and more. Torch-bearers rush about the antechamber in disarray. Some of the torches are inserted in the pillar rings. People are shouting.

— Look, Algista is here!

— The tortured Queen is risen!

— And her son too.

— Woe is us. Was it not an evil thing that we did?

MALGISTA. Yes, woe. You have done an evil thing—you have broken the beautiful vessel and spilled the precious wine.

The antechamber grows brighter and brigher from the light of the torches. Algista and her son stand at the bottom of the staircase, the rest cluster about the walls and pillars. The King, Bertha and Ethelbert appear. Clodoveg and Bertha have dressed hurriedly, but their crowns are on their heads. The King carries a naked sword. The noise subsides. Everyone except the King stands motionless and silent, eyes fixed on Algista.

MALGISTA. Algista, dearest daughter, speak to him sweet words of love.

ALGISTA. King, it is an evil thing you have done, but my love forgives you. Leave this stranger and follow me, follow me to a life of freedom and joy.

KING. Who are you? Why have you come here? If you are alive, hide yourself from our just anger. If you have risen from the dead, return to your slumber and do not trouble the living with your nocturnal visitations.

MALGISTA. Algista, dearest daughter, summon him to follow you.

ALGISTA. Clodoveg, dear lord and husband, I am your Algista. I love you. I have come to summon you to me. Come to me, follow me.

KING. You deceived me.

ALGISTA. I was true to you, I shall remain true to the end.

BERTHA. King, kill the sorceress.

ALGISTA. Clodoveg, tell me, did you love me?

KING. I did.

ALGISTA. Tell me, do you love me?

KING. I do.

ALGISTA. Then follow me.

KING. Have the torments of your just punishment darkened your reason? Or have you come to us raised from the dead by evil charms? Who are you?—tell us. A night-wandering ghost or the living Algista?

BERTHA. Why is your sword in your hand, King? Thrust its iron into the evil heart of the impostor.

MALGISTA. Algista, dearest daughter, enchant him with sweet words of love, whisper secret incantations in his ear.

ALGISTA. My lord, I have come to you—take me as you will, living or dead. By the might of my infinite love, by the power of my unbearable suffering, by my will, triumphant over life and death, I have bought from heaven and earth and the dark subterranean world your body and your soul and your night-wandering shade. Here I stand before you, neither living nor dead, the breath all but gone from my body, yet still untouched by corruption; I hesitate at the terrible crossroads, my blood in the damp earth and my voice rising to the witching moon—and I summon you: come to me, of your own will choose for us a path to life or death. Come with me living, love me; or remain here—but here too you shall be with me, dead. Love me, lord and husband, mine forever, love me.

KING. You cheated your way into my bed, you stole the Queen's name and honor.

BERTHA. She is a sorceress. Quick—run her through with your sword.

ALGISTA. When you loved me, when you showered me with caresses, when you whispered tender words to me, what did we care about the glitter of your crown or your sovereign might? Did I not make you drunk with all of love's delights? Did I not sweeten your every joy with carefree mirth? Did I not dissolve your every sorrow in my tears? Was I not the bright sky to you and the cool shade, and twittering of birds and the stream's bright babble? White and naked, my arms rested on your weary shoulders more lightly than the necklet of royalty. Sweeter than Falernian wine were the sultry kisses of my scarlet lips. My eyes shone upon you more brightly than the rich-hued diamonds and rubies of your crown. Was I not more beautiful than any queen? Was it not you who said that I was the wisest of women, that my words fell like gold on the worthless ashes of the speeches of your most venerable nobles?

KING. You were beautiful and wise, and I loved you. But what is past is past. Go.

BERTHA. Run her through with your sword.

ALGISTA. I will not leave you. We are united forever by the mysterious power of my love.

KING. Here is my wife, Queen Bertha—our son and heir, Charles, sleeps in his chamber, guarded by faithful servants. You and your son have no place among us.

ALGISTA. But do you love me?

KING. I do.

ALGISTA. Then let Queen Bertha and young Charles remain here. Yield your crown to him and follow me. I shall reveal to you a free and happy world, I shall lead you to a valley amid distant mountains where there are no rulers and no slaves, where the air of freedom is light and sweet.

KING. You speak madness. I am the King.

BERTHA. Kill her.

ALGISTA. Clodoveg, your fate is in your hands. Look—the torches are going out. Listen—the quick-eared dogs are howling outside, scenting mysterious traces in the fine dust of the roadway. See, King: everything around you is quiet and dark and still. Listen: no one speaks and my words fall into the darkness before you.

KING. Go, madwoman. Pages, take her away.

All those around the King stand motionless, their eyes fixed on Algista.

ALGISTA. Here I stand alone, all life and death within me. Yours is the choice, Clodoveg, dearest lord and husband. The final moment draws near. Destiny will not wait. For the last time I say to you: follow me, go forward with me into life—for only with me is there life; and there, where you grow rigid, King, beneath the madness of your crown, beneath your robes of blood, is death. Take off your crown, follow me.

KING. I shall not follow you. I am the King. Begone, mad-woman.

The ringing of churchbells is heard outside.

ALGISTA. The hour has come. Clodoveg, your choice is made. You will not come with me? You will not?

KING. No.

MALGISTA. He stands before you, a cold stone among stones, Algista. Algista, my serpent-eyed daughter, with terrible words cast a spell upon him, condemn him to eternal stillness.

ALGISTA. You stand before me, a cold stone among stones. Become a stone then, King; stand, a cold stone, until time devours you too.

Algista falls at the King's feet. Her son falls across her corpse. The King and the others stand motionless. A dispassionate voice is heard:

— See, Algista is dead, Chilperic is dead. Her mother kneels over them, eternally inconsolable. See, Clodoveg and those about him have turned to stone. See, they stand like the carved figures in a stone frieze. See, before your eyes life petrifies to a flat tableau; the moon grows dim, and all light flees this place, and the proud castle's immensity is hidden by the black cloud of death. Believe, then: by Death Love conquers—Love and Death are one.

NOTE

The substance of this tragedy is taken, in its general outline, from the legend of Queen Bertha of the Big Foot, the mother of Charlemagne. The name of the king has been changed deliberately in order to remove the tragedy from the realm of history, and even from the legend, which ends somewhat differently from my play. This is how the legend is summarized in G. N. Potanin's book *Eastern Motifs*, pp. 5-7:

The Frankish King Pepin wishes to marry; his nobles journey to Hungary, to the city of Buda, and ask the Hungarian king for his daughter's hand. The king is very flattered by the proposal, but fears that Pepin will reject his bride because she is deformed: one of her legs is longer than the other. However, the nobles, though aware of this, stand by their original decision. The parents send their daughter on her way in the company of two serving-women, one old and one young; the old one is Margista and the young one is her daughter Algista. The bride is received with due ceremony in Paris. Night falls; Bertha must go to the marriage bed. Margista expresses the fear that Pepin may kill her mistress; Bertha is troubled; Margista agrees to let Algista go in her place in order to save the princess. Bertha passes the night in Margista's room and in the morning steals into the royal bedchamber, intending to change places with Algista, unbeknown to the king. When she enters, Algista wounds herself with a knife and accuses Bertha of attempting to kill her. The king, taking Algista for Bertha, is outraged and orders the supposed Algista to be put to death. Bertha is taken into a forest, where she loses her way. She wanders about in the forest for a long time, until at last she comes upon the house of a miller, who gives her protection. Suspecting no deceit, the king lives with Algista, by whom he has two sons. Bertha's parents decide to visit their daughter; they arrive in Paris and see Algista in the queen's place. The Hungarian king suspects that Pepin himself is responsible for the substitution. He prepares to return to Hungary and gather an armed force to punish Pepin. Before his departure, however, Pepin persuades his father-in-law to go hunting with him. During the hunt Pepin loses his way and comes upon the house of the miller in whose care Bertha has been living. The miller has two daughters, and that evening Pepin asks the miller to send one of his three girls to spend the night with him. The miller sends Bertha, having prepared for the king a bed of leaves in a cart . . . Bertha tells the king who she is and how she came to be living with the miller. The fact that one of her legs is longer than the other convinces Pepin that she is the true Bertha and that the woman he took for Bertha is an impostor. He takes Bertha to Paris and makes her his queen, puts the false Bertha to death and is reconciled with the parents of the true Bertha. Bertha gives birth to a son, who, either because he was conceived or born in a cart, is given the name *Charro mano*—Charlemagne.

MIKHAIL KUZMIN

Mikhail Kuzmin (1872-1936), poet, novelist and short-story writer, dramatist, composer, critic and translator, was born in Yaroslavl, where his family belonged to the local gentry. Failure to complete his studies (1891-94) at the St. Petersburg Conservatory, where Rimsky-Korsakov and Liadov were among his teachers, led to *Wanderjahre* in Italy and Egypt. Returning home, he became absorbed in Russian antiquity, accompanying Old Believers on their expeditions to the provinces in search of ancient icons. These early experiences found expression in the largely autobiographical novel *Wings* (1906) and the free verse poems of the *Alexandrian Songs* (1907), both first published in the Symbolist journal *The Scales. Wings*, with its bold defense of homosexual love, gained its author some notoriety—there was even an attempt (fortunately unsuccessful) to organize a boycott of his work. *Nets* (1908), Kuzmin's first book of poems, established him once and for all as a new and individual voice in Russian poetry. A skilled performer of his own songs at the piano, Kuzmin was the favored entertainer of artistic and bohemian St. Petersburg. Close to Diaghilev and his *World of Art* circle of aesthetes, painters and musicians, Kuzmin was also a frequenter of Viacheslav Ivanov's "Tower"—which became between 1907 and 1912 his permanent residence. Kuzmin's initial enthusiasm for the October Revolution was of short duration; he remained in the Soviet Union, however, scraping a living as a translator (of, among others, Apuleius, Boccaccio, Shakespeare, Mérimée, Henri de Régnier and Anatole France). As late as 1929 he contrived to publish the wonderful long poem *The Trout Breaks the Ice*, in which he remains quite uncompromisingly himself. We may suppose that he was fortunate to die in a hospital bed, since his companion of more than twenty years, the writer Yury Yurkun, was arrested and shot two years later.

"Kuzmin is a writer unique of his kind. There was no one like him in Russia before, and I do not know whether there will be in time to come"—Blok's words, written at the outset of Kuzmin's literary career, still seem valid. His early poetry, deliberately "minor" in its celebration of evanescent everyday pleasures, had a welcome lightness of heart and touch amid the portents and prophesies of Symbolism. His prose, with its tendency toward stylization and turning away from psychology, had a sophisticated simplicity that seemed to hark back to Pushkin. It would be wrong, however, to stereotype Kuzmin—as literary histories have tended to—simply as a poet of exquisite trifles and exponent of the "beautiful clarity" he advocated in a famous manifesto; his later work—dense, elliptical, oblique—is often difficult and demanding.

Much of Kuzmin's work for the theatre (and the list runs to over thirty items) had the nature of divertissement—pastorals, operettas, pantomimes, ballets, masquerades, children's plays, plays for puppets. Many of these pieces (some of which survive as no more than intriguing titles) were intended for St. Petersburg's little experimental theatres, such as Meyerhold's House of Interludes, or the intimate cabarets frequented by poets and artists, such as the Stray Dog and its successor, the Players' Rest. Admitting that Kuzmin's plays, for all their mastery of dialogue and scenic grace, had failed to gain a foothold outside the little theatres, the drama critic of *Apollo*, writing in 1916, awarded them "the leading place in our theatre of underground classics."

Kuzmin's first attempt at playwriting, the amorphous "dramatic poem" *The History of the Knight d'Alessio* (1905), a potpourri of reminiscences from *Faust, Peer Gynt, Tannhäuser,* Pushkin's *Little Tragedies, Die Zauberflöte, The Tempest* and no doubt other things beside, is an ambitious failure. But by the *Three Plays* of 1907 Kuzmin has clearly found his characteristic style; fragile miniatures that mingle verse with prose and song with dance, these entertainments—*The Dangerous Precaution, Two Shepherds and a Nymph in a Hut, The Choice of a Bride*—are subtitled respectively "comedy with singing," "pastoral for a masquerade" and "comedy ballet" and suggest the stylized rococo of such *World of Art* painters as Somov, Sapunov and Sudeikin (all close friends of Kuzmin's). *The Dangerous Precaution*, an adroit minuet of sexual identities, was found shocking enough by the censorship to cause the little volume's confiscation.

The *Three Comedies* (1908) are perhaps Kuzmin's most consummate achievement as a dramatist. Blok pronounced *The Comedy of Eudoxia of Heliopolis* (a treatment of the favorite *fin de siècle* theme of the saintly courtesan) to be "the most perfect creation in the field of Russian lyrical drama," and Mirsky has called *The Comedy of Alexis* "the most exquisite" of Kuzmin's plays. Kuzmin here is using the word "comedy" in its archaic sense of "mystery play," and like Remizov in his mysteries he draws on Russia's ancient holy tales—but to very different effect: at once lucid and enigmatic, the Comedies hold refined irony and naive piety in perfect equipoise.

"The Venice of Goldoni, Gozzi and Longhi" is the setting specified by the author for his comedy *The Venetian Madcaps*. For Meyerhold and his circle, late eighteenth-century Venice was the golden age of pure theatricality they were seeking to revive. Venice and the *commedia dell'arte*, particularly in the fantastic aspect represented by Gozzi, became the object of a cult. It was Kuzmin who originally composed the music for the culminating production of

Meyerhold's *commedia dell'arte* phase, that of Lermontov's *Masquerade*, on which the director worked from 1911 until 1917 (a new score was later commissioned from Glazunov), and it may be that work on Lermontov's melodrama of jealousy and murder, fate and retribution in a setting suggestive of Venice inspired him to produce one of his own (curiously, Blok too at this time was contemplating a drama set in eighteenth-century Venice with "cards and candles"). Written in 1912, *The Venetian Madcaps* was staged two years later at the Moscow mansion of the Nosovs, wealthy patrons of the arts, with music by Kuzmin himself, decor by Sudeikin and choreography by Mordkin. Something of the extravagance of the occasion is preserved in the limited edition (555 copies) of the play published in Moscow in 1915, in which the actors are depicted by Sudeikin in the guise of porcelain figurines—one of the most beautiful of all Russian books.

Though strictly outside the bounds of the present volume, Kuzmin's later plays deserve some mention. Like his later poetry they tend toward complexity, unexplained juxtapositions, and a deliberate confusion of time and place. *Mary's Tuesday* (1921) is described as a "spectacle in three parts for live or wooden dolls" (recalling Maeterlinck's plays for the puppet theatre). *Hull's Stroll* (1924), described by its author as "half scenario, half lyric, half short story," reveals the influence of the German expressionist film. *The Death of Nero* (1929), a three act play, is also suggestive of a film scenario, cutting back and forth between modern and Imperial Rome; Nero's career, as seen by Suetonius, is juxtaposed with a modern, somewhat Dostoevskian love triangle. Neither of the last two plays has been published in the Soviet Union.

Kuzmin was active in the theatre as a composer as well as a playwright. Sometimes he combined both talents to produce musical plays and operettas such as *Dutch Liza* (1910), a charming pastiche of Russian *opéra comique,* or *Maidens' Pleasure* (1911), the oriental theme of which drew from Sudeikin some of his most gorgeous theatrical designs. On other occasions he wrote music for other men's plays; his music for Blok's *Puppet Show,* "piquant, highly spiced, disturbing and voluptuous" to the ears of a contemporary hearer, seems to have contributed significantly to the play's success. In addition he wrote music for Ernst Hardt's

Tantris der Narr, Znosko-Borovsky's *The Transformed Prince*, Grillparzer's *Die Ahnfrau* (in Blok's translation), Krylov's *The Frantic Family*, Ernst Toller's *Hinkemann* and Plautus' *Menaechmi*.

Among the essays collected in *Conventions* (1923) are to be found a good many on the theatre. As a theatre critic, Kuzmin keeps to the positions staked out by Meyerhold: the theatre must above all be theatrical, and the enemy of the theatrical is vulgar naturalism—"the real sausages of Antoine's theatre; the Gothic chairs of the Meiningen troupe and the notorious 'crickets' of Stanislavsky." Impatient with social drama, he insists that "the time we live in, it is clear, calls for tragedy, for high comedy, for fantastic Aristophanic comedy, for an exaggerated and simplified psychology (i.e. melodrama), for pantomime and magic."

MIKHAIL KUZMIN

THE COMEDY

OF ALEXIS, MAN OF GOD[37]

OR

THE LOST SON TRANSFORMED

DRAMATIS PERSONAE

ALEXIS, *man of God*
EUPHIMIAN, *his father*
SEXTON
SHOPKEEPER
SERVANT
NARRATOR
AGLAIDA, *Alexis' mother*
MASTRIDIA, *Alexis' wife*
MAIDSERVANTS
HARLOTS

The action takes place in Rome and Edessa.

PART ONE

Rome. Mastridia's bedroom. Mastridia, Aglaida, maidservants.

MASTRIDIA. I keep trying to remember that song the girls were singing; there's something in it about carpenters.

AGLAIDA. We celebrated the wedding in the old-fashioned way, keeping in the country songs that you, as a maiden of royal birth, had never heard before.

MASTRIDIA. Were they pagan songs?

AGLAIDA. Yes, pagan songs. The one you mean begins:
The garland has let fall a flower.
The carpenters raise the bridal bower.
Of weeping and wailing we have no need:
Joy we summon—joy's our creed.

MASTRIDIA. Joy's our creed.
I think I can remember the next verse:
Soon shall the carpenters' work be ended—
A new-gathered rose with the old be blended.
Such is eternal destiny.
Demeter . . .

AGLAIDA. Demeter weeps, and Persephone.

MASTRIDIA. And Persephone.
If the flower perish . . .

AGLAIDA. The fruit's in time's womb.
Carpenters, build the virgin's tomb!
Soon shall the sacred fortress fall,
The clamor of birds shall breach the wall.

MASTRIDIA. I don't quite understand the last words.

AGLAIDA. There's a lot more to the song, and what goes before is clear from what follows. Nothing can be understood by itself.

MASTRIDIA. I still can't get used to the idea that I'm married to your son. How long is it since I left my father's house, my careless romps? I'd never set eyes on Alexis before the wedding, before that moment in the blessed church of St. Boniface. O how beautiful his eyes were when I lifted my own and saw them gazing from beneath the wedding garland—being too big for him, it had slipped down onto his forehead!

FIRST MAIDSERVANT. The young master has grown so thin lately; I'm always afraid the golden girdle will slip from his waist one of these days.

AGLAIDA. That will pass. Health returns with love.

MAIDSERVANTS. Amen.

AGLAIDA. He was always frail and sensitive. Look at his picture. Wouldn't you say it was a girl dressed as a boy?

MASTRIDIA. Holy apostles, how thin his neck is! Those rings seem too heavy for those emaciated fingers.

FIRST MAIDSERVANT. The young master seldom wears them.

AGLAIDA. He will wear them. With love return good cheer and joy.

MAIDSERVANTS. Amen.

MASTRIDIA. How pale his cheeks are, and how the blue veins on his temples stand out! How faint is the pink of his half-open lips!

AGLAIDA. The roses will come to those cheeks, the skin of his temples will thicken and purple will stain his lips—my child, my one and only child, will be happy, healthy and joyful, in accordance with the wishes of God, who created him, of nature, and of myself, who gave him birth; for who will have a man's welfare at heart more than the mother who gave him suck?

MASTRIDIA. I love him, dear Mother, and I am most grateful to you for choosing me as his bride; give me again your tender blessing.

AGLAIDA. May God be with you, pure and noble maiden. Farewell; await his coming. The sacramental hour of marriage is at hand. May Love be with you!

She goes out. The maidservants attire Mastridia for the night.

SECOND MAIDSERVANT. There you go, my lady, getting sad again; a bride should be joyful.

MASTRIDIA. How I can be joyful when I do not know the fate in store for me? When I know neither my husband, nor his house, nor his parents.

SECOND MAIDSERVANT. Only one who does not think ahead can be joyful.

FIRST MAIDSERVANT. Why should you worry about the future? Your father-in-law's house is hardly less wealthy and abundant than your father's.

THIRD MAIDSERVANT. The noble Euphimian has as many as three

thousand servants, and all of them wear silk and girdles of gold.

FIRST MAIDSERVANT. And there's scarcely a house in Rome more noted for piety and good works: are not three tables set up every day—one for beggars, one for widows and one for orphans?

THIRD MAIDSERVANT. Does not the lord Euphimian himself, in his humility of heart, partake of food with itinerant monks?

FIRST MAIDSERVANT. Does he not fast until the ninth hour?

THIRD MAIDSERVANT. And what of the alms he distributes? And what of his prayers?

FIRST MAIDSERVANT. Of the young master I say nothing: he's a saint!

MASTRIDIA. How am I to live with him?

FIRST MAIDSERVANT. He's a saint! No one can compare with him in feats of fasting and godly exercises.

THIRD MAIDSERVANT. They say he wears a hair shirt.

MASTRIDIA. How am I to live with him?

FIRST MAIDSERVANT. From his childhood on he's studied grammar, rhetoric, choral singing and church law.

SECOND MAIDSERVANT. It's a delicate flower you're plucking, fortunate Mastridia.

MASTRIDIA. O I am wretched, wretched. What does fate have in store for me?

A knock at the door and a voice: "The noble Alexis, son of the most worthy Euphimian, wishes to know whether the noble Mastridia is prepared to receive him."

FIRST MAIDSERVANT. The noble Mastridia is ready to receive, joyfully and submissively, her husband and her lord.

Enter Alexis. The maidservants leave.

ALEXIS. So, lady—you are my wife.

MASTRIDIA. My lord . . .

ALEXIS. You are my wife before God and man. The will of my parents is fulfilled. A long life shall we walk hand in hand together, supporting each other. Do you understand the solemnity of these moments?

MASTRIDIA. My lord . . .

ALEXIS. Do you understand the solemnity of these moments? Should they not be dedicated to prayer, as the first fruits are dedicated to God? And in the silence of night, in solitude, our spousal prayer, joined although still pure, will the more surely take wing into the starry sky.

MASTRIDIA. My lord . . .

ALEXIS. I will not hinder you from fixing your thoughts on holy things; I shall return in an hour, at your service.

MASTRIDIA. Don't you love me then? Or do you love another? Or do you find me repellent?

ALEXIS. I don't understand what I have done to deserve such questions. As a Christian, how can I fail to love anyone? I shall leave you for a short while only.

Goes out.

MASTRIDIA. What an affront! And this sanctimonious goody-goody is to be my husband? How shamefully I have been deceived. But I shall work my wiles—I'll make his eyes, accustomed to reflecting only the winking of altar lamps, burn with love! Let's see, what's to be done? The wise man takes advantage of the moment to forge his future fate. I shall put on my finery and I shall sit in this golden chair—he's not a stone, he can't remain indifferent to one who is of royal blood and far-famed for beauty.

She adorns herself and sits down.

O my beauty's decaying,
My finery fraying!
Who may gaze, cares not.
Who would gaze, dares not.

To a fine lord and master
Has cruel fate cast me!
Is not my breast tender,
My neck white and slender?

But wasted is beauty
On blind man and eunuch:
Not for them the sweet kernel,
The rose eternal.

But what we desire shall be granted,
Patience and will are not daunted:
The sage casts his line with the dawning,
The sluggard lies snoring all morning.

The sower dreams, sowing,
Of harvest's growing;
I'll wait for Alexis.
Come—I'm no ogress!

See, my beauty's decaying,
My finery's fraying:
Who may gaze, cares not,
Who would gaze, dares not.

She falls asleep. Alexis enters.

ALEXIS. How am I to choose between God's will, which commands us to obey our parents, and the voice that sounds in my very ear, urging me to flee, to save myself? And who knows—may it not be that he who thinks to heed God's word works his own will? But I shall not yield to temptation; our own feeble desires cannot alter the pre-ordained pattern of fate. Farewell, my father's house, farewell, our household icons, and you, unhappy Mastridia, a widow among brides, a maid among wives—farewell! I shall leave you this ring and this girdle, wrapping them first in a purple kerchief. When the lark awakens you, Alexis will already be far away. And so I kiss you for the first and, God grant, the last time.

He kisses her on the forehead and goes out.

Knocking at the door. Aglaida's voice: Are you still sleeping, my daughter? It is morning already. Leave your husband's embraces.
MASTRIDIA. Is it you, my lord? Come in.

Enter Aglaida and maidservants.

AGLAIDA. Well then, my daughter? Has the holy and longed-for consummation come to pass? But what do I see?—you are confused, downcast? Where then is my son? Has he gone so early to pray?
MATRIDIA. Mother, I do not know what is the matter with him: he has

not been with me. He is there.

AGLAIDA. You disturb me, Mastridia. Alexis! Alexis!

She goes out.

MAIDSERVANTS. This bodes no good. Who ever heard the like? Who ever did such a thing? It's just what I expected. And the bed is untouched—I changed two creaking boards on it for new ones. Poor darling, we weep with you. It is hard to go against the will of heaven: what do our desires signify? Weep, weep!

AGLAIDA. *(entering)* Unheard-of! Incredible! What a disgrace to our house: he is not there! What's in this purple kerchief?

FIRST MAIDSERVANT. A ring and a girdle! Saints Gurias,[38] Samonas and Abibus preserve us! He has left you.

AGLAIDA. Nonsense! We'll see whose will is stronger. Summon Euphimian—I shall pursue him to the ends of the earth. Do not weep, my daughter; all is not yet lost.

MASTRIDIA. I can't bear it! I can't bear it! To be abandoned in this way. Give me musk! . . . Everything is going dark before my eyes . . . O!

She falls down in a swoon.

PART TWO

NARRATOR. Roar, you waves, as we fly through the foam!
Farewell, belovèd, lovely Rome!
He must not weep who takes in hand
The pilgrim's stave.
Be of good cheer and dry your tears—
Set forth, be brave!
"I dreamed this night, Mastridia says,
A fearful dream—
In church I stood at a requiem,
But for whom, for whom?
Who lay there cold and glassy-eyed?
Alexis—dead!
In terror I woke, my heart weighed down
With darkest dread."

Roar, you waves, as we fly through the foam!
Farewell, belovèd, lovely Rome!
Money he had for the sailors' pay,
And some to spare—
To beggars he gave it, himself entrusting
To God's good care.
Who trusts in the Lord walks ever the way
Of righteousness,
With angels for guides and the Mother of God
To shield and bless.
To Edessa town he comes at last,
Stands at the gate,
With hair unshorn and beard unkempt—
A sorry sight!
Roar, you waves, as we fly through the foam!
Farewell, belovèd, lovely Rome!
At the cathedral door he stands,
Ragged, unshod,
In poverty soul-resolute—
A fool in God!
In the harlots' den he spends his nights,
Quiet as a stone.
"My body is known to the harsh hair shirt,
To love unknown."
Through nights of passion he stands in prayer,
The women wait;
But he steals away when the east grows red,
Inviolate.
Roar, you waves, as we fly through the foam!
Farewell, belovèd, lovely Rome!
All sorts of virtue are pleasing to God,
He thinks no ill:
If a saint be reputed a profligate,
He's saintlier still.
Wider and deeper is the soul of man
Than the salt sea:
Change is our law, let pass but an hour—
We are not we.
Foolish the man who rails at fate—
So madmen rave!
Scarce is our fate revealed to us

In the damp grave.
Roar, you waves, as we fly through the foam!
Farewell, belovèd, lovely Rome!

SCENE ONE

A street in Edessa. Evening. Alexis and harlots.

HARLOTS. Alexis! Alexis! Who are you going to visit today? Me! Me! My sweetheart, my poppet, my pretty—come and visit me! There's a pot of rue on my windowsill—it's blooming wonderfully. And I have bed-curtains with a maiden and a unicorn and fighting warriors embroidered on them. I don't have any curtains, but I can sing you songs all night, and never the same one twice, and I'll give you an amulet to ward off the evil eye. Me, visit me!

ALEXIS. My sweet sisters, I wouldn't want to hurt the feelings of any one of you, so I'll go somewhere I haven't been before.

FIRST HARLOT. You'll soon get through us at that rate.

FOURTH HARLOT. Have you heard, ladies, that a new saint has been proclaimed at Antioch?

FIRST HARLOT. What, does he get barren matrons with child?

FOURTH HARLOT. No, he isn't a hermit—he's a stonemason.

FIRST HARLOT. A stonemason?

FOURTH HARLOT. I heard about it from fat Ephrem—the one who used to be my protector. They were building a house there after the recent earthquake, and while they were taking a rest, Ephrem *(he was overseer)* suddenly noticed a pillar of fire over the head of one old man. They made enquiries, and it turned out that this man was a bishop who had quit his office of his own free will to labor in obscurity with the common folk.

FIRST HARLOT. He's a great fool, your bishop! To cover himself with grime in the heat of noon when he might be lying in a fragrant bath or riding a white mule.

SECOND HARLOT. Anyway, what has all this to do with us?

THIRD HARLOT. What are you looking around you like that for, Alexis?

FIRST HARLOT. He's looking to see whether there's a pillar of fire over his head.

SECOND HARLOT. Perhaps you're a bishop too?

THIRD HARLOT. Or even a pope?

FIFTH HARLOT. *(sings)*

> Cries merry Lisetta:
> "A sea-trip! What better?
> Let us fly through the foam
> Till we come to eternal, seven-hilled Rome."
> Says the lady Omphale:
> "The sea waits, my darling,
> But we also need sails
> And a cap for your pigtails;
> Listen to me, we'll cut our hair,
> Our feet will be bare
> And jerkins will flatten our breasts—
> On a voyage a sailor's disguise is best.
> Ah the delight
> Of the caraway-scented Palatine night . . ."
> "O mother, be silent I pray:
> Call not to mind what is far, far away."

Alexis weeps.

FIFTH HARLOT. What's the matter, friend—why are you weeping?

FIRST HARLOT. Let him be. Each of us has her little cell where she can be alone when the time for tears comes—but where can he go?

They go out.

ALEXIS. O Rome! My poor deserted ones, do you still live as you used to? Have you forgotten me?
"Call not to mind what is far, far away."

Enter a sexton.

SEXTON. Are you the holy man?

ALEXIS. In the light of dusk one man looks much like another. I think you're looking for someone else.

SEXTON. You're the Alexis they call "the harlots' friend," aren't you? Let me kiss your hand.

ALEXIS. I am the one they call "the harlots' friend," but I see no holiness in that.

SEXTON. Enough of these denials. You will soon learn that everything is known: your virtue and your humility both. This night the Queen of Heaven appeared to me and said: "The holy man must live in My house, not stand with penitents in the galilee." "But who is he?" I ventured to ask, and she said to me: "Alexis, the harlots' friend." And so, brother, I beg you to let me reveal you to the lord bishop and lead you into the temple. I came purposely at the twilight hour to speak with you, lest I should offend your humility.

ALEXIS. I cannot oppose the Voice of Heaven: go, light the candles, prepare to welcome the servant of the Queen of Heaven.

SEXTON. We shall expect you at once.

He goes out.

ALEXIS. Surely I did not leave my father's house and my love that I might be honored here? I must flee, I must flee. The Lord will forgive me: the tempter too sends visions. I do not wish for worldly honors. I do not want them!

He goes out.

SCENE TWO

Rome. A street.

NARRATOR. A mother planned marriage—
It was not well:
It profits us little
To have our will.
His wife he abandons—
And what of it? What?
Who's to determine
Where truth is, where not?
The plum being eaten,
The stone's cast aside—
Yet the traveller shall rest

In the plumtree's shade.
Vice or virtue
Are hidden in vain:
At the hour appointed
All shall be plain.
In vain to seduce you
The harlot schemes
Your holiness haunts
Another's dreams.
Scorning all honor,
You braved the sea-foam,
For joy or for sorrow,
Your path leads to Rome.
The path that is destined
You may not gainsay—
Then shoulder your bundle
And go your way.

ALEXIS. Can I be in Rome?! O fate, who can argue with you? How well I remember everything, even though it has changed in these seventeen years! Here's the bend in the street, halfway home from school; here's the shop where I used to buy cakes from fat Titus—is he still alive? Someone is coming out of the shop: can it be he? No, no—he was fat with three folds of flesh at the nape of his neck . . . I'll speak to him, all the same . . . Respected sir, I bid you good day.

SHOPKEEPER. And to you, passer-by, a day no less good . . . Have you come from afar? Your feet are covered with dust, your face is sunburned, your clothes are shabby: perhaps you come from the holy places?

ALEXIS. No, I do not come from the holy places; I'm very tired, that's all.

SHOPKEEPER. Is there no one that you know in town?

ALEXIS. I very much doubt it.

SHOPKEEPER. You might seek help from the noble Euphimian; his charity is known far beyond the bounds of Rome.

ALEXIS. Indeed? I don't remember ever hearing of him . . . where is his house?

SHOPKEEPER. If you came through the square, you must have seen it: by the gates there is a fountain with bas-reliefs depicting the story of the prophet Jonah.

ALEXIS. Are there two big planetrees at the entrance?

SHOPKEEPER. That's right . . . You noticed them? But you needn't trouble yourself after all: here comes Euphimian himself on his way home from the senate.

ALEXIS. Really? Be still, my heart, be still!

SHOPKEEPER. Yes, I'm sure it is he. Why have you turned so pale, traveller? Are you afraid?

ALEXIS. Yes, very afraid. Which of them is Euphimian: the curly-haired one with the gray beard?

SHOPKEEPER. You have guessed aright.

ALEXIS. Gracious heavens! His very features!

Falls to his knees, sobbing.

SHOPKEEPER. You *are* in a state, though indeed a humble posture befits a supplicant.

Enter Euphimian with two friends and several servants.

EUPHIMIAN. I shall talk with Titus Claudius tomorrow about the matter you mentioned at matins. You may consider your petition all but granted . . . Who is this man? What is it you seek, thus abasing yourself? You're sobbing? Have you been shipwrecked? But where is the tablet depicting your misfortune?

ALEXIS. My lord, be merciful, give shelter to one who has no roof over his head, feed one who hungers, succour one pursued by fate! If someone dear to you is on a journey or roving abroad, remember him and take pity on an unhappy wanderer!

EUPHIMIAN. Who taught you these words? Or are you a seer?

ALEXIS. No one. No one.

EUPHIMIAN. Follow me; in my house you will find shelter; pray for God's servant Alexis.

ALEXIS. Alexis, God's servant, is happy, is blessed.

EUPHIMIAN. Do you mean he's dead? Do you know him?

ALEXIS. No, I know nothing, nothing . . .

They move on.

PART THREE

SCENE ONE

The courtyard of Euphimian's house; Alexis' cell by the gates, the window of Mastridia's chamber opposite.

ALEXIS. Lord, I thank Thee that Thou hast permitted me to spend the last days of my sinful life in my father's house, although unrecognized and in a lowly guise. My humiliation, the mockery of the menials, the disdain of visitors and passers-by are sweet to me. I thank Thee. I see poor Mastridia every day, and her tears give me hope for her salvation. But I do not wish, dying unrecognized, to leave my kin in ignorance and to be deprived of the requiem masses and funeral rites which, perhaps, have already been performed for me in my lifetime. I shall write the story of my life on a long scroll and let them find it when I am no longer among the living. I feel that God will soon call me to Himself. Mastridia is late appearing today; she is dallying behind her painted windows. Already it is evening; swallows soar screeching above the earth; the shadows lengthen and the earth flushes pink, like the blood-stained sand in the arena.

Mastridia throws open her windows.

There she is! Who knows, wife, this may be the last time I shall see you.

MASTRIDIA. *(addressing a cage visible through the open window).*
Little bird, little sparrow mine,
Of what do you sing all day long?
Misery past measuring
Brings ever the selfsame song.
Two beds, O two beds in my chamber are,
Between them I numbly grieve.
Through wearisome days of widowhood
I drag my slow steps to the grave.
What joy do we know, the two of us?
Gray sadness has made us his own.
Unknown to men are our melodies—

And let them remain unknown!
Gaily you chirruped at liberty,
Drunk with earth's heady spring.
But now you hang here my prisoner,
My companion in sorrowing.
O I wouldn't constrain and torment you,
Hang your cage by a green grassy plot,
But I am weary to death of this misery,
This wearisome widow's lot.

What boredom! What a wretched life is mine! What do I care if I am honored by all and first among widowed matrons if I am deprived of the joys of love and family? O Alexis, my dear husband, why did you forsake me? Are you pining, too, eh, little bird? If you like, I'll open your cage, but I won't let you out, no I won't . . . You're used to captivity by now, aren't you? You're happy in your tight little house . . .

She opens the door of the case; the bird flies away.

O! Has he flown away? Would you believe it! Quick, girls, catch my bird, my little bird! What are you standing there for, old man? Run—catch him! Look, now he's perched on the wall, now he's flying from the bush to the gravel! Did you catch him? No? But he's forgotten how to fly. He's flown away? What? You nasty, lazy old man—you couldn't even manage to do that for me. Does my father-in-law feed you for nothing then?

Weeps.

ALEXIS. If I were a cat, then no doubt I would have been able to return your plaything to you, lady, but I am only a feeble old man.

MASTRIDIA. You couldn't even do a little thing like that for me, you disgusting old sponger. I'll tell Euphimian to throw you out: I can't bear to look at you.

ALEXIS. Lady, do not weep, be comforted. Suppose your husband were to return—your eyes must not be red for the joyful welcome.

MASTRIDIA. And when is he going to return, I'd like to know. Perhaps he is no longer among the living.

ALEXIS. All the same, he may return. Everything is in God's hands. There's one thing I wanted to ask you—only you mustn't be offended—but I've heard it said that the features of the missing lord somewhat resembled mine.

Mastridia laughs.

ALEXIS. Even I was young once.

MASTRIDIA. What rubbish! He was taller than you. And how dare you say such things to me? You are becoming insolent; you deliberately allowed my bird to escape and now you rub salt in my wounds. You're a malicious, idle, filthy, disgusting old man. Your cell stinks too.

ALEXIS. Lady!

MASTRIDIA. All our visitors turn away when they pass to avoid breathing in the stench.

ALEXIS. Not everyone can smell of ambergris.

MASTRIDIA. You send me evil dreams! You're a sorcerer! You torment me! I don't want to set eyes on you. Get out! Take that, take that!

She throws the empty cage at him and goes out.

ALEXIS. My God, my God, it's not enough that the servants mock me and beat me and throw slops over me—now even my own wife is treating me cruelly. The time has come for you to die, wretched Alexis.

SCENE TWO

Mastridia's chamber.

NARRATOR. To his setting the sun rolls swiftly,
And deathward we sink with the sun.
When death comes, can brother help brother?
That prison-house no man may shun.
Sweet are the ills of our dotage
When the terrible caller comes by.
Dear is this life—must we leave it?
In silence the blind reaper scythes.
Soul weeps to be sundered from body,
The sun sinks to earth, crimson-rimmed.
Be your lot happy or hapless,
The light of your eyes must be dimmed.
Fall the white hands and lie listless;
Journey's ended, and are you content?

All in vain is Niobe's weeping:
Her young are beyond her lament.
When the righteous die, we see wonders:
Their lives are a chalice of gold.
Through the heavens, by paths paradisial
They mount to a better world.
Thing of clay, the body lies lifeless,
But soul's wings like dove's wings are spread.
Weep, brothers weep, cast your eyes down,
For saintly Alexis is dead.

Mastridia, Aglaida, maidservants.

AGLAIDA. How stuffy it is, though it's only March; should we open a window, Mastridia?

MASTRIDIA. I don't want to see the sun; I find painted glass more comforting.

AGLAIDA. Well, the heat is killing me.

FIRST MAIDSERVANT. It's been hot for days; a great cloud of stifling dust hangs over all the Campagna—the acacias on the Appian Way have turned gray from the early heat. I can't remember such sultry weather in March.

SECOND MAIDSERVANT. Did you hear that on Friday, on Saturday and again on Thursday, in the cathedral, the pope and all the clergy and congregation heard a voice from the altar—always the same voice?

MASTRIDIA. And what did it say?

FIRST MAIDSERVANT. "Come unto me, all ye that labor and are heavy laden." The whole city knows about it.

MASTRIDIA. I don't know—I hadn't heard.

SECOND MAIDSERVANT. The Holy Father spends all his nights in prayer.

AGLAIDA. How stuffy it is, Mastridia! O how stuffy it is!

FIRST MAIDSERVANT. Today I saw the young master in a dream. I was walking along the road by the sea and I saw a man, clothed all in gold, sitting in a pine tree; I asked someone nearby, "Who is that?" and he replied, "Alexis." And the man gathered his robes about him and flew up into the air; his golden sleeves covered half the sky.

AGLAIDA. A phoenix! A phoenix!

MASTRIDIA. And you recognized my husband?

FIRST MAIDSERVANT. I recognized him by his eyes: they're hard to forget.

AGLAIDA. I saw eyes like that somewhere not long ago. But where? Where?

MASTRIDIA. Yesterday my little bird, my catamite, flew away. That blockhead who lives at our gates couldn't manage to get him back for me.

AGLAIDA. Bells. Do you hear bells?

MAIDSERVANTS. We can't hear a thing. It's the heat making your ears ring. Rest awhile, mistress, you're not well.

MASTRIDIA. He couldn't catch him. Someone should tell Father to throw him out. He's insolent, coarse and lazy.

SECOND MAIDSERVANT. You should be more compassionate, mistress.

AGLAIDA. Open the window. Don't tell me you can't hear bells now.

They open a window.

MAIDSERVANTS. Yes, yes. And singing too. Look, look: crosses, banners . . . choristers, clergy, bishops, the pope, the synod—and they're all coming here, right into our courtyard. What does it mean? They're going into the old man's cell.

Enter a servant.

SERVANT. Ladies, a miracle, something unheard-of. Today at matins, when the pope celebrated mass after praying unceasingly for three nights, there came a miraculous voice, saying: "A man of God has entered my dwelling," and he made it known that the saint should be sought in your house . . .

MAIDSERVANT. *(at the window)* Look: the lord Euphimian is coming from the cell holding a scroll; he's reading it, he's staggering, he's fallen down in a faint. Other people are reading it; the singing has ceased, incense billows from the censers. What's this—they're coming over to the window? What? Louder! They're calling Aglaida and Mastridia. What can it mean?

LOUD VOICE FROM THE COURTYARD. Noble Aglaida, give heed! Your son Alexis has been found dead: it was he who for so many years hid in the cell at your gates.

MASTRIDIA. *(shrieking)* Oh no! Oh no! That filthy, crazy old man! O my widowhood!

MAIDSERVANTS. Shhh, what are you saying? It is God's will! A miracle!

AGLAIDA. Alexis! Phoenix! They are carrying him out. My son! My son! How beautiful his face is! What radiance! The sky is filled with light! What fragrance! Where is the dust cloud now? And the stifling heat? Alexis! Alexis! Alexis!

NARRATOR. Angels and archangels, thrones and powers
Watch sleeplessly over the affairs of men,
God's faithful servants, faithful to His word.
"Who is the new-departed come among us,
Leaving behind the suffering and dreams of men?"
They whisper, gazing wonderingly about them.
"Saintly Alexis, our brother, has left the world
behind him,
Disdaining the sweets of earthly love.
Now do you hear the heavenly choir?"
"I hear, I hear."
"In vain were you your sainthood's own oppressor;
you reached that verge
Where human pride and power are powerless;
Have you learned at last to know their worth?"
"I have, I have!"
"Howsoever we may strive, the will of God
Shapes with hand invisible the fate of men.
Swift is our lot, and finds us out."

EXIT LUDUS

April-June, 1907.

MIKHAIL KUZMIN

THE VENETIAN MADCAPS[39]

Comedy

DRAMATIS PERSONAE

FINETTE, *an actress*
THE MARQUISE MARCOBRUNO
MARIA, *her servant*
AN ACTRESS
COUNT STELLO
NARCISETTO, *his friend*
HARLEQUIN
HARLEQUIN'S APPRENTICES
GROBUFFI, *the Marquise's son*
THE ABBE, *his tutor*
GONDOLIERS
BLACKAMOORS
LAMPLIGHTER

PLAYERS IN THE PANTOMIME

COLUMBINE
PIERROT
HARLEQUIN
FRIENDS (WOMEN)
A HERALD
DEATH
FRIENDS (MEN)

The action takes place in eighteenth-century Venice, the Venice of Goldoni, Gozzi and Longhi.

ACT ONE

Night. An embankment. Music.

SCENE ONE

Enter servants with lanterns; two blackamoors carry on a mirror. Enter Count Stello and Narcisetto, embracing. They pause before the mirror.

COUNT. O beauty, say, why is thy hour so fleeting?
Wherefore, O love, so quick to spread thy wing?
O might a youthful heart be ever beating
Within this breast, and time's unerring sling
Not dare take aim at this inviolate brow
Until my soul shake off life's here and now.

NARCISETTO. See: cheek pressed to cheek and hand to hand,
This mirror shows us in a ghostly guise;
These shadowed forms that float before our eyes
Dwell surely in some far, enchanted land.

COUNT. But I have found a prize none may surpass:
A heart more true than any flattering glass.

They step into a gondola.

SCENE TWO

Enter players, Harlequin and his apprentices, Finette.

FINETTE. Can that be that strange man Stello? The one they say is a stranger to love and tenderness for all his wealth and fine looks? As far as I can judge, he *is* very attractive.

ACTRESS. People talk about nothing but his odd whims.

FINETTE. Yes, I know . . . His detestation of love is enough in itself to make one consider him an extravagant melancholic.

ACTRESS. An actress with the troupe that was here last year did her best to seduce him—but without success.

FINETTE. Obviously she didn't know how to go about it. Ah, that's a great art, and there's not many have the secret of it. I'd only have to lift my little finger and he'd be at my feet.

Finette, Finette,

Who can escape your net?
Gray old bird or cock sparrow,
You'll fall to my lure—
When I loose love's arrow
My aim is sure.
Wise man and dullard,
Court breed and street—
A carpet bright-colored
For these dainty feet.
Finette, Finette,
Who can escape your net?

ACTRESS. Aren't you a little bit overconfident? And wouldn't Harlequin be jealous?

FINETTE. Harlequin—jealous? What an absurd notion! . . Would you like me to ask him? Harlequin, Harlequin!

HARLEQUIN. Now what is it?

FINETTE. You won't be jealous, will you, if I make the good Count fall in love with me?

HARLEQUIN. You can fall in love with him yourself, for all I care. I'd as soon be jealous of you as I would of my left foot.

FINETTE. Not a very flattering comparison.

HARLEQUIN. A good little cow always comes home, wherever she wanders—and so do you.

FINETTE. You're becoming insufferably coarse lately, Harlequin—but you know that I love you.

HARLEQUIN. Well that's just dandy!

ACTRESS. Ladies and gentlemen, time to step into our gondolas!

FINETTE. I'll attend to Count Stello en route.

HARLEQUIN. I have to warn you that I won't be coming along, as I still have matters to settle on shore. We'll meet there.

FINETTE. Another of your unsavory affairs?

HARLEQUIN. Take yourself off, there's a good girl. You can kiss your precious count to your heart's content and I won't get in your way—just leave me in peace.

FINETTE. You don't love me, Harlequin.

ACTRESS. Do let's be off, Finette. They'll all be waiting for us.

HARLEQUIN. I'll stay behind with my boys, but you'd better hurry, Finette—I see just the people I need coming this way. Goodbye!

The players step into a gondola.

SCENE THREE

Enter the Abbé and Grobuffi

ABBE. *(boxing Grobuffi's ears)* I'll teach you to gawp at girls, you wretched boy! I'll teach you to go sneaking into Maria's bodice! For shame, a boy your age shouldn't have the least notion of such things.

Harlequin's apprentices laugh loudly.

GROBUFFI. *(bawling)* But I don't understand what you're talking about, signor Abbé!

ABBE. *(boxing his ears)* I'll give you a whipping when we get home—then you'll understand!

GROBUFFI. But I thought you said that I shouldn't have the least notion . . .

ABBE. What's that? I didn't say that you shouldn't have any notion *at all*, I was simply trying to eradicate your baser instincts. *(Indicating Harlequin's apprentices)* Ask these boys whether they would dream of doing such things, even though their mothers were not, in all probability, marquises. *(The apprentices laugh)* Take them as your example—they've never even heard of such things!

APPRENTICES. We don't go sneaking into bodices—we're not fleas!

ABBE. There you are, you rascal! *(boxes his ears.)*

SCENE FOUR

Enter the Marquise, Maria and servants.

ABBE. *(changing his tone)* You acted rashly, my son, in leaving off your scarf. It may be spring, but the nights get chilly. Of course the Lord watches over his creatures, but we should never put his mercy to the test by failing to respect the laws of nature.

MARQUISE. I must say I'm surprised to find you tagging along: surely you don't imagine we're going to take you to the pavilion with us? There'll be nothing for you to do there—you'd better stay home with the Abbé.

GROBUFFI. Mama, if only you'd let me . . .

MARQUISE. Don't argue . . . go to Maria.

GROBUFFI. There, you see, signor Abbé, Mama herself tells me to go to her, and you said . . .

ABBE. What did I say? I didn't say anything . . . I have, however, written some verses in honor of this evening's events, and I'd be disappointed not to have the opportunity of delivering them at the appropriate time. I venture, therefore, to intercede on Grobuffi's behalf and to beg that, since he cannot remain in town without my supervision, he should at least be allowed onto the balcony surrounding the delightful pavilion of love.

MARQUISE. Very well, that might be possible, but only as long as you keep an eye on him—he's such an impressionable boy. As for your always charming verses, it would give me great pleasure to give them a preliminary hearing, just to assure myself that you are not too free in your expressions. You may be an abbé—but you're a naughty man all the same!

ABBE. I assure you, madam, that my priestly office guarantees the propriety of my inspiration. I'll be happy to read them to you this very moment.

MARQUISE. I'm listening. Maria, put your hands over Grobuffi's ears.

ABBE. *(reads)* Venus assumes her pedestal,
Freed of her last constraining fetter,
But lo, at her feet, revealed to all,
Another Venus, and a better.
Two pretty, wingless amorets
To assist love's purposes make haste,
And dazzled night, whom rage besets,
Her dusky veil o'er earth has cast.
Forget, O Venus, thy caprices,
Crease not with envious frown thy brow:
The loveliest of all marquises
Love may not boast that he doth know.

MARQUISE. Most touching, signor Abbé—but why isn't Harlequin here yet? Did you convey to him my gratitude and my purse?

ABBE. Set your heart at rest, Marquise; indeed, he is already here, as are his diligent apprentices.

MARQUISE. Delightful boys! I can hardly wait to get to our pavilion. Ah, what a delicious evening is in store for us!

HARLEQUIN. *(coming forward)* Marquise, I am entirely at your service, but I find that I have somewhat underestimated our expenses.

MARQUISE. Never mind, never mind—here are two more purses for you; dispose of them as if they were your own. These cupids will be coming with us as we agreed, won't they? I have decided to bring my maidservant Maria with me so that she can stand on the pedestal in the person of Venus, the goddess of love—just imagine how poetic that will be! Our good Abbé has composed some perfectly charming little verses, which you shall hear in due course—but now to our gondolas and away! Away on our voyage to Cythera! *Allons, allons.* Ah, those boys of yours—quite, quite delicious!

HARLEQUIN. Marquise, your hand. *(To his apprentices)* Quick march, you rascals!

GROBUFFI. Signor Abbé, don't forget to take me with you.

ABBE. Hurry up then, my child, hurry up!

All climb into gondolas.

GONDOLIER. *(sings)*

Over the sleeping waters
(We two in a world that's still),
The salt-breathed zephyrs waft us,
We glide at our own sweet will.

Hate is paid no heed to
And jealousy is far
When we glide toward the Lido
And love's hand guides the oar.

Now let the rower quicken
His smooth, melodious oar,
Now let love's longing waken
And bear us far from shore.

Hate is paid no heed to

And jealousy is far
When we glide toward the Lido
And love's hand guides the oar.

The salt-breathed zephyrs waft us,
We glide at our own sweet will
Over the sleeping waters
(We two in a world that's still).

Finette dances in her gondola in an attempt to capture the count's attention. The gondolas glide on, stopping at last by the two pavilions.

SCENE SIX

Inside one of the pavilions.

COUNT. Look, Narcisetto, at that amazing lacemaker, the moon! See how she spreads her golden lace over the sea's deep mourning, sewing the indigo veil of the heavens with golden stars. No costumer more cunning than she, Narcisetto! And what is nobler in life than to find beauty in all things, to take delight in them and to lose oneself in a lover's revery? Everywhere the subtlest beauty lies hidden, to be revealed only to the eye of the elect—in night and in day, in autumn and in spring, in the fading leaf and the first violet, in the voice of the lute and the trumpet's snarl, in passionate embraces and in hopeless love . . .

NARCISETTO. And in death?

COUNT. O silent sister death, uninvited but ever welcome visitor! . .

SCENE SEVEN

Enter Finette.

FINETTE. Excuse me, I've made a mistake . . .

NARCISETTO. Uninvited but ever welcome visitor! . .

FINETTE. I thought . . . I thought that the pavilion where my friends were supposed to land . . . I didn' t expect to meet you here . . .

COUNT. Perhaps fate is giving us a sign, and you will consent to remain with us, all the more as there is no one to escort you to your pavilion.

FINETTE. You are too kind.

Narcisetto brings up a chair for her and goes out.

COUNT. You are, I believe, one of the town players?

FINETTE. Yes, I'm their leading actress. My name is Finette.

COUNT. I have heard your name—it's quite a well known one.

FINETTE. You are gracious, Count, but your name is no less familiar to me than mine is to you and, to speak frankly, I am grateful for the chance, if not to make your acquaintance, then at least to talk with you.

COUNT. You wanted that?

FINETTE. I can't deny it.

COUNT. But, tell me, what for?

FINETTE. I won't speak of your looks, your wealth and your whims, but I have heard that you are a stranger to love. Can such a thing be possible? To live without smiles, without meetings, without kisses—is that not to live without breathing?

Were all the world's great store of riches mine,
The privilege and power for which men pine;
Did some great poet, crowned with deathless fame,
Make me his muse and glorify my name,
Yet would I count my state of little worth
If loveless passed my days upon the earth!
To love, I ask no more, although in vain,
Only to feel that pleasurable pain,
With beating heart await the appointed tryst
When the green star glimmers through a veil of mist,
When trembles all the drowsing, moon-blanched glade
With murmur of a distant serenade!
Can Stello, beauty's lord, unmovèd move
And shun the soft captivity of love?
Nor yield his liberty to her sweet thrall
Who, like the fabled siren, lures us all?
Who can but pity, who but heave a sigh
To see a loveless traveler pass by?

COUNT. Very prettily declaimed. But if you imagine that any passion resembling love can be aroused in me, you're very much mistaken. I am an observer, nothing more.

FINETTE. But when you see lips and eyes that please you, when you see spring clouds and translucent leaves, a calm sea and a starry sky, surely you feel an emotion for which there is no other name than love? When you read Petrarch or listen to Paisiello, do you not experience a joy that can only be defined as the joy of a man in love? This hand—do you not find it graceful? Should it touch you, would not a delicate flame shoot through your veins? Can it be that you feel nothing when the gondolier sings:

"The salt-breathed zephyrs waft us,
We glide at our own sweet will"?

And when you kiss your friend Narcisetto—do you feel nothing then?

COUNT. You're a very cunning girl—they didn't call you Finette for nothing. But I assure you that I'm no simpleton either, and quite cunning enough to resist you.

FINETTE. To resist me? You imagine that I have some sort of scheme in my head? Oh Stello, look at me: do I have the look of a scheming woman? Flighty and frivolous I may be, but I am always, always truthful.

COUNT. And you consider that a great virtue?

FINETTE. I'm not saying that—I'm only saying what happens to be so, regardless of whether it pleases you or not.

COUNT. And you expected me to respond to that? I who live for dreams and beauty and care no more for truth than I do for the stones that pave the embankment?

FINETTE. I know that, but I also know that I can make your most ardent and fantastic dream a reality. All the enchantment of love's play, love's fancy and love's smiles I can pour into this goblet like a foaming wine and raise it to your beautiful lips, as I do now.

Pours wine and lowers the curtain of the pavilion.

SCENE EIGHT

Grobuffi and the Abbé tiptoe along the balcony of the pavilion to the left. Narcisetto stands on the balcony of the pavilion to the right.

ABBE. Careful you don't trip up, my son—the moonlight is so deceptive. How dreadful if I were to miss the moment for reciting my poem.

GROBUFFI. *(peeping through a gap in the curtain)* I don't think it's time yet, signor Abbé: Maria is still undressed.

ABBE. What, she's undressed already? A wondrous sight! And are the two little cherubs ready?

GROBUFFI. But what's Harlequin going to do? Isn't he going to take his clothes off?

NARCISETTO. What's the matter with me? What's the matter with me? This woman, this actress has cast a spell on me with her beauty, her voice, her charm. I never experienced anything like it before. And what is she doing with Stello? A cloud hangs over our friendship—or can it be the beginning of love?

GROBUFFI. Hee-hee! You should just see what those two little fellows are up to, and Maria's already on her pedestal. Oh that *is* interesting. Signor Abbé, signor Abbé, hurry up or you'll miss your entrance.

ABBE. True, child, I think it is time we made an appearance.

The curtain opens. Maria is standing on the pedestal, the Marquise half-reclining; one of Harlequin's apprentices is positioned on either side of her and Harlequin stands behind her. The curtain descends as the Abbé and Grobuffi enter the pavilion.

SCENE NINE

GONDOLIER. The salt-breathed zephyrs waft us,
We glide at our own sweet will.

NARCISETTO. O cruel love, O love most fair,
I pierce your mystery at last.
All things I am, all things I dare;
Reborn, I shuffle off the past.

Finette comes out of the pavilion and halts.

NARCISETTO. I love you, Finette, I love you.

FINETTE. Is that you, Narcisetto?

NARCISETTO. Yes, it is I, Narcisetto, who never knew until now what the word "love" meant, who never smelled the smell of seaweed, who never saw orange sails, who never heard the songs of the gondoliers. You have revealed to me the beauty of life. If you reject me, I shall die.

FINETTE. You're a pretty lad, Narcisetto—it's dangerous to listen to you on a dark night.

NARCISETTO. I love you, Finette.

FINETTE. You're a great friend of Stello's, aren't you?

NARCISETTO. When you are close to me I forget everything.

FINETTE. He's heartless and ill-bred, your Count.

NARCISETTO. What does it matter?

FINETTE. Are you listening to me, Narcisetto? Tomorrow at dawn, wait for me outside my door. Do you understand?

NARCISETTO. I understand, but I can't believe it. Say it again, Finette.

FINETTE. Tomorrow at dawn, outside my door.

NARCISETTO. Do with me as you will, Finette; I am yours, utterly and forever.

Goes out behind the pavilion.

SCENE TEN

The Abbé and Grobuffi are thrown out of the pavilion, the curtain of which then descends. The Abbé and Grobuffi peer through a cranny, laughing loudly.

GONDOLIER. Hate is paid no heed to
And jealousy is far
When we glide toward the Lido
And love's hand guides the oar.

ACT TWO

A street corner. A bridge; Count Stello's palace; facing it, the house where Finette lives; below, a gambling den.

SCENE ONE

The windows of the gambling den are thrown open and laughter is heard; the window closes and all is quiet again. Harlequin enters, turning out his empty pockets.

HARLEQUIN. Not a bad game—not a penny of the old woman's money left! The devil take the man who invented cards! I'll have to go through the comedy with the painted Marquise all over again. Another thing: I haven't the least notion of what Finette's up to—not that it interests me much; she's a woman I can absolutely rely on, after all. Of course, she's trash like the rest of them, but for some odd reason she loves me. And here she is—talk of the devil.

SCENE TWO

Finette appears at the window.

FINETTE. Harlequin, I'm cross with you.

HARLEQUIN. Oh, why?

FINETTE. The old Marquise—that's why. What kind of tricks have you been getting up to with her?

HARLEQUIN. What kind of tricks *could* a man get up to with her?

FINETTE. I know what kind . . .

HARLEQUIN. Well that's just dandy.

FINETTE. You're a terrible gadabout, Harlequin. I'm jealous of every woman you look at.

HARLEQUIN. Quite unnecessarily.

FINETTE. There's another thing I'm cross with you about.

HARLEQUIN. And what's that?

FINETTE. Why aren't you jealous of the Count? Of Narcisetto? It's as if you don't care what I do.

HARLEQUIN. I care who you sleep with, but as for the other nonsense—whispers, sighs, glances, verses, even kisses perhaps—all that, to tell you the truth, doesn't interest me in the least.

FINETTE. You talk like that because you don't love me, Harlequin.

HARLEQUIN. If you're not careful, I'll come up to your room and drag you down by the hair, just to stop you getting silly ideas.

FINETTE. *(joyfully)* Just you try, just you try!

She moves away from the window, and Harlequin enters the house. It begins to grow light.

SCENE THREE

NARCISETTO. *(sings, standing on the bridge)*

O moon, with bow of silver
Dissolve the mists of night.
Reach in thy silver quiver
And put love's fears to flight.
    Finette, my dove, my darling,
    Wake up, you sleepyhead!
    Finette, my dove, my darling,
    It's time to quit your bed.
The window rattles—listen!—
The door squeaks merrily;
A foot that's light and lissom
Comes tripping down to me.
    Happy the step she touches
    As she goes flitting by
    (Rosy with sleep, she stretches
    And rubs a drowsy eye).
But I who watch this dwelling
Am happiest of all:
Her beauty is past telling
Who lives beyond this wall.
    Finette, my dove, my darling,
    Wake up, you sleepyhead!
    Finette, my dove, my darling,
    It's time to quit your bed.

SCENE FOUR

FINETTE. *(at the window)*

Take comfort, Narcisetto,
You have not long to wait,
Finette, your dove, your darling,
Is up and won't be late!

She moves away from the window.

NARCISETTO. Finette! Now she's running a comb through her golden hair, losing her temper with wayward pins, pulling her stockings over her adorable feet. Now she's running down the stairs, now she's carefully turning the key in the lock. O Finette!

Finette enters. Narcisetto rushes to fling his arms round her and kiss her.

FINETTE. Darling boy—how soft your cheeks are!

NARCISETTO. At last, Finette, I can look at you, hold you in my arms, kiss you—I can't believe my happiness!

FINETTE. What would Count Stello say if he saw us together, Narcisetto?

NARCISETTO. What do I care what he would say? He means no more to me than last year's snow or the vanished moon that brought you to me, my darling, as it led away the tedious night. Why must you constantly be reminding me of that man?

FINETTE. Because you love him, Narcisetto.

NARCISETTO. I love no one but you; I wish to see no one but you, to hear of no one but you.

FINETTE. Now it's my turn to distrust you, Narcisetto. If your memory is so short, by tomorrow I too may mean no more to you than last year's snow.

NARCISETTO. I shall never forget you, never—I swear it.

FINETTE. There's no need to swear, Narcisetto—oaths are the most easily forgotten of all. Did you not swear an oath of eternal friendship to the Count?—and he's already forgotten!

NARCISETTO. The Count won't stand between us, Finette, I assure you.

FINETTE. Does he stand between us then? If only he did!

NARCISETTO. Finette, Finette!

FINETTE. Don't be cross, dear boy! Though it suits you extremely well when you flush and pout and knit your brows, and your eyes gleam. One wants so much to comfort and caress you, to do everything one can to bring cheer and contentment back to that sweet little face.

NARCISETTO. You treat me as if I were a little boy.

FINETTE. But you *are* a little boy—a little boy I find quite delightful.

NARCISETTO. You don't love me, Finette.

FINETTE. Love! Ah, what magic in those four letters!

SCENE FIVE

Harlequin appears in the doorway.

NARCISETTO. Finette, I'll do anything you want to make you say "I love you."

FINETTE. If I didn't, Narcisetto, why would I agree to meet you, why would I come to you, why would I be speaking to you now?

NARCISETTO. Tell me, tell me that you love me, Finette.

FINETTE. Perhaps Count Stello is awake by now and is waiting for you, Narcisetto. You know he can't bear to be without you for a moment, the good Count.

NARCISETTO. Damnation! You'll take a different tone with me this evening, Finette.

He runs out.

SCENE SIX

Finette rushes toward Harlequin, throws her arms about him and kisses him.

FINETTE. Harlequin, my Harlequin, kiss me, hold me, squeeze me, bite me, beat me—I am your thing, a thing that will never leave you, however badly you treat it.

HARLEQUIN. Was there ever such an insane woman? Stop it, Finette, or I really will give you a beating.

FINETTE. Beat me, beat me!

HARLEQUIN. Where did that halfwit run off to? It's true what they say—love deprives men of their reason. Stop it, I say, Finette—here comes another madman, in love with himself or with his own shadow by the look of him. He wants to speak to us—lay off, Finette.

SCENE SEVEN

Enter Count Stello.

COUNT. I'm glad to see you, my friends—you can help me act out a caprice that came into my head last night. It will be both charming and fantastic.

FINETTE. As your caprices invariably are, my charming Count.

COUNT. Is it true that you are to perform a pantomime here today?

HARLEQUIN. You have not been misinformed. I trust that we shall have the pleasure of seeing you among the spectators?

COUNT. Much better than that: you shall see me among the performers.

HARLEQUIN. What? The Count wishes to do us the honor of acting with us?

COUNT. That's exactly what I wanted to discuss with you. Naturally, you are not to know that my friend Narcisetto and I are no mean dancers—anyone who has seen us will confirm that. My idea, then, is that Narcisetto and I should take part in the pantomime—incognito, of course. We'll put on your company's masks; I would like to be dressed as Mademoiselle Finette, and my friend will be dressed as Harlequin. We shall imitate your gestures and steps, so that no one will be able to tell who are the real Harlequin and Columbine and who their doubles. That will be amusing, don't you think?

FINETTE. As everything is that our dear Count contrives.

HARLEQUIN. And your friend dances too?

COUNT. No worse than I.

FINETTE. A pretty lad, your Narcisetto. If I were you, I wouldn't let him out of my sight, I'd be so jealous. Ah, love is so fleeting, so fleeting.

COUNT. True—but what can jealousy do about it?

FINETTE. Jealousy can do a great deal.

HARLEQUIN. Then we'll go and get some costumes ready for you and prepare for the performance in general.

Harlequin and Finette go out.

SCENE EIGHT

COUNT. *(alone)*

We revel until break of day.
The festive masks we wear are gay.
E finita la commedia,
But we must play, and play, and play.

SCENE NINE

Enter Narcisetto.

NARCISETTO. Stello, I must talk with you.

COUNT. Not now, Narcisetto, not now. The day and night before us are to be given over to folly and gaiety! If you knew what I've thought up!

NARCISETTO. Stello, I absolutely must talk with you now.

COUNT. But what has happened? Does not my house stand where it has always stood, do not the pigeons coo on the Piazza San Marco, do not the gondolas glide, do not I love you as before? What is there for us to talk about?

NARCISETTO. Something very important happened today.

COUNT. Has a bad dream disturbed you, my friend?

NARCISETTO. You seem in a carefree mood today, Stello.

COUNT. Indeed I am! Let's go—I'll tell you about my scheme. You'll be charmed with it!

NARCISETTO. I beg you to listen to me, Stello.

COUNT. Later, later!

He goes out.

SCENE TEN

Enter the Marquise Marcobruno, the Abbé, Grobuffi and Maria.

MARQUISE. It's absolutely essential that I see signor Harlequin before the performance begins.

ABBE. I'll do everything in my power, but I doubt whether your endeavors will be crowned with success . . . Grobuffi, get away from Maria! . . I hear music approaching.

MARQUISE. You must be suffering from auditory hallucinations, Abbé: there is no music approaching, everything is quiet, and I absolutely must see Harlequin in order to arrange another rendezvous.

ABBE. Surely Madame la Marquise was not dissatisfied with the first one?

MARQUISE. In the first place, if I had been dissatisfied I would not wish for a repeat performance; in the second place, certain details remain unclear in my mind.

ABBE. With regard to Harlequin or to his apprentices?

MARQUISE. I was speaking in general, you naughty man.

ABBE. This time I'm certainly not suffering from auditory hallucinations: I can hear music quite clearly, and I trust that you can hear it too.

MARQUISE. Yes, I can hear it. How vexing that I didn't have a chance to speak to Harlequin.

PANTOMIME

A procession of players comes into view, followed by the crowd. Dances. The Count and Narcisetto appear in the costumes of Columbine and Harlequin. A game of shuttlecock. The procession moves back across the bridge. Narcisetto and the Count make up the final pair; as they cross the bridge, Narcisetto silently stabs his friend, kisses him and throws the body noiselessly into the canal. A burst of laughter comes from the window of the gambling den and then dies away. Narcisetto runs down from the bridge and Finette runs forward to meet him.

SCENE ELEVEN

HARLEQUIN. Respected patrons, we are called travelling players for the reason that we are unable to remain in one spot even for a single performance. The prologue, so to speak, of the play will be given here, but the pantomime itself will be performed elsewhere. In that way our audience will not get tired of standing or sitting in one place and will feel more at their ease. Silence! We are about to begin!

SCENE TWELVE

FINETTE. What have you done? What have you done, Narcisetto? Have you killed him?

NARCISETTO. Yes.

FINETTE. Did you do it for love of me, Narcisetto?

NARCISETTO. Yes.

FINETTE. You love me then?

NARCISETTO. I love nobody but the Count. I never loved anyone but him.

FINETTE. I see. So that's your great love for me, Narcisetto!

NARCISETTO. I hate you, Finette—get away from me! Stello! Stello!

SCENE THIRTEEN

Enter Harlequin, the players and the crowd.

HARLEQUIN. Where did you disappear to, Finette? You and the Count and Narcisetto? We can't carry on the show without you.

FINETTE. Sssh, Harlequin, ssh! We can't carry on the show anyway. *(softly)* Narcisetto has killed Count Stello—we must leave at once.

HARLEQUIN. Can that be possible, Finette?

FINETTE. It's more than possible. Let's leave, Harlequin, please let's leave quickly.

ALL. What's happened? What's happened?

HARLEQUIN. *(loudly)* Respected ladies and gentlemen, nothing at all has happened—it's just that time is short and we have to leave for Verona at once. It had completely slipped our minds that we were due to appear there so soon that we'll hardly have time to get there. We thank you for the gracious welcome accorded us and for all the attentions you have shown us. We hope that you will remain loyal to us in the future. Good-bye. I trust that we shall meet again soon!

FINETTE. *(sings)*

Let not our deeds discomfort you or daunt,
You honest burghers, pups and poppinjays.
What is our life if not a merry jaunt?
Actors all of us in plays.

Verona today, tomorrow Rome,
We dance, we sing, call everywhere home.
Clear skies today, tomorrow rain—
Wring joy from today, lest tomorrow bring pain.

Stand not amazed at altered circumstance.
In life we all play parts, some well, some ill,
But in the giddy whirl of change and chance
We serve Another's will.

Verona today, tomorrow Rome,
We dance, we sing, call everywhere home.
Clear skies today, tomorrow rain—
Wring joy from today, lest tomorrow bring pain.

We do not forge ourselves unneeded chains
From life's encounters, be they grave or gay.
Players are we, ready to take our gains
And go our careless way.

Verona today, tomorrow Rome,
We dance, we sing, call everywhere home.
Clear skies today, tomorrow rain—
Wring joy from today, lest tomorrow bring pain.

Should our indulgent patrons be content,
Clap hands—we give you leave—and cry "bravo,"
And should tomorrow find you pleasure bent—
Come see tomorrow's show.

Verona today, tomorrow Rome,
We dance, we sing, call everywhere home.
Clear skies today, tomorrow rain—
Wring joy from today, lest tomorrow bring pain.

1914

INNOKENTY ANNENSKY

Innokenty Annensky (1856-1909), poet, playwright, critic, translator, classical scholar and pedagogue, was born in the Siberian town of Omsk, the son of a senior civil servant. His life was not rich in external events. Having completed his studies in the philological faculty of St. Petersburg University, he spent the rest of his life in education, first as a teacher of classics, then as a school principal (notably, from 1896 to 1906, at the *gymnasium* in Tsarskoe Selo) and finally as an inspector of schools. Annensky made a late entrance into the literary world. His first collection of poems, *Quiet Songs*, appeared pseudonymously in 1904 and drew little attention, his second, *The Cypress Chest*, appeared in 1910, shortly after his death, and a third collection, *Posthumous Poems*, edited by his son, was published in 1923. It was only at the very end of his life that Annensky began to win the recognition that was rightfully his, assuming the role of "elder statesman" to the burgeoning Acmeist movement, in whose literary journal, *Apollo*, critical articles from his pen began to appear.

Behind the façade of the classicist and pedagogue, the beautiful, somewhat old-fashioned manners, the unvarying starched collars in which he once jokingly expressed a willingness to sleep, dwelt a subtle and original poet whose "buried life" found expression in lyrics of polished form, disquieting imagery and distinctly modern sensibility. Standing somewhat apart from Russian Symbolism by reason of his age and background, Annensky was of all the Russian Symbolists the closest in spirit to Baudelaire, the poet of Spleen and Ideal. A neo-Parnassian and aesthete, Annensky was out of sympathy with the mysticism and hierophantic pretensions that characterized the second phase of Symbolism in Russia. In words that recall Gautier, he called upon the poet to "carve a shining chalice for perfectly achieved impressions"—advice entirely in keeping with the Acmeist aesthetic. It was natural, then, that the more traditional post-Symbolist poets who grouped themselves under the banner of Acmeism (Gumilev, Akhmatova and Mandelstam among them) should have acknowledged him as their master. Annensky's influence on some of the best Russian poetry of this century is indisputable.

Annensky was a classicist of great erudition who wrote on such recondite topics as "The Language of Lycophron" (an Alexandrian poet of notorious obscurity). The last fifteen years of his life were devoted to Euripides, "the most tragic of all poets," all of whose nineteen extant dramas he translated into Russian. There was nothing coldly academic in Annensky's approach to his favorite tragedian; a friend records that "he would defend the dear deceased as if he were making a plea on behalf of a dear and living friend." Annensky's translations sometimes upset purists by introducing the piquant anachronisms and vivid impressionistic stage directions we find in his own plays.

Annensky's interest in the drama extended far beyond the bounds of the classical theatre. Among the remarkably perceptive and original criticism collected in the two *Books of Reflections* (1906 and 1909) we find essays on Pisemsky's *A Bitter Fate*, Tolstoi's *The Power of Darkness*, Gorky's *Lower Depths* and Ibsen's *Brand*; particularly interesting are what might be termed the lyrical reorchestrations of *Three Sisters* and *Hamlet*. Annensky's Hamlet is an artist whose "aestheticism lies at the roots of his nature and determines the tragic outcome of his story." "Hamlet's chief argument against his mother is his father's beauty," observes Annensky, and goes on to suggest that the Prince's infirmity of purpose stems from the terrible doubt that he may be the son not of the "beautiful" King, but of the "ugly" Claudius, begotten in an adulterous affair. But perhaps, after all, Hamlet is the only "real" character in the play and "all these Osrics and Ophelias" are figments of his imagination—a bold thought that transforms Shakespeare's play into a Symbolist "drama of the single will."

Annensky's long creative involvement with Euripides led him to the conclusion that "certain devices of the classical stage await their turn on ours"—not, he hastens to add, "masks and buskins," but "lyricism and mime, which have been so long and so unjustly estranged from tragedy." Although Annensky's tragedies are likely to remain limited in their appeal, they have some claim to be considered the most impressive achievement of the Russian Symbolist drama in their unique fusion of ancient and modern, their wan autumnal beauty and genuine dramatic qualities. Three of the four—*Melanippe the Wise* (1901), *King Ixion* (1902) and *Laodamia* (1906)—are based on subjects treated in lost plays by Euripides; the last, *Thamyris Kitharodos* (completed 1906, published 1913), takes its theme from Sophocles. Yet they are in no sense "reconstructions." Discussing his dramatic method in the preface to *Melanippe*, Annensky rejects the easy way of "archaeological stylization" for the "mythic" method, which, "permitting anachronisms and the fantastic, enabled the author to enter more deeply into psychological and ethical questions and to fuse more effectively the world of antiquity with the modern soul." This modern soul, "so incommensurate with classical antiquity," still yearns for the "dim rays bequeathed to us by the beauty of antiquity." These last revealing words point to a link between Annensky's poetry (which rarely touches on classical themes) and his dramas—the aesthete's foredoomed quest after a beauty not to be found in this world.

Thamyris Kitharodos, Annensky's last and most personal play, differs from the rest in being described as a "bacchic drama" rather than a tragedy. Clearly the comic element—the bibulous Silenus and the chorus of satyrs—was suggested by Euripides' *Cyclops*, the only surviving satyr play, the Dionysian ecstasies of the bacchantes by the same writer's *Bacchae*. At the play's center stands a poet-aesthete who has much in common with Annensky's Hamlet. The poet admitted that into the conception of *Thamyris* had entered "*Grenzfragen* that fascinate me in the area of musical psychology and aesthetics."

Thamyris was the only one of Annensky's plays to reach the stage, in a celebrated production at Tairov's Kamerny Theatre in 1916. No doubt the production owed something of its success to Aleksandra Ekster's brilliant "cubist" sets and costumes. One wonders what Annensky would have thought of these—his careful notation of changing light suggests impressionism, his etiolated Nymph, with her winding tresses and frond-like draperies, art nouveau.

INNOKENTY ANNENSKY

THAMYRIS KITHARODOS[40]

A Bacchic Drama

MCMVI

Dis manibusque sacrum

The narrative framework of my new drama "Thamyris Kitharodos" is as follows: Thamyris, or Thamyrides, the son of the Thracian king Philammon and the nymph Argiope, won fame by his playing on the cithara; such was his overweening pride that he challenged the Muses to a contest; defeated, he was deprived of his sight and his musical gift as a punishment.

Sophocles wrote a tragedy on the subject in which he himself performed, on occasion, the role of Thamyris, but the tragedy has not come down to us.

My play was conceived a long time—six years—ago, but it was only during the last five months that I began to give particular thought to the subject. A. A. Kondratiev did me the honor of dedicating to me his beautiful story dealing with the same theme, in which the Muses put out Thamyris' eyes with their hair-pins. He told me of his intention a year and a half ago, while I in my turn informed him of my idea of writing a Thamyris tragedy; about the nature of the tragedy itself I told him hardly anything, however, as I never tell anyone about my plans for future works—at all events, apart from mythical names and the narrative framework mentioned above, my "Thamyris" has nothing in common with Mr. Kondratiev's story, or, in all probability, with Sophocles' drama. I have also departed considerably from the classical theatre. The chorus leaves the stage, and in one scene the characters, or at least some of them, abandon verse. For this, however, there are weighty artistic reasons.

DRAMATIS PERSONAE

NYMPH
OLD NURSE
CHORUS OF MAENADS
THAMYRIS KITHARODOS
DADDY SILENUS
TWO SATYRS, *one with blue ribbon, the other with a pink ribbon in his hair*
CHORUS OF BACCHANTES, *uninitiate*
CHORUS OF SATYRS
LANGUID SATYR
SHADE OF PHILAMMON
HERMES

Dawn glimmers. Transparent shadows still lie upon the ground, but in places they are beginning to waver. In the distance are great piles of rock—dun-colored, red or overgrown with forest. Stray boulders, some dark, some white, some fantastic in shape, have rolled down from the mountains and seem to be crawling downwards. Nearer to the forestage is a wretched dwelling, something between a house and a tent. On the trampled grass are scattered crude household utensils of clay, sponges, a reed basket with bread, pitchers and bowls. The low hill, on the slope of which Thamyris' dwelling stands, merges into meadowland splashed with the scarlet and gold of flowers. A hushed silence. There is a smell of cumin in the air.

SCENE ONE

Cold and Pale

The mist clears, releasing the Nymph. She is dark-haired and somewhat thin. Her face, with its fugitive, despairing smile, is youthful and rosy-cheeked, but has a tendency to turn pale suddenly, as if drained by her eyes, in which the light has a way of being extinguished in a moment. The triangle of brow visible between two smooth swatches of hair is tormentingly white. Her movements are nervous. She wears a loose robe the color of sea-water. Her grassy veil is translucent with silvery glints and her girdle resembles the stem of a plant. Her feet are white and very small, but they leave a print that is somewhat broad and flat-soled.

NYMPH. *(looking about her)*
That's what Silenus said.
And here's the rock
Shaped like a bull's head.
But what can it all mean?
This house of leaves is not a nest for birds,
But a dwelling, and a royal one. Bread?
Can this be bread? How black it is. Pitchers
Full of water, topped with leaves for shade . . .
What poverty in all of this . . .
But wait—

Bending down, she picks up something and examines it with a womanly earnestness that causes a crease to appear between her brows.

A woman must live here . . . Look, a hairpin
Dropped . . . by some old woman.
She peers into the hut.
A couple of sheep
Beneath this puny shelter. No, Silenus
Must have lied or been confused. I shall find
No son here, but a sullen goatherd
Tending his ten black goats—or does some ragged
Trapper pass the night here with his wench? . .
Is anyone at home? Hey, answer me!

SCENE TWO

Nymph and Old Woman

From somewhere in the depths of the hut emerges a big-boned old woman, her hair unbound; she is carrying washing over her shoulder and in her arms; she wears glittering earrings, but her clothes are shabby and dingy. On seeing the stranger, she hurriedly puts down her load, and then, standing in the doorway of the hut, she gazes intently at the Nymph, clearly struck by her rare beauty.

OLD WOMAN. I can't see who it is. Forgive me, lady.

As if to herself.

A visitor from court, that must be it . . .

More loudly.

Women like you are a wonder in these parts,
Only flowers bloom here so pink and white,
And in gardens at that—and water them
Three times a day as well.

The Nymph smiles and takes a step toward the Old Woman.

Sit down, my girl,
And let me wash your feet for you . . .

Goes to pick up a basin.

NYMPH. Oh no,
I'm not tired, nannie . . . and the highway's dust
Has not begrimed my feet. My thanks to you.
Tell me, who lives here? Surely not Thamyris?
OLD WOMAN. Thamyris, lady, yes.

Gives her a searching look.

NYMPH. Where is he then?
OLD WOMAN. You wish to see Thamyris? He does not like
To be disturbed.
NYMPH. He won't mind seeing me.
I won't outstay my welcome.

OLD WOMAN. *(moving away with a reverence)*
Pardon me,
I humbly beg of you, princess or queen,
My eyes are weak.
Perhaps I've said
What I should not have: our mountain eyrie
Sees few visitors.
NYMPH. Oh, not at all.
But why, old woman, are you with Thamyris?
Were you his nurse?
OLD WOMAN. Yes, this breast it was
He clung to when the heart within him yearned
To taste of consolation.
NYMPH. Then you're a slave?
OLD WOMAN. Yes, I was bought . . . Alack, alack the day!
NYMPH. The child grew up without a mother, then?
Or was it but a little while ago
You hid her in some rough-hewn resting place?
OLD WOMAN. You want to know all that?
NYMPH. *(impatiently)* I do indeed . . .
OLD WOMAN. But what am I to tell you? In Philammon's
Palace never a word was spoken

Of Thamyris' mother . . .

Gloomy our king is,

And stern . . . And gold he loves in ingots,
And not in women's tresses.

NYMPH. Then Thamyris

Is his only son?

OLD WOMAN. And no one knows who bore him . . .

NYMPH. Philammon, though, did not disown the boy?

OLD WOMAN. How could he disown him? Father and son
Are like as twins. And there were omens too
That Philammon, no one else, begot him.

NYMPH. Ye gods—a foundling! Was it long ago?

OLD WOMAN. O evil memory!

Covers her face with her hands.

These twenty years

I've had the care of him . . . A babe, he was,
Scarce in the world a week.

I tell all this

Without a notion whom I tell it to.

NYMPH. I am a nymph. Argiope's my name.

OLD WOMAN. *(trembling)*

A nymph?

And here to see Thamyris?

NYMPH. Yes . . . He cost me much in suffering.

OLDWOMAN. *(completely baffled)*

Suffering! A nymph . . . and suffer . . . for Thamyris? . . .

NYMPH. On a bed—a bed of wood, much like your own . . .

Dumb show. The Nymph covers herself with her veil, while the Old Woman gazes at her wide-eyed and whispers something but to herself.

OLD WOMAN. *(pulling herself together and speaking softly, breathlessly)*

You are pleased to mock a wretched bondwoman,
Celestial one! . .

But if the prince were truly

Goddess-born, he'd never have been left

A homeless waif, and never, you gods,
Would you have given him into the care
Of a bondwoman with ring-pierced ears to love
So blindly, so devotedly.

A moment of silence.

NYMPH.
(*with a suppressed sigh*) Great Zeus,
My father, so ordained . . . What could I do?
But why this wretched dwelling? Philammon
Holds no court? Or was Thamyris banished?
And where are slaves to serve him? . . What, I say,
Should not a prince's bed, though in a forest,
Be made by two white hands more soft than yours?

OLD WOMAN. (*hurriedly*)
Goddess . . . I'll tell you everything. Our prince
Has quarrelled with his father . . . Neither warrior
Nor merchant would he be . . . He cannot bear
The sight of blood, be it of humankind,
O nymph, or forest deer . . . What need has he
Of slaves? . . Thamyris' bread I bake for him,
His cithara he serves alone: I dare not
So much as touch it. As for womenfolk—
Search as you will, lady, you'll find no others . . .

NYMPH. One more thing . . . Tell me . . . Why do I ask?
Too well I know the answer. But the sound,
The question's very sound, comforts my heart.
Did he never in his sleep utter the name
"Argiope," never call upon me?

OLD WOMAN. The prince was always a poor sleeper. I guard
His slumber as amid the briny waves
The sailor guards his store of pure spring water—
But never in the stillness of the night,
Half-drowsing, did I hear him call upon
Argiope—but who am I, a slave,
To argue with the gods? . .

With impetuous entreaty and a sudden rush of tears.

Pity my old age . . .
I beg you, by the sanctity of those knees,
By the softness of those fragrant tresses—
Have you come here to take away from me
My child?
Ah no, tell me that cannot be . . .
Through their tears my eyes can see the tenderness
That lurks about your still unanswering lips;
The rose has risen to them . . .
(softly) Are you his bride?

NYMPH. From suffering, mortal, we are not exempt,
But, unlike you, we have no need of lies:
I come not as a temptress, but to weep . . .

She makes a gesture of dismissal; the Nurse gathers up her washing and goes out.

SCENE THREE

Of Beams yet Crimson

The Nymph sits down on a stone and wraps herself in her translucent veil. The sun has now risen. Sounds of tambourines, copper cymbals and bacchic cries are heard offstage. The chorus comes running into the orchestra from the right. The opening bars of their song are heard off stage. The Nymph remains unseen by the Maenads. She sits so still that she might be taken for a carven figure. The flowery meadow presents a strange contrast between the ecstatic Maenads, with their flying thyrsi, necks bared to the bosom, tossing tresses, running, whistling laughter and music, and the motionless Nymph, who seems sunk in slumber on her white stone.

CHORUS. Zing . . .
Distances beckon . . . And would you go home?
Evius, sweet one, mine thou art, mine . . .
Ah where art thou, Evius? We conjure thee, come,
Evius, Evohe . . . Evan . . . Evan . . .
By day none may claim thee
Save the blue rays alone . . .
Ah then be mine

In the stillness of night
With the hotter a flame.
Shall mist be our bed-curtain,
The white, curling mist?
Evius! Evan!
Zing . . . Distances beckon . . . I love thee, I love thee.
I'll endure thy blue flame . . .
Evius, O Evius, Evan-Evohe,
Evius—Evohe,
Shall I call thee my own?
Strength to the rudder,
A rose to the stem,
Arrows for battle,
And I with thee only,
With thee and no other
Sleep and sleep not . . .

Waltz. First variation—row by row.

What though the flame of the rose has consumed us,
Though the sun has drunk deep of the purple-blue grape?
Dragonfly wings will flame rose in the sunset,
And purple-blue stars in the heavens will flame . . .

Second variation—a circle. In the middle of the circle, a scene with thyrsi and veils; the circle moves slowly, languorously.

1

Evius, god, rend our circle asunder,
O Dionysos!
See how the ring of our fevered hands joined,
See how it falters, the ring of white hands,
O Dionysos!

2

Bend, we beseech thee,

        O Dionysos,
Bend to our veils—
Our mouths will not wound thee,
        O Dionysos . . .
White as the lily,
Touch, O touch only,
Thou wafter of fragrance,
Our vestments most holy,
        O Dionysos!
Softly responsive,
With rich dyes inwoven—
In a moment we'll mingle
Like twin strands of ivy,
I with leaves golden,
Thou of leaves naked . . .
In a moment we'll mingle,
Thou wafter of fragrance,
On a soft bed, O Evius,
Breast white as lily
And jubilant body.

3

Evius, god, rend our circle asunder,
        O Dionysos!
For thee does it falter, the ring of hands joined,
For thee and none other, the fevered hands joined.
Evius, come . . .

The tempo slackens. The Maenads make ready to lie down.

White hands flutter earthward,
White shoulders sink swardward.
White breasts would be freed of their robes,
        O Dionysos!

With an effort, yawning.

Evius, god, rend our circle asunder . . .

Suddenly they are alert; one of the Maenads has caught sight of the house, and possibly of the Nymph.

A MAENAD. Here mortals be, Maenads! . . To the forest, away!
The dimness of dawn has deserted the heavens,
And blazing the sun gazes down . . .
See where the satyr's eye gleaming
With urgent desire looks upon us,
And beckons and burns . . .
Onward, O Maenads!

ANOTHER MAENAD.
Or are you awaiting another summons?
Onward!
Look lively—no noise now . . .

They begin to climb the mountain slope, quietly at first; suddenly one of them lets out a wild:

Zing!

A MAENAD. *(coming to a halt, she lays her cymbal to her breast and draws her girdle tighter)*
Be still, thing of copper . . .
Lie cool on my breast, be still as a stone.

ANOTHER MAENAD. *(pointing to her tongue)*
And thou, thing of scarlet, be dumb,
Click not, nor whistle . . .
Let us flee . . .

They run off and are soon lost to view. A moment of silence ensues. But the noise of day grows ever more distinct. The late birds awaken. Bees, dragonflies and butterflies are in the grass, on the flowers, inside the flowers. The Nymph throws back her veil and goes down into the meadow; she picks up an abandoned thyrsus, tosses it from one hand to the other, lets it fall, sits down, gets up again, plucks flowers and bites the petals. During all this, the distant sound of singing is heard from the forest.

Zing! . . Distances beckon . . .
Lulla, O lulla!
O thou of the deep blue eyes!
Command, I implore thee . . .

Zing . . . Distances beckon . . .
O distance, O blue . . .
Forsaking all others . . . be mine . . . be mine . . .

NYMPH. *(stretching out her hands imploringly)*

Like acrid smoke of midnight visions,
Of roses wild and love's disquiet,
Dissolve, O joyous shades, and vanish . . .
Bright rays will seek you out and harass . . .

CHORUS. *(from the forest)*

Zing . . . Distances beckon . . .
Thine—I am thine . . .
My heart is fast melting,
Harboring fire . . .

NYMPH. Such bitter sorrow have I suffered,
Such depths of shame for that "I love thee" . . .
With the longing that consumes you
Afflict me not, I beg, O veiled ones.

CHORUS. *(from the forest)*

Evius, god, rend our circle asunder,
See how the ring
Of white hands has faltered . . .
O Dionysos!

NYMPH. Is heaven's expanse too narrow for you,
The world too poor in lips for kissing? . .
I am Thamyris' mother, Maenads,
No more than mother—let me be . . .

CHORUS. *(from the forest, growing faint)*

We shall not pursue you—
Drop your veil if you fear us:
The feeble we sting not,
The weary we wound not . . .

NYMPH. *(passing a hand over her face)*

Like acrid smoke of midnight longings,
Of roses wild and love's disquiet,
Begone, O joyous shades, begone—
Unwanted and misunderstood!

She goes into the hut.

SCENE FOUR

Pale blue enamel

Thamyris. Young, beardless, white-handed, thin and fragile, he looks even younger than he is. He is meanly dressed and quite unconscious of his clothes; he carries no weapon of any kind. A lyre hangs at his shoulder, a switch at his belt; he carries a staff.

Thamyris alone, then with the Nymph.

THAMYRIS. Turbulent are the hearts of men. I love
The hoary mountain stones.
And here's my haven—

(lays his staff and switch on the stones)

The end of the dusty road at last.
But why,
Thamyris, did you go to them? Did you crave
Bracelets of gold? These strings, did they demand
Eyes moistened with emotion and bodies
Wasted with longing?
Or was it hen-birds
The nightingale hoped to lure, disturbing thus
The mountain air—pent in the turtle's shield—
That weeps with the desire of distant stars?

The Nymph appears in the doorway.

A woman . . . ha! What business has she here?
My talents, it would seem, have gained admirers—
Lascivious Maenads; forget to beat your cloak
And moths will breed in it. I know that kind.
(to the Nymph)

Leave my house. I am a poor lyre-player:
You sought some other door.
We have no flutes
Or garlands at our feasts.
Are you hungry?

There's bread there in that basket; I do not play
To women, but to the stars alone.

NYMPH. It is my child! My own beloved child . . .
Among thousands I'd have known him. The pangs
We bear are not in vain. A little while
He stayed with me . . . until the mists of madness
Swirled round this wretched nymph—for twenty years,
Twenty long years, blotting out the world from her.

THAMYRIS. *(less confidently)*
We have no cure for madness here—begone.
You're mad, of course I see that now.
But why
You call me son I cannot understand . . .
I have my reason still.
You think you can
Infect me with your madness, poison me
With melancholy's pain?
(taking a step toward her) Who are you?
Who?

NYMPH. Argiope, a nymph of heavenly birth,
Yet outcast.

THAMYRIS. *(meditatively)*
What should you immortals
Know of tears? Is this not some cunning trick
To make me captive, playing on my heart?

He stands with downcast eyes while she gazes at him hungrily.

NYMPH. Strange feelings trouble me, although I shed
No tears.

THAMYRIS. You claim me, woman, as your own?

NYMPH. I gave you birth. Why did I desert you?—
The question's in your eyes. My tale is full
Of pain, but hear me out. Give me your hand.

She takes his hand. Thamyris follows her submissively.

Here on this stone we'll sit apart, Thamyris:
I will confess myself to you alone.

THAMYRIS. I'll willingly sit down with you. I love—
Not you—but legends wrought of rose and pearl.
I love the strangeness of the words you breathe.

NYMPH. Have you heard tell how the immortal gods,
Pierced by desire, have taken on strange shapes?
Bull, swan and shower of gold—in such disguise
Has Zeus caressed his brides; as Death itself
He lay with Semele, consuming her . . .
But this white hand, whose gentle clasp arouses
Fear in you, was resolute to keep him
From this breast . . .
Well I remember—the day
Was very sultry. Wearied with the chase,
We laid us down among the hills. The buzzing
Of a wasp caught in my hair made me start up,
And in a trice two black and bulging eyes
Had worked their spell on me . . . The thing's green length
Lay basking in the sun . . .

A lizard runs out from beneath a stone.

Ai—there it is—
Look! . . The very one—again . . .

THAMYRIS. What foolishness—
Are lizards to be feared?

The Nymph rises.

But do not cease to charm my ears. I love
The sounds your strings breathe. They are like
The gradual breaking of the dawn—a dawn
All wreathed about with mists. The rest's a dream!

NYMPH. *(sitting down at his side)*
Filtering down through leaves, the light's caress
Robbed me of will, and once again I drifted
Sleepwards. If Chronos' son had found me then
I could not have resisted him. No man
Had then unloosed these tresses, soft as down.
But again caught in the tendrils of my hair,

The wasp grew frantic, driving its sting
Hard into my flesh. I gave a wild cry,
Leaped to my feet and with my hand drove off
The cunning one. I saw the emerald tail
Vanish among the stones, and in a moment
From the great bowl the sun had overturned,
First draining it, two balls of unconsuming fire
Went whirling past me with a thunderous crash;
I thought some glassy vault had shattered—ringing
And groans and billowing smoke filled the ravine.

THAMYRIS. How terrible this dream, and beautiful:
A veil of white pierced by a blood-red ray.

NYMPH. Zeus has not pardoned me. O never yet,
Meeting his eyes, have I seen anger in them—
He looks upon me with a tender smile . . .
O the smile of Zeus! *Later*, mortals,
You shall come to know its meaning—ages hence
We shall impart it to you, in that gray stone
Where, carved by cunning masters, we shall sleep
With hands tight-clasped upon your tombs, our eyes
Fixed, vacant, on the vacant heavens . . .

THAMYRIS. Is the tale so quickly done? . . A pity . . .

NYMPH. The telling's painful—ah, Thamyris, how
I long to turn aside from this black path
I am foredoomed to . . .
(lowering her veil, softly) The hour had come—
The nymph knew love. A melancholy fate
Philammon's was and mine. I had forgotten
His face. But you so vividly bring back
My marriage to me—the memory of that night
Amid salt spray, my unavailing pleas,
The howling waves, the winds among the pines,
My scarlet shame, and of my yielding hands
The lacing and unlacing.

Her eyes gleam through her veil, which she half-raises as she moves toward Thamyris; he fixes upon her an earnest, questioning gaze.

Before me now

Father and son are merged . . .
Yet each is clear . . .
He conquered men, he gave commands, but you
Were born to waken unconsoling love,
Dream-like, to charm and, wraith-like, slip away.

THAMYRIS. The dawnlight fills the sky. I see the sun—
Its bright gold blinds me. No, I'll hear no more,
I'll go . . . Or sing a song less harsh, you strings!

NYMPH. Nine joyless moons that followed on that night
Did I unloose my virgin cincture.
A son was born. Again a black, black night—
To nymphs are given two such nights, no more.
In the woods, alone, I bore my pangs. All
The rest is darkness.

(giving Thamyris a strange look and smiling enigmatically)

Yet you remained
With me in memory, if memory
Indeed it be, and not delirium—
Delirium that abides when memory fades . . .
Or are these twenty wandering years too few,
O Zeus, to satisfy thy lust for vengeance?
Yes, twenty years, tormented by the wasp,
Shelterless, I roamed distractedly
The forest's desolation, barren steeps,
The sandy shallows and the open sea:
Perhaps for the sailor in his wave-tossed skiff
The forlorn beauty of the brainsick nymph
Sweetened the aftermaths of Phrygian vines.
One day—one endless, gray, oblivious day,
Encompassing a multitude of nights
And days—those years seem to me now. Ancient
Silenus found me, drove his goatlings off
And nursed me back to health, giving me to drink
Potions of fragrant herbs—but first he killed
The accursed wasp by luring it to light
Upon his shaggy arm.
I know Philammon

Lives to this day, though punished by the gods
For taking an immortal to his bride.
No woman solaces his lonely bed,
And in Philammon's halls no children play.
Of you, Thamyris, too I've heard report:
How you won garlands at the games, how all
The land of Greece pays homage to your lyre.
But why did you leave your father's house?

THAMYRIS. *(in an altered voice)* Can you
Really wish to listen to my words?

NYMPH. Your words, and words that tell of you.

THAMYRIS. Or in
This wild delirium, Nymph, do you intend
To make a player of the lyre your slave?
What capers could he cut for you? Silenus
Of the hinged joints could quite outcaper him.

Pause.

My mother, are you? Rather say my daughter—
You speak of torments, but about your lips
A smile plays always.

NYMPH. You see a mask,
My child, no more. Can goddesses grow old?
O we are young in face, our skin is smooth—
If you could see our hearts!

THAMYRIS. Philammon's
Court you'll have no trouble finding—there
You can repeat your tale.
For the lyre player
It holds no further interest.
Destiny
Denied me mother, sister, father,
O melodious one: for the heights, the black,
The starry heights I live; they alone
In language lingering and tender,
Like the bright-streaming air of evening,
Sing to me sometimes. All my striving is
To catch those secret harmonies and fill

My song with them; but with longing only
My strings reverberate—my heart's own longing.
I do not need you, woman, and between us
There can be no past.
This tale of yours—
Its rhythms will remain with me, perhaps
I'll grow to love them, yet the moonlit splash
Of fish at play in some secluded creek
Is no less dear to me. My soul is wide
To all the world, not to the nymph alone,
However great her suffering.
Farewell!

He makes as if to enter the hut.

NYMPH. *(holding him back, impetuously)*
A moment, wait . . . You have no love for me—
That's understandable: you can't forgive
The brainsick nymph a loveless childhood
Void of tenderness, deprived of all
Those boyish pranks so dear to memory,
When first our mother scolds, then has to laugh,
Then weeps as she caresses us, while the trees
Peer through the windows—green and vast, wafting
Such fragrances as they never will again.
You do not trust me.
What am I to do?
Philammon will not hear me.
If my tears
And travail cannot melt Thamyris' heart,
How shall I touch Philammon?
Or do you think
He'll want a nymph by shaggy satyrs nursed
On sodden leaves to grace his royal halls?
Life's sweetness is unknown to you—it's not
Too late to taste of it: childhood's delight
I shall restore to you, make live again . . .
Who knows such tales as I! . .
A moment, stay!
Perhaps you are in love, but modesty

Ties your tongue.
You frown? I'll say no more . . .
You spoke of music. Mastery of your art
Leaves your proud soul unsatisfied. I could
Gain access to the Muses.
What do you say?

THAMYRIS. *(brightening)*
You'll promise me the Muses?
Wondrous dream!
But do the Muses play for such as I?

A pause. Suppressing a sigh, rapidly.

Ah Nymph, could I but hear Euterpe's song,
Not as a transient gleam, not fitfully,
As birdcalls echo in the wakening woods—
Would she but tune her flute of gold for me
Alone, then I would love you.

(Strangely agitated)

Even now
I love you for that word, all tremulous
With melody that begs to be set free—
Thamyris shall untie its swaddling bands.
Come here, give me your hand.

NYMPH. *(clinging to him with a moan)*
O my Thamyris!

THAMYRIS. *(ecstatically)*
All wrongs endured from mother, men and gods
I here forgive—let them in time to come,
If they will, make sport of me; grant only
My ravished eyes to view the lyre, my heart
To beat as one with the celestial strings,
The tremor of the seven celestial strings!

NYMPH. *(caressing Thamyris convulsively)*
O my Thamyris! O my son! My soul's
Awakening! My light, my god, my idol!
My longing and my heart's incessant ache!

THAMYRIS. *(freeing himself from her embrace)*
Enough, I say. Leave me. I am afraid.
Is this how mothers love? I have heard tell
Their songs are calm as curtained sleep; but you—
Your words and your caresses are fierce wine
To sear the skin and darken memory.
The wood's more free. The nightingale loves there,
And the gnat. The doe there licks her young.
Man sings, or offers prayers, or meditates.

He disappears into the forest.

SCENE FIVE

Deep Sapphirine

The Nymph remains on stage. She is unable to regain her composure immediately and gazes after Thamyris, wringing her hands. Suddenly voices are heard in the distance, and a new chorus—composed this time of the uninitiate—enters the orchestra. The women are clad in fawnskins; they carry thyrsi, and their hair is entwined with ivy and vine; nevertheless, their movements are as yet devoid of the ecstasy of the nocturnal Maenads. They have about them a dreamy air.

CHORUS. Leaving walls of white behind us,
Scorched by sun, by blizzard frozen,
Trudging long through many a meadow,
Came we to the snow-giant's kingdom.
Nothing dulled our ardent longing—
Noontide heat or dew of evening.
Not in vain we left our cradles
In the custody of house-slaves.
Not in vain we lashed our frenzy
In palestra and in pasture.
Not in vain we left our household
Altars unrefreshed with lilies.
Those the gods afflict with madness
Know the lure of distant forests,
Lure of cumin-scented grasses.

Grasses with the dewfall heavy,
Grasses intertwined with flowers,
Grasses glistening with moonlight
Lure us through a haze of incense.

BACCHANTE. *(catching sight of the nymph)*
Ha . . . a woman! Are you of our company?

NYMPH. Bacchus you serve. Another god I honor:
His curls fall calmly on his open brow,
Deep are his eyes and stern the stare of them.

BACCHANTE. He'll not make sport, this god?

NYMPH. What foolishness!
Make sport with whom?

BACCHANTE. With you, as our god does.

NYMPH. Swan-straight he is in anger and in joy;
His lips are fine: he is Kitharodos.

BACCHANTE. Where is his temple, woman?

NYMPH. In this house.

BACCHANTE. And does he sleep here too?

NYMPH. On straw, alone.

BACCHANTE. Strange god indeed!
Is he your lover then?

NYMPH. My son, no more . . .

BACCHANTE. Both god and son . . . Oho!
Like me, you are a woman . . .

NYMPH. Are you sure?

BACCHANTE. If not a woman, what?

NYMPH. A mountain nymph.

BACCHANTE. Goddess, forgive! Forever may you thrive!
But if the question be not overbold,
What god is it you cherish in this place?
You call him son, O nymph, yet offer him
Your prayers. I cannot understand it, no.

NYMPH. How should you understand one mad as I?
You have abandoned, I have found a child,
You kindle in this hour your midnight torch,
While mine is burnt out, maenad, burnt out quite . . .

BACCHANTE. You've found a child? Where is he then, this child?

NYMPH. Alone he grew—forlorn, exquisite, proud;
He summoned me, but madness held me fast;
He hid his heart—his heart is lost to me.

BACCHANTE. May you not name him then?

NYMPH. Thamyris is
His name, and I am called Argiope.

BACCHANTE. *(making an obeisance to the Nymph)*
O mountain nymph! Thamyris' need is peace:
The games, the mob say nothing to his heart . . .

NYMPH. You've seen him then?

BACCHANTE. Hidden one day
Behind the feathers of a fretted fan,
I listened to his playing, and the tears
Fell one by one, fell sweetly, endlessly—
Slowly they came, welling from tight-closed lids,
As in the midnight hour's oblivion
A broken fountain lets its slow drops fall.

SCENE SIX

Unnoticed at first, an odd-looking man makes his appearance among the Bacchantes. He is an old satyr, ruddy-faced, chubby—almost obese—gray-haired; locks of curly hair cover his small horns, which he is obviously attempting to conceal. His mien is modesty itself—that of a being who has long since attained irrevocable respectability. The agitation of the chorus soon gives way to curiosity at the sight of the embarrassed smiles of this goatskin-clad old man with his gnarled, hairy hands, which have, however, nothing of the aggressor about them.

SILENUS. *(with a bow)*
I beg your pardon, ladies.
Your attire
Relates us somewhat. Willingly indeed
I'd fall into your soft captivity,
Had not, alas, so many years gone by
Since maenad called me anything but brother—
Daddy Silenus at your service.

(catching sight of Argiope and peering at her in astonishment)

Well . . . well . . . Do my eyes deceive me? . . We're old friends . . .

(to the chorus)

A most impressive mansion, is it not?

NYMPH. Daddy Silenus . . . What good luck . . . Ye gods . . .

SILENUS. Always at hand, and yours to command.

(in an undertone)

But first let's get these bacchic beauties settled . . .

(claps his hands)

At this sign two boyish satyrs come running out of the forest. They are as like as two peas, the only difference between them being that one wears a blue ribbon in his hair and the other a pink one. Their appearance is hardly such as to inspire confidence, although in Silenus' presence they do their best to conduct themselves in a dignified manner. They stand in such a way that one masks the other.

SCENE SEVEN

The same, plus the two satyrs.

SILENUS. *(loudly, to the Bacchantes)*
Allow me to present my nephew here—
A gadabout, I fear, though long betrothed.

BACCHANTE. Betrothed? Which one? They seem to be a pair . . .

SILENUS. Now, goatlings, what's all this? . .
(he rubs his eyes) You' re right—a pair.
Well, the more the merrier, that's what I say . . .
And merry lads they are . . . Ladies, look out—
A trice, and you'll be prancing in the rout!

Pause.

SATYR WITH BLUE RIBBON. *(bowing to the Bacchantes)*
Allow me, for the sake of daddy here,
To make the basis of our friendship clear.

My partner stammers—
not to the extent
That he won't best you in an argument—
I'm quick of tongue, his fingers are like eels,
And so I make the speeches while he steals . . .
That's how we live, as close as flesh to bone,
But when it comes to love—to each his own.

SATYR WITH PINK RIBBON.
Yes, w-w-when it c-comes to l-love—
to each his own.

Laughter. Exeunt chorus and satyrs.

SCENE EIGHT

White Clouds

NYMPH. *(going over to Silenus, she lays her head trustingly on his shoulder)*
Daddy Silenus, help me—you must help me . . .
Or give me some herb that I may wake as mad
As ever I was. My case is desperate.

SILENUS. *(in mock terror, but nevertheless holding the Nymph to him and humoring her)*
Avaunt, avaunt! Don't mention madness here—
The bacchic rout's at hand with all its din.
I might run mad myself in the whirl of it.

NYMPH. Silenus, I am a mother, yet unloved.

SILENUS. Mistrusted rather—so it seems to me.

NYMPH. He has no need of me. I tell you, he needs
No one. That's the dreadful thing, Silenus.
He lives in dreams. His heart is proud, unfeeling . . .
Music's his malady.

(prostrating herself at Silenus' feet)

O you who healed

My afflicted soul! What power is it that makes
Me love Thamyris as I do? Why do
Thronging desires thicken to fog about me—
A fog so dense that the heavens' blue
Is murdered by them. O that a storm would break,
But there's no hope . . .

Pause. The Nymph covers her face.

SILENUS. I understand. No words . . .
You must rejoin the rout—I wish it were
Not so, Nymph, but you must . . . Come then, let's be off!
Those cursed strings!—they make the blood run cold,
Yes, like a fog they poison you with dreams
That may not be . . . The flute's more suitable
For womankind. The lies of the flute are light
As those a fickle lover tells.

NYMPH. I won't
Be parted from my son.

SILENUS. No, not until
He drives you out . . . How stubborn women are!
What is it you want to prove? . .

NYMPH. The altar's here,
And here my house shall be . . .

SILENUS. Old subterfuges
Of an old desire.
Some plan is hatching
In your head, that's clear . . . You're fondling now
This shaggy carapace of mine that hides
A sentimental heart . . .

NYMPH. I have promised
My son the Muses . . . Dear Silenus,
Do not deny him, be his guide. Ah why
Did you restore my mind to reason?

SILENUS. Of that I see scant evidence as yet.
Which Muse would he have sing?

NYMPH. Euterpe.

SILENUS. A cold goddess. There, I fear, the scythe
Will strike on stone. Of course, who may not be

Deceived? And though Euterpe be a Muse,
She's nonetheless a woman. How to hide
Thamyris, that's the rub. That pride of his:
He won't crouch in a barrel . . .

NYMPH. No, Euterpe
Must sing *for him alone*—such is his dream . . .

SILENUS. Let him then engage the Muse in contest.

NYMPH. Ah satyr, but the reckoning? . . Such as he,
Shall they oppose the gods? How many of us,
Cherished of Zeus, have given heroes birth?
Achilles, Memnon, Rhesus—all of them
Were glorious, yet of them could you name
A single happy man?

SILENUS. Well, we can choose
Our own conditions, and it would do no harm,
I'd say, to take him down a peg or two.

NYMPH. Daddy Silenus, I'm a woman—dim
Is my mind's sight, but my heart is tremulous
As a doe's. I see no flowery meadow:
I see a quagmire, bottomless beneath
Its cloak of flowers, O satyr . . .

SILENUS. Like enough
You're right.
Pause. So be it. Let's to the mountains then.
We'll find sequestered places there—moonlit
And passion-lit; scarlet the mouths are there,
Lips swollen from the flute; the shoulders there,
How white they are . . . the dancing, how abandoned . . .
What if the fumes of wine envelope you
Like morning haze?

NYMPH. The morrow—what of that?

SILENUS. The morrow's still far off.

NYMPH. What shall I say?
What can I say? My mind is clouded . . . Have
You heard Thamyris play, old man? If
A tournament's arranged, who will be judge? . .
Might it be you? . .

SILENUS. There's little chance of that.

NYMPH. And did you like Thamyris' playing?
SILENUS. He's gifted, certainly.
NYMPH. Well, and the Muse?
SILENUS. Never heard her, though I've seen her more than once.
She's high and mighty—when she walks our way
She picks her skirts up. Her hands are delicate,
And rings look well upon her long pink
Fingers. Only they must be cold, those hands
Of hers—she's always looking down at them
And smiling: she's delighted with herself.
NYMPH. And is there no one that she loves?
SILENUS. No one,
And suitors never a one: your Thamyris—
In a peplus. Here he is, though. Quick,
Decide. Shall I arrange the business then?
NYMPH. *(in a whisper)*
Yes, yes, Silenus. I rely on you.
You don't mind if I listen while you talk?
SILENUS. No, not at all—I won't seduce the boy.

SCENE NINE

Tortoiseshell Clouds

Silenus and Thamyris.
The Nymph listens, unseen by Thamyris.

SILENUS. Most honored sir! Accept our heartiest
Congratulations on your latest triumph . . .

(as if suddenly recalling something)

Your latest—not your last.
THAMYRIS. My thanks to you.
Alas, I am no Orpheus . . .
SILENUS. You wish
To bring the stones to life, as he did?

THAMYRIS. Silenus, no. Even had I the gift
Of mighty Orpheus, never would I
Inflict such torment on my grizzled friends.

(tenderly stroking a stone)

Move white stones? What need have they of motion?
The life of stones is different from ours—
Different and better. Their lives are passed
In deepest contemplation. Only the moon
Can sometimes with its gliding shadows touch
Their ancient wrinkles—touch, and steal away.
Stones hold their peace and trouble nobody.
They care for nobody, and no man asks
That they should care for him.
To bring to life
My grizzled stones? For whom? For a bladder
Of warmed-up blood; thrust a knife in—so—
And cart your bladder off before it stinks.
Orpheus lacked a heart, though demigod.

SILENUS. We live by moments—the felicity
Of minerals is beyond my ken. You've been
Beguiled by centaurs' tales, ephemeron.
Proud minds fear happiness that flies; the fruit
That must be eaten thoughtlessly they scorn.
So fame's not to your liking. Very well—
Your taste's impeccable . . . What's fame but dust? . .
But have the strings you master yielded up
Their plenitude of joy? A sweeter prize
Awaits your lyre than palm or fatted ox
Or pot of beaten bronze, a prize more sweet
Than the promise in a pair of sly blue eyes . . .
Tell me, have you heard the Muses play?

THAMYRIS. *(diffidently)*
There was a woman here just now who claimed
To be my mother, and she promised me
The Muses.

SILENUS. Promised you the Muses. Well now . . .
Ha ha ha . . .

(guffaws)

THAMYRIS. Why do you laugh, Silenus?
SILENUS. I'll stop for reason's sake, although your words
Seem not a whit less foolish than before . . .
You missed your mother's meaning; even the gods
May seldom hope to hear the Muses' song.
THAMYRIS. O Silenus, why was I moved to kiss her?
He kisses—I'm supposed to say what for!
Her beauty, I suppose, and tender care,
And because, most worthy sir, wise though you be,
You're still a babe in arms—a flaming torch
Will draw the moth.
THAMYRIS. What must I pay, Silenus,
To gain Euterpe?
SILENUS. Brightly burns the torch—
Poor foolish moth, so soon to be consumed . . .
THAMYRIS. Enough of moths and flames—I'll flatter her,
I'll serve her as a satyr.
SILENUS. You hardly
Have the build, my son. Players of the lyre
And satyrs both are pleasing to the Muse,
Each in his own way and in his proper hour.
Euterpe cannot be your singing partner,
But compete with her you may. Offer her
A wager . . .
THAMYRIS. O delicious madness!
But where shall I find her? Let's be on our way!
SILENUS. No so fast, my friend . . . What about conditions?
You've heard of Marsyas? I recommend
You take a glance in your Herodotus.
THAMYRIS. If you'll be go-between, I'm ready now
To sign a contract: all Thamyris
You may dispose of—let me only keep
My lyre, a hand to pluck its strings and, yes,
My heart—the rest is yours.
SILENUS. Tut tut, such haste.
Let us reflect awhile. Who's to play first?

THAMYRIS. Who first? Why she, of course—the Muse.
SILENUS. The time?
THAMYRIS. I'm ready now.
SILENUS. And who's to be the judge?
THAMYRIS. You—if the choice be mine.
SILENUS. A sorry choice . . .
No bodily harm to be inflicted then—
A needful precondition.
And the prize?
THAMYRIS. That, Silenus, let the Muse decide . . .
SILENUS. And if the victory be yours, what then?
THAMYRIS. You've seen her face to face; tell me about her:
Tall she must be, and slender—very pale,
Her dusky tresses gathered in a knot . . .
SILENUS. Then add: the clasp worn high on her left arm
In which a jacinth burns, and fingers pink
And tapering . . .
THAMYRIS. Enough—I'll marry her;
We shall beget an Orpheus, old man.
SILENUS. Wait for me in this place. I won't be long.

He goes out.

SCENE TEN

Dark Gold Sun

Thamyris. Chorus in the distance.

CHORUS. Soon the dance shall set us whirling,
Feet of white in moonlight flying;
Drowsing only with the dawnglow,
Rising with the noontide only.
THAMYRIS. With darkest blooms the rose is ensanguined,
The rose is ensanguined . . .
O joy!

Kitharodos, come!
O thou golden-tongued, smile on us!
O joy!
Let her heart know desire,
Thy white-throated votaress . . .

CHORUS. There, to fierce desire submissive,
We'll slay a doe at streamside drinking,
And the doe's forsaken youngling
At our own white breasts we'll suckle . . .

THAMYRIS. Long hast thou guarded the flock of Admetus,
The flock of Admetus,
O joy!
And wilt thou, Kitharodos,
Abandon thy friends?
O joy!
Tune thy pipe, yield thy pipe
To the white-throated votaress . . .

CHORUS. Then shall tambourines' harsh clamor
Echo through the troubled forest:
Days shall melt away like shadows,
Nights shall be as honied kisses.

THAMYRIS. Half-buried in grasses, the carapace glitters,
The carapace glitters . . .
O joy!
Of my longing, Kitharodos,
Of my longing it sings,
O joy!
Will she care for my songs,
Thy white-throated votaress?

CHORUS. Shake your tambourines in frenzy—
Even beds of down will surfeit.
Heart to flute will prove unfaithful—
Become Kitharodos, O Bacchus!

THAMYRIS. Dionysos has born the dark roses away,
The dark roses away . . .
O joy!
Touch thy bow, O Kitharodos,
To the strings lightly . . .
O joy!

And the rose she'll forget,
Thy white-throated votaress . . .
CHORUS. Rise, O Bacchus, moonlight-fickle,
Of the deep blue eyes gold-glinting,
Gently wafting, far resounding,
Diamond-flickering thy mantle.
THAMYRIS. Tresses of black—she is pale, she is stern,
She is pale, she is stern,
O joy!
She cares, O Kitharodos,
For thy meadows only . . .
O joy!
And what are my longings to her,
To thy white-throated votaress?

He goes out singing.

SCENE ELEVEN

Dry Lightning

As the last strophes resound, the Nymph, who has been listening to her son's conversation with Silenus and to his singing, walks slowly toward the hut. She stands for a while in silence, head bowed, toying with a corner of her veil. At length she lifts her head.

NYMPH. His soul is troubled, and the tempest shakes
The unaccustomed strings. Now roses haunt
His dreams; he cries aloud, with burning lips
He seeks that white-stemmed, melody-enfolding
Rose, that double rose . . . The Muse—what's she to him?
I erred. That siren is his rival. To
Humiliate her, that's what he intends . . .
But how, but how?
By pressing a kiss upon
Her neck's white stem?
Thamyris and the Muse?

And I must yield? Shall I relinquish him
To anyone in all the world. Nine moons
He passed with me . . .
(softly) but not the honeymoon . . .
Leave me, O dreadful dream . . . O let me be,
Unchain my will . . .
(buries her head in her hands) I have forgotten
How to pray.
O Zeus, my sovereign lord,
Thy lightnings I endure, yet joyless flames
Lay waste the heart, parching the spring of tears.
Philammon was as he is now . . . ah yes . . .
But twenty years . . . His curls are silvered now—
That's not for me, nor purple veins, nor rough-
Skinned, passionless embracings.
Hold your peace,
Accursed madness! Thyrsi, and the scent
Of musk and fawnskins mingled . . .
Mother,
Come to your senses. What do you want? To push
Your child into a fray no less insane
And vicious than yourself? But who is not
So here? Even he—a prey to love's remorse,
Though undefiled as yet.
For what am I
To pray? Thamyris' victory? The Muse
Surrendering to his will—is that my wish?
Or would his shame be sweeter to my heart?
Yes, yes—Thamyris' shame . . . Such words are fearful,
Hoarded in the mind—the air shall have them . . .

(raising her hands)

O son of Chronos, if by thy will this flame
Of madness and of longing burns within me,
Grant that my son Thamyris . . .

(her hands fall to her sides; in a louder voice)

I lack the strength
To voice the conjuration—mother's milk
Grows turbid from the poison of the grape
That neighbors it . . .

(with suddenly awakened energy)

I'll make one potion of them . . .

Rolls of thunder grow nearer and more powerful.

The all-powerful one would drown my words. But no,
Desire in me is stronger than all fear.
Let not his life be forfeit, Chronos' son . . .
Yet do not yield to him the victory . . .
By thy Cretan cavern, king,[41] I conjure thee.

The stormclouds disperse; somewhere in the distance rain falls, gleaming and vaporous. Silhouetted in one of the radiant clouds appears the smiling face of Zeus.

SCENE TWELVE

Voices are heard from the direction in which Thamyris went off, and he himself now appears. He is followed by his lamenting nurse.
Thamyris, Nymph, Nurse.

THAMYRIS. *(who has not yet noticed the Nymph)*
Well, that's enough of it. She lied to me—
What then? Why should she invent it all,
I ask you, nurse? If it's a fairytale,
I like it—why should I be annoyed to find
Myself so well connected?

NURSE. O my lamb!
They'll dupe you, sure as day! Get away from them,
Or they'll eat you, skin and bone!

(catching sight of the Nymph, she draws back)

THAMYRIS. *(also catching sight of the Nymph, but calmly)*

You hear her, Nymph?
You've frightened my old nannie. Look into
Her eyes, dear nurse . . . Do malice and deceit
Lurk there? Now do they?

(holding his hand out to the Nymph) Mother, although

I came of age a stranger to your love,
The Nymph has made amends by giving me
A happiness undreamed-of. Yes, I'll be
A Titan stealing fire from heaven—though
I'll bring to men a purer, gentler fire . . .
And later, when my son . . .

NYMPH. *(drawing away from him impatiently)*
Thamyris, no,
You must not gaze into the future. Why
Were you so quick to challenge her?

THAMYRIS. *(drawing the Nymph to him)*
How else
Shall her celestial melody illume
My heart?
There, let me see you smile! No time
For stormclouds now. My love for you is such—
For everyone, for everything—that my heart
Is like to burst my breast, though once the stars
Breathed there and the empyrean burned.
(the Nymph weeps, covering her face with her veil) I know
What makes you weep. What's to be done? Until
Its own good time fate hides its will. I won't
Reproach you, dear, wherever fate may toss
My tremulous cup. No more of this . . . Satyr!

SCENE THIRTEEN

The Sun Breaks through the Clouds

The same plus Silenus. He carries a wineskin on his back, and goblets dangle from his belt. At the sight of him the old woman gives a cry and runs off into the house.

Silenus, Thamyris, Nymph.

Without a word, Silenus sits down on the ground and slowly, one by one, sets about untying the wineskin's thongs. His face streams with sweat.

NYMPH. Silenus! What did she say to you?
THAMYRIS. Daddy Silenus, can we go?
SILENUS. *(continuing his work)*
The wineskin's still to be undone,
And he's imploring, "Fill the cup!"
THAMYRIS. Minutes are few. For heaven's sake,
Her answer! I can wait no more.
SILENUS. *(continuing to busy himself with the wineskin)*
Minutes are plentiful with us,
Though never, never in excess.
What's joy to you? Delirium—
A flare that leaves the night more black.
Ah, but for us, Kitharodos,
Ah, but for us, Kitharodos,

(finally he manages to undo the knotted thongs; he unties one of the goblets that hangs from his belt and pours some wine)

It's in the hymeneal knot . . .
What's happiness to men? A shadow
Cast by a leaf on shifting dust.
A moment, and the cup is filled;
The lips are dry—what more's to ask?
THAMYRIS. Silenus, answer me . . .
SILENUS. *(drinks, then unties two more goblets and slowly fills all three of them, admiring the streaming liquid. Then he raises one of them with a bow)*
Your health . . .
A cup for each of you, my friends?

(He offers a goblet to Thamyris, and then to the Nymph)

THAMYRIS. I don't drink.

Silenus drinks with a bow.

NYMPH. *(smiling)*
You'd better empty mine as well.

Silenus drinks and kisses his fingertips.

SILENUS. A shame, but even the sun has spots . . .
I understand why you refuse—
You make the answer "I don't drink"
As I might say "I do not sing,"
If, offering me his lyre, the Delphic god
Suggested that I partner him in song.

(he drains the goblet with deliberation and relish)

And now, my loves—a bite to eat.

The Nymph gives Silenus bread; he eats and drinks.

We'll give the drinking cups a rest.

(washes the goblets)

I'll just give one of them a parting kiss,
One little kiss,

(pours and drinks) and I'll be at your service.

(stands up, brushing off crumbs)

Thamyris, are you ready?
Briskly we'll
Stride the journey out.
(gazing at the sky) Phoebus still stand high . . .

THAMYRIS. Silenus, are you joking?
SILENUS. Listen to him . . .
And who kept saying "Now, let it be now!"
Your terms are granted. Pan will be chief judge,

Terpsichore and myself the jury.
Whew, such a heap of news I've dumped!—
I'll leave you with the wineskin, children.

Lays the skin on the ground and begins folding it. Thamyris makes as if to help him.

Wait a moment . . . Let me leave it dry.

(drinks, wipes his lips and follows Thamyris out)

SCENE FOURTEEN

Rosy Sunset

Groups of satyrs come running into the orchestra. A dumb show—they look for bacchantes in the grass and among the bushes. A flute. Castanets. Wild dancing. The sun is close to setting. The clouds in the west are flushed and fiery with the last rays.

A VOICE. Day-long have I sought you,
An endless blue day—
But leave my cup empty:
You alone slake my thirst.

SATYRS. The night to our darlings—an hour to the flute,
An hour to the flute,
My lips burn with fever . . .
Ah nymphs, show us kindness,
Ah nymphs, show us pity!
Come kiss us then, darlings . . .

A VOICE. A weary doe—I,
An icy spring—you,
Only gleam, only glance,
And we'll mingle as one.

SATYRS. We are weary of heights, we are weary of space,
We are weary of space,
Of blue, vacant space . . .
O would you but yield us,

But yield us, sore-stricken,
    Your honey-sweet lips.

ANOTHER VOICE.

But hide not your eyes:
You're the wrong—I'm the knife.
My embrace shall enfold you
Like flames that devour . . .

ARIOSO OF THE LANGUID SATYR.

In the red sky of sunset
My gaze cannot fathom,
Can the gods be unsoftened
By the fate I'm condemned to?
Ever an athlete
Impatient for battle,
Like a husband forsaken,
I long for your presence.
Are you not the flame's flutter?
In the high smoky vastness,
Invisible, pearl-like,
Do you not have your being?
No, flame were you never,
Not there in the star-shine,
And not by spells muttered
Amid ripening clusters,
In the fragrance of flowers—
Not thus shall I find you . . .
And in some meadow
All sweet with the dewfall,
To a maenad I'll whisper
(silken her tresses)
That in the blue distance
A fawn haunts my vision;
That longing consumes me
More fiercely than ever,
That, hungering greatly,
I'm wasting to nothing,
That sweeter than honey
Is my heart's expectation,
That fair Amimona
To my hands should surrender

Her twin moon-white lemons,
Her ripe-swelling lemons.
In weather so sultry
The nights can be chilling
And leave you enfeebled.
O merciless Parca!
With these eyes I have witnessed
Too often thy vengeance,
O merciless Parca!
Yet this night, I swear it,
We shall not be parted,
This night, I swear it,
We'll lie hot together.

SCENE FIFTEEN

Blue Moonlight

Night is at hand. One by one the satyrs cease their sport and music-making and lie down in the grass to sleep. The moon is visible in the east. Dusk gives way to a bluish glimmer. Only the trees, massed and heavy, loom blacker still. The Nymph appears, adorned with large and luxuriant white and yellow flowers. Her arms are bare.

NYMPH. "To nymphs are given two such nights, no more."
O nymph, can that be true? Why then these flowers,
These flowers you wear? This night? Was ever
Maenad more troubled that the shade of night
Should creep so slowly? Those livid hags
That wait on Hecate—were they more swift
To hide their snakes and yellow poisons
Deep in their lady's black and stifling coils
Than was this heart to gaze through burning eyes
Into the eyes of innocence, to merge
Untrammelled with another heart, and so
Infect it with irresolute unease?

SATYR'S VOICE. *(softly)*
A woman, brothers . . .

ANOTHER, DEEPER VOICE. One of ours?
HIGH-PITCHED VOICE.
It's dark, dad, I don't see too well.
DEEP VOICE.
Push your way through scrub and bushes
And find out—is she ours or not?
But just be careful—if you cough
Or sneeze, I'll let you have what for.

A rustle in the grass, then:

HIGH-PITCHED VOICE.
Not a maenad . . .
But an oread . . .
Come to keep some lover's tryst,
Decked out with flowers from head to foot.
ANOTHER HIGH-PITCHED VOICE.
And with Kitharodos, Kitharodos!
Look, here he comes—straight from his grove . . .

SCENE SIXTEEN

Dusty Moonlight

Thamyris and the Nymph. The chorus, scattered about in the grass and bushes, is invisible. Thamyris is about to approach the Nymph, but, embarrassed by her attire, draws back; mastering himself, he goes over to her and holds out his arms in an embrace. But the Nymph stands motionless. Her whole being is in her eyes.

THAMYRIS. Dear one . . . Have you forgiven your Thamyris?
While you in your heart's pain confessed to him,
He stood and heard you out with cold mistrust . . .
I need no token.
Only a mother
Could give such happiness unenvying
And not recall her tears . . .

NYMPH. *(in a husky voice, almost inaudibly)*
I claim a share
In your success, my son. The victor's crown . . .
THAMYRIS. Success, you say? What is the victory
On which I am to be congratulated?
NYMPH. *(more smoothly)*
You did not shirk the battle . . .
THAMYRIS. No, I went
To fight as men fight in the arena
And bring you back my sweaty armor.
But
The tournament did not take place.
NYMPH. *(with a quick movement, in a voice that has regained its former vigor)* You withdrew?
THAMYRIS. Yes, I withdrew.

From the grass, softly.

He's fooled us—and how . . .
Thamyris, take a bow!
NYMPH. *(again somewhat huskily)*
But you were the challenger,
And said that you were happy . . .
THAMYRIS. Utterly . . .
NYMPH. You'll wed the Muse then?
THAMYRIS. Why do you say that?
NYMPH. *(sarcastically)*
What of the songs you sang, the dreams you dreamed? . .
When visions filled your mind with rosy fingers,
Jacinths . . .
THAMYRIS. That brief intoxication
Shames me now. Sweet is the trouble kisses
Stir the blood to, yet from them harmony
Grows pale—distressed, she wrings her hands and flees
To forest fastnesses—to mossy roots,
To the eagle-owl's hoarse cry . . . I shall not wed.

Quiet talk in the grass.

— The fiddler's still a bachelor then?
— What a speaker too! . . And brainy!
— Quiet then, let's listen to him!
— A treasure-house of wisdom—yes,
An inspiration to us all.
— Now that's what I call eloquence . . .
— Fine enough, but highfalutin':
Maybe he's telling the moon his dreams.
A scentless flower, if you ask me.

NYMPH. Tell me, Kitharodos, where does it lie,
This special happiness? And is the Muse
More beautiful than I?

THAMYRIS. I paid no heed.
The sunset held my gaze; I saw the path
Of heaven strewn with roses, while the sounds
Her lyre made like an exhalation rose
And hung, a mist, athwart the path . . . They seemed
Myself and not myself. I have no words—
Shadows are not so fine. Or were they souls
Awaiting birth? Or had the shaping hand
Shattered the forms it wrought, and in despair
The shaper slit his throat? Above me there
They filled the roseate and aery way,
Assuming first the shapes of constellations;
Then imperceptibly their choirs began
To move, as Serpent, Fish, as Ring and Lyre,
And one by one above each dream of mine
A soft star kindled, spinning and dissolving
Into the ether with my dream, keeping
A perfect rhythm. All that was left at last
Were aery points of light, and craving eyes
To link them up through tears with threads of gold.
Delirium, you'll say? . . Yes, even now
I can't explain what I experienced:
I looked—or did I listen? Did the clouds
Reverberate above me, or did the strings
Beget those forms? And the sunset, was it
A tender scale, no more? . .

CHORUS. *(in the grass, softly)*

FIRST VOICE. Lord, what a fog of words!

SECOND VOICE.

To asses' ears, maybe . . .
I'd call him a crater
Burning beneath its ashen shell . . .
For once I'm sorry that we're goats
Or that he isn't one of us.
That's where we'd learn to conquer hearts . . .
Where everything's as clear as mud—
That's where a woman sees a god.
Just look—the Nymph's quite overcome . . .
A good thing, lads, we chanced to come this way!
One more such speech, and all that loveliness
Will melt and leave two charming pits—her eyes—
And twenty vain chrysanthemums.

During this pause, Thamyris stands gazing at the sky, as if trying to recall something. Fanning herself with a large, pale leaf, the Nymph gazes at Thamyris with burning eyes.

THAMYRIS. *(repeats)*

O the sunset
Was a tender scale, no more.
Consummate
Was the bliss I knew. And knew it waking . . .
My heart's blood courses to my fingertips.
The golden bees are pining for the strings—
Long have their light wings vainly brushed my heart—
But they shall not prevail.
Let them to the hive,
There to prepare the house—and let it be
A golden house of rare delight . . .

A RUSTLING IN THE GRASS.

Upon my soul, he turns a pretty phrase!
Such words may serve a melting moment.

THAMYRIS. *(repeating)*

O rare delight . . .
I see the meaning now
Of all I lived by, all I thought. I played,
Yes, well enough at times . . . But like a boy.

WHISPERING IN THE GRASS.
Our shrinking violet's quite ecstatic . . .
NYMPH. But
The tournament? Thamyris, were you beaten?
THAMYRIS. I did not play. O never think that fear
Undid me. Can judgment be pronounced
Between Muse and mortal man? I'm beaten, yes—
You see, my lyre is gone. Let them decide
My fate. Silenus will deliver strings
And verdict both—or say the reckoning
To pay for bliss, for the sweets of unsuccess.

SCENE SEVENTEEN

Bright Moonlight

Silenus arrives in some haste. Goblets dangle from his belt, as before; on his back is another full wineskin, in his hands a lyre. Thamyris, the Nymph, Silenus and hidden chorus.

SILENUS. Your instrument . . . in perfect shape . . . It's yours
To keep in memory.
THAMYRIS. *(for some reason he does not take the lyre immediately, but stands gazing at it intently)*
Friend of my heart,
Long has our parting been! Have you pined for me?
Or did Silenus wake to melody
Responsive strings?
SILENUS. *(querulously)*
As if I've nothing better
To do than scare the crows by twanging on
That celebrated instrument of his . . .

Thamyris takes the lyre and examines it with a surprised expression; his gestures are strange; he seems reluctant to touch the strings.

Why are you staring? Isn't that your friend?

Thamyris puts down the lyre.

SILENUS. *(drawing closer to Thamyris, confidingly)*
Dear Prince . . . you really think that happiness
Is all in music? . . When you're supple-limbed
And above your curly head the sun has half
His course, and more, to run. You think the world,
The gorgeous world that breathes upon your lyre,
And trembles in the butterfly, and burns,
And shifts from hue to hue, and hangs in mist
Above the fountain's jetting urn, and sings,
And laughs with joy in roses and in pearls—
You think that world is fit to live and sing
And waft its tender breath and bring us joy
Only because you snapped the golden thread
That linked a turtle's slow-paced hours and strung
The empty shell with calf-gut?

THAMYRIS. *(who in the course of this speech has at last ventured to pick up his lyre, now plucks some strangely inharmonious chords on it)*
I cannot
Understand these words of yours . . . Silenus,
Do you know what's happened to me? What is
This broken thing you've given me?

SILENUS. It was
No broken thing I gave—the faithless one
No longer recognizes you.

THAMYRIS. *(in alarm)*
Listen:
Are these not fingers and are these not strings
Beneath these fingers? Rouse me from this dream,
Old man . . . We have no need of toys . . . O give
Me back my heart—this is some cruel joke . . .
I have forgotten all I ever played.

At the beginning of Thamyris' speech the satyrs get up; they gather round the Coryphaeus and listen to Thamyris with curiosity, examining his lyre and following with close attention his unsuccessful attempts to play.

Or have I lost my hearing?
Nymph, can you hear

My playing? *Am* I playing? Am I?
Please, someone, tell me . . . Listen, satyr,
I know your kind are skilled in music. See
If you can draw a tune from this dull block.

Taking the lyre from him, Silenus begins to play. The satyrs applaud.

Aha, do you hear, old man, do you hear, I say?
You call it music that your fingers wake?
Oh no—some bat, some midnight-flitting bat,
Has strayed beneath a vault and blindly beats
Its wings against the moss-encrusted walls.
You're dancing to it, goatlings? Ha ha ha!
What rhythm's there?—Oh now I know for sure
You're making fun of me . . . Are you content?
Take back your instrument and give me mine . . .

Silenus continues his measured and expressive playing. Thamyris seems to be trying to analyze the music or to recall something that has slipped his mind. He buries his face in his hands.

Or, satyr, break this trance that binds my heart!

(with a gesture of entreaty)

My plight is desperate—pity me!

The music ceases. A buzz of voices. The satyrs congratulate Silenus.

Why do
I hear your words so clearly . . . while the strings? . .
Silenus, where is music?

SILENUS. *(with gentle gravity)*
You are young
To know betrayal, boy. The gods themselves
Perforce endure it. Night and Day alone
Are faithful to each other, and the Pole
Star, which may not be moved.
Submit you must
To universal law. After happiness

Comes night, as after day: the judgments passed
By gods are fixed as the celestial pole.

NYMPH. *(softly)*

What sentence has the god pronounced on him?

SILENUS. *(no less softly)*

To music he must be forever deaf.

The Nymph and satyrs express the sympathy that overwhelms them by noises and piteous exclamations; Thamyris, in contrast, becomes calm and stands motionless, like a man thinking something over. There is a prolonged silence.

SILENUS. Bless us! Is it so dreadful, after all,
To live in the wide world sans pipes and strings?
Now if he were a satyr! . . How can we
Dance if there's no music? Here's a wise man—
Yet for his strings he weeps.

THAMYRIS. Silenus, no,
I do not weep. The wave broke over me,
Broke gently and was gone. My head is deeper
In the sand, the taste of salt remains
Upon my tongue—that's all.
The same dream
Still enthralls this heart of mine . . . I do not mean
To wake, old man.

SILENUS. I wish you pleasant dreams,
Most reverend Thamyris. Zeus himself
Could find no better remedy. But sleep
Is comfortless unsweetened by the thought
That it is only sleep, the end's not here—
I will it, and the torpor falls away . . .
Pluck from your heart that thought, and what remains?
A hoop of lead about the skull, a dull
Envenomed daze, a sorcerer's foolery?
Young men sleep ill without a woman or
A cup of wine, Thamyris—say the word,
And I'll oblige, we'll drain the cooling draught,
Judge and condemned together, and the skin
We'll sacrifice to Themis—pretty it's
Not, but then they say the lady's blind.

THAMYRIS. Leave me, Silenus . . . As it is, my heart's
Befuddled. Let oblivion's mold grow there.

SILENUS. Mother and nymph! You've lurked there long enough
Amid the dappled moonlight and the flowers—
You must have some advice more serviceable
Than mine to give Thamyris. Otherwise
I find your silence quite unpardonable . . .
Silvery vibrations by the dozen—
So far, that's all we have to thank you for . . .

NYMPH. Thamyris, son. Music has other means
Than trembling silver strings to reach men's hearts.
On yonder mountain tops the flute-god's breath
May heal your spirit.
Say but the word,
We'll join the rout. I'll beg my sisters' aid—
There's none to match their skill. We'll deck you out
As a bacchante. Well will they become you—
Fawnskin and vineleaves, the green of ivy
And the green of yew twined in your hair!
You call on sleep—surrender of the will
Is sweetest, child, in mountain coppices
Washed by the amber moon. It's early there
For sleeping.
Think what it must be to yield,
Yield utterly, to some impassioned will.
And later—who can say?
I have the art
To soften Dionysos—by what means?
By feline blandishments, the serpent's clinging,
The fluttering of the dove: from the high gods
I'll wrest your happiness, my son . . . But let
A night pass first, and then a day, and then
Another night with me . . . Come, let us go!

CORYPHAEUS *(addressing the Nymph)*
Black mystery prolongs the nighttime,
By mystery of roses honied—
But Thamyris' heart is stony,
If perhaps it be not wooden . . .

For the summons of his mother
Cares he nothing, all unheeding—
So runs wild the forest fledgling
From its nest untimely fallen

One of the satyrs, who had been listening enraptured to the Nymph, begins to accompany her on his flute, hesitantly at first, then more loudly and confidently. The Nymph's words become musical declamation. Finally, both flutist and Nymph are captivated by a particular phrase, which is taken up now by the voice, now by the flute, each tenderly supporting their common longing.

NYMPH. I'll weary you with mind-distracting pleasure,
I'll find a way to part you from your pain—
We two shall sleep beneath a single fawnskin,
Like sisters twain.
Only beware the day does not betray you:
Teeth are sharp there, hearts brook no disdain . . .
And free at night we'll lie beneath our fawnskin,
Like sisters twain.
Let Iris with her bow make bright the heavens,
Or let them be obscured by mist and rain . . .
What's heaven to us? We'll lie beneath our fawnskin,
Like sisters twain.

THAMYRIS. Like sisters twain . . . Would that not be too cramped,
Too hot, too close? Such sleep will never bring
Oblivion upon the heart through nights
And months and years . . .
This scheme won't do for us,
Woman. With a moment's happiness you locked
Our lips eternally. And never think
To hear a word from me in praise or blame.
But do not call the flute to breathe upon
A soul that's dead. That breath defiles the heart.
The veins stand out upon the flautist's brow,
His lips are like a beast's—how shall such lips
Be consecrated by the word? I loathe
Them, swollen, red as blood.
If anything
Remains to take from me, then take the shades
That beckon me—whither I do not know . . .

O to be blind to them, as I am deaf
To music . . .
                                        If I could hollow out,
More black, more deep, the pit of night . . . Ah yes . . .
The air is filled with turmoil . . .
                                                        You, nymph,
With your beauty and the shades that shift
Across that pallid face, across those flowers,
Move me to pity and to horror . . . Go.

(a pause; quietly)

Or can you be Thamyris' fate? Is there
No other place in the world for you? . . . The sun
Will flame and night return once more—and you
Will never leave my side . . . and I must learn
To love this fate of mine.
                                                Your eyes infuse
My soul with subtle poison . . .
                                                        Not to see—
Not hear—not love.
                                        But what if love itself
Be deaf and blind? . .

He goes over to the Nymph and takes her by the hand; she follows him as if spell-bound.

                                                        O music's last
And all but silent ray! Descend into
My eyes and thence take refuge in my heart,
Despairing, dumb. And after you have passed,
I'll not admit a shadow.

The Nymph tries to press herself to him, tries to speak, but Thamyris gently frees himself.

                                                        Roses . . . lips,
O never open more. Your words I do
Not need, nor you yourselves . . . These tresses soft

As down . . . this hand . . .

(he lifts one of the Nymph's pale hands, then lets it fall)

These cheeks . . . the tears
on them
Still wet . . .

(he draws away as the Nymph makes a movement toward him)

You must not touch me, no I say.
I long for rays, for rays alone. In them
Is music . . .

(he runs off)

SCENE EIGHTEEN

Whitish

General consternation. Everyone is silent for a moment. A gust of wind, followed by another, and yet another. From the forest a cloud of dust comes flying, whirling leaves within it; branches creak. In the soughing of the wind can be heard, faintly at first but ever more distinctly, a sound between a howl and a moan. Meanwhile, the moon has disappeared behind a cloud and the stage is lit only by a whitish gleam. Between Silenus and the Nymph appears the Shade of Philammon. There is a rope around its neck. The face has not lost its bluish tinge and in the moon's absence seems almost black.

Turning toward the Nymph, the Shade bares its teeth, then it raises a hand as if it wanted to loosen the rope about its neck; but the hand, transparent, with black, swollen fingers, drops back limply, like a tendril; the Shade repeats this gesture several times as it approaches the Nymph—as if it were seeking her aid. The satyrs huddle together in fear. No music, no exclamations. The Shade emits a howling moan of vexation, not as loud as those which the wind carried. All is quiet now—the wind has dropped. The Shade of Philammon, the Nymph, Silenus, chorus of satyrs.

NYMPH. Is someone playing pranks? . . . Silenus? . . . Satyrs? . .

SILENUS. *(softly, not taking his eyes from the dead man)*
These are no pranks. Some ghost has sought you out,
Whose, I can't say. Don't you recognize it?

NYMPH. *(also very softly)*
I fear to name it . . . fear to be mistaken . . .
Thamyris?

(she approaches the Shade, which retreats)

No . . . O no—it cannot be!

SATYR WITH BLUE RIBBON.
(goes over to the Shade with a businesslike air; it makes signs) I can help you, gentlemen . . . at least, I think I can. *(addressing the ghost)* Now what's all this? No one can understand you, you short-weight fly-by-night, you wingless bird, old would-if-I-could. Well, you can start by telling us who you are and why you got cut off from the herd. What kind of behavior is this? *(looks round at satyrs, but no one laughs)*

NYMPH. Daddy Silenus . . . Is he fooling us,
Your goatling? Where can he have learned the tongue
Men speak beyond the grave? Is it contrived,
This apparition? . .

SILENUS. Like enough you're right . . .
Goatlings . . . this is . . . your handiwork . . . Shine, moon—
Let's see our visitor.

The moon emerges for a moment from behind the clouds, bathing the phantom in its light. Quivering all over, it raises a hand to its eyes as if to ward off the light. Instantly everyone realizes that this is no charade.

SILENUS. *(to the Nymph)*
He's an old man.

The Shade takes its hand from its face and makes signs.

SATYR. Nymph, this man died by hanging, and he's a king, and he's your husband . . . he was your husband.

The Nymph fixes an unwavering gaze on the phantom, at the same time pulling the chrysanthemums from her hair with one hand. The Shade shakes its fist at her. Then, groaning, it makes a sweeping circular motion with one arm.

SATYR. Tell me, mother—what have you done with our son, with my . . . my son? . .

NYMPH. *(loosening her hair, as if in delirium)*

Philammon . . . yes, Philammon . . . How I see
My son in him . . . The reckoning has come.

SATYR. *(dispassionately)* Instead of giving him suck, you abandoned him, and for twenty years he lived without you. And now, wanton, you appear from the blue and destroy him in a single day. Criminal and evil creature! There is no name for you, but you shall be punished . . . yes, you shall be punished. You deserve to be turned into a bitch, wasted with desire—a bitch in a back yard that on some clear spring night cannot tell which of the suitors that crowd about her has lain heavy on her . . .

He has difficulty in speaking; they prompt him: "breast."
Yes, that's it—her breast . . .

Signs of consternation and horror in the chorus. The ghost advances on the Nymph. Barely conscious, she is supported by Silenus, who makes a sign to the satyrs; they surround the dead man and, singing and dancing, raise a fearful din. It does not last long, however; gradually the glassy eyes (two fugitive moons are reflected in them) in the blue face have a chilling effect on the artificial gaiety. General silence. No one knows what to say.

CORYPHAEUS. And where, dear brother goatling, did you learn
This art? . .

SATYR IN BLUE RIBBON. There was a time when three of us
Were bound to Hermes as his errand-boys,
And ten whole days I wandered in the wake
Of a multitude of shades like this one here—
O some of them were far more terrible—
And then it was I learned to understand
A few words of their tongue. This fellow here
Was breathing not long since—he's yet to learn
The knack of storytelling. Hey there, friend!
How come you have a rope around your neck?

(to the chorus)

I hanged my self-self-self—that's what he says

The Shade emits sounds resembling "self-self-self" with a disgusting smirk.

What made you do it then?—Life was a bore . . .
And the money—where's the money?

The Shade makes no response.

SATYR WITH PINK RIBBON.
If I m-may say so, th-that's the n-n-nub. He was
A m-moneybags and a skinflint too . . .
And n-now,
You'll see, Thamyris will do wonders . . .
But
It's up to you to put the question plainly . . .

SATYR WITH BLUE RIBBON. *(somewhat piqued)* Do me a favor then, brother—*you* ask the questions. I refuse—well, it's not that I refuse, but I just can't make out a word he says. He must be hiding something. They do that sometimes, you know, gentlemen. He'll dig his heels in, and that'll be that. I knew one that had been executed—no head on his shoulder and still wasn't saying whether he was guilty or not. Let's try this:

Philammon! Most mighty lord!
A drop of blood then? Or some milk and wine?

No—he's just not talking. Well then, let him be. He kept saying the same thing: it's hidden, it's no good trying to find it . . . Yes, but where's it hidden, blockhead? He said something—some kind of garbled word: in the water, it could have been, or in the forest, or under a rock, or in a house—it might mean "nowhere," come to that. To put it in a nutshell—forget about the money. Well, there you are . . . Now he's asking for something to drink. You know, when they've had a drop, they really get talking—sometimes they even prophesy.

Daddy Silenus! May I beg of you
A little wine?—libation for the dead.
I'm too devout to touch the stuff myself.

SILENUS. *(catching his tone)*
Now don't go plying him too liberally—
Two ounces should suffice. We'll make it up
With milk. It's not that I begrudge the wine—
To make the dead dead drunk's a grievous sin,

And I've a conscience, though my name's Silenus.

The crowd of satyrs come running to Silenus' aid. In spite of all Silenus' vigilance, they are soon noticeably flushed. Only the interpreter goes to the milk.

LANGUID SATYR. *(his cheeks are very red; he is wearing the chrysanthemums thrown away by the Nymph)*

I simply can't endure the sight of milk—
It brings the isle of Sicily to mind,
The monster and his dreadful eye. To be
So young and to have born so much!

(whimpers. Then in a cooing voice)

Silenus!

Can't I have a thimblefull of liquor?
I'm not myself. This dampness . . . makes me queasy . . .

Silenus makes a threatening gesture, pulling at his ear. The chrysanthemums disappear into the crowd. Meanwhile, the Shade has flung itself on the milk and wine, which it gulps greedily.

SILENUS. *(softly but meaningfully)*
Quick—while he's drinking—into the rout, my lads!
NYMPH. No, no, Silenus . . . Let him have his say . . .
SILENUS. Better not, my dear . . .

The Shade gets to its feet; it speaks, but its lips move soundlessly.

SATYR WITH BLUE RIBBON.
No, I won't pass that on for anything, because it can't be true.

A cry from Thamyris is heard offstage, followed by another, which breaks off, apparently suppressed by an effort of will.

ALL. *(to the satyr, who stands dumbfounded, pressing a hand to his rapidly beating heart)*

What's all this? Secrets? From us?

Several thyrsi go flying over his head.

SATYR WITH BLUE RIBBON. (*trembling*) Accursed carrion. He prophesied that Thamyris would put out both his eyes with a burning coal. Satyrs, who was that cried out just now?

Without a word, without even a sound, the Nymph collapses into Silenus' arms. The satyrs prepare to flee. They lay the Nymph on a hurriedly rigged-up stretcher. At this moment the satyr with the blue ribbon shouts:

Wait, wait! . . he's speaking again . . . Nymph!

She opens her eyes.

Because you didn't love the one you should have, because you loved the one you shouldn't have, the gods will now turn you into a bird with a red neck . . . I can't make out the name.

Uproar. Confusion. One of the satyrs shakes his flute threateningly at the phantom, a second his tambourine, a third his thyrsus. They chase the phantom; it ducks, glides and every now and then rises a few inches above the ground with the ungainliness of a hen attempting flight. Suddenly a small bird flutters up from this turmoil, and the whole crowd, including Silenus, run away in horror.

SCENE NINETEEN

The Shade and the bird are left alone on stage. For some minutes the Shade pursues the bird, threshing about terrifyingly with its arms. While this is going on, Thamyris can be seen groping his way from stone to stone with the faltering gait of a blind man as he descends toward the hut. Now and then he pauses by a stone to rest. His face is bloody and terrible to look at. At last he approaches the hut. Reaching the last white stone, the one that resembles the head of a bull, he bends down and silently embraces it. The bird alights on his shoulder. Not daring to come closer, the phantom stands at a distance; its folded arms are pressed to its chest, and tears run down its darkened face. Meanwhile, the morning mist has arisen. The moon has faded. Only a few pale stars remain in the brightening sky.

THAMYRIS. The final step . . .
Soon I shall reach the hut,
And peace, and sleep. This day's work is done.
A mist is rising. I can feel—my clothes

Are moist with it. O my white stone, my sole
Companion! How shall I know you now?
Your whiteness is invisible to me . . .
And what's this lying at my feet?
(picks up his lyre) My love . . .
O come to me, my love. The blind man holds
You dear—it was not you betrayed him,
And witchery no longer lays its spell
On your responsive strings.
Even now, perhaps,
One ray of music lurks within my heart . . .

He attempts to play, straining to remember something. Blood, mingled with tears, streams down his face. The phantom shakes its head. The bird remains motionless on his shoulder. Thamyris carefully puts down the lyre.

The wineskin's worn—the wine's all leaked away.
Pause. But there are voices here.
Now I can hear
Nobody. Only the impetous beat
Of someone's heart . . . beside me . . . Child or bird
I cannot tell . . . I felt a sudden warmth
Upon my cheek . . . Day glimmers in night's wake—
I thought the coal had seared the last of sight.
O tender one, who are you? Here, are you,
On my shoulder?

(he carefully picks up the bird, which offers no resistance)
Some fledgling chick, it seems . . .
And tame, so very tame. Where are you from,
My little bird? How come these bleeding pits
Arouse no fear in you?
Ha . . . but what is this?
An icy gust—from where? The dead breathe so
On living hearts . . . O . . . if it be a shade . . .
But whose, but whose? Answer, I conjure you.

The Shade utters a groan, but it is very faint, auroral; a lisping "self-self-self" is heard.

THAMYRIS. *(he moves in the direction of the voice. He carries the bird on one hand; the other calmly and unconsciously brushes Philammon, who falls at his feet and kisses them)*

You gods . . . I have rendered to you all I have—
The debt is paid—with interest. But Thamyris
Did not come alone into this world. If
You see his father and his mother now,
Grant him one prayer in this his bitter hour
Of desolation: for the agony
That he has freely born, condemn him not
To solitude—but let his father
Or his mother, weeping, cleanse his wounds.

SCENE TWENTY

Dawn

Hermes appears in the distance, surrounded by an aureole of divine glory. His words fall in clear and measured cadence.

HERMES. Your parents are with you, Thamyris.

THAMYRIS. *(suddenly alert)*

I feel the radiance of divinity;
My agony abates. I bow before
Thee, though I may not view thy countenance.
Forgive a blind man, lord . . . What god art thou?

HERMES. The son of winged Maia, by morning
Delivered, the shepherd uncaring
Of sorrowful flocks—Hermes I.

Your parents are with you, Thamyris,
Both mother and father. The bird in
Your hand is the Nymph metamorphosed.
To you I entrust her safekeeping . . .

Your father's disconsolate spirit—
He longs to embrace his Thamyris,
But cold he is, cold and enfeebled,

By dawn's rosy fingers held fast.

Philammon's shade dwindles until it at last vanishes.

And you—are doomed to live; long shall you live,
Thamyris, though a beggar. Do not hope
Ever to cross again your father's threshold . . .
Philammon died by his own hand, having cast
His treasures to the waves.
Your bondwoman
Shall be brought to you, Thamyris.
(pointing toward the hut) There she lies
Sleeping, the nurse who fed you at her breast—
Enchantment binds her, but she hears my words,
And tears creep down her ancient wrinkles. You
Shall follow her to Athens, Delphi, Argos,
And to the famous fortress where Poseidon
Crowned you victor; the bird shall have her task:
To win you alms by tender song.
Your lyre
Take with you too. Lots shall be cast therein—
Merchants delight to have their fortune told—
Which with her beak your mother shall remove.
Thus let her feed her son until his dotage,
Until his dying, many a long year . . .
When earth is scattered on your eyes, the Nymph
Shall charm in her old guise. About your neck,
O sightless one, shall hang a sign with these
Four words: "Behold the Muses' rival."

(motions to the bird with his finger)

Wipe clean his face, Nymph . . . He is pitiful . . .

The bird flies off and returns with a wet sponge. Thamyris moistens his face. The deep, blackening pits and the scattered white hairs in his beard are more clearly visible. It is now light. The glow of dawn has faded into the morning sky. Hermes is on the point of vanishing. His outline grows dim. Thamyris gropes for his staff, then picks up the lyre, no longer touching its strings. The bird sits meekly on his shoulder. She is now mistress of the situation.

THAMYRIS. Blessèd are the gods, for they preserve
Our consciousness even in torment.
But the spider of oblivion that spins
A web to veil the past . . . is kindlier.

Hermes vanishes. The nurse runs out of the house and rushes toward Thamyris, lamenting.

Summer 1906
Tsarskoe Selo

ALEKSEI REMIZOV

Aleksei Remizov (1877-1957), prose writer, dramatist, artist and calligrapher, came from a background of book-loving Moscow merchants and factory owners. In 1897 his presence at a Moscow student demonstration led to a prolonged period of exile in the provinces under police surveillance, bringing his formal education to an abrupt end. In 1905 Remizov was granted permission to take up residence in St. Petersburg, and his literary career began in earnest soon after, his first stories appearing in Symbolist journals in 1906. Although he greeted the October Revolution with a "Lament for the Ruin of the Russian Land" (a title that awakens echoes of the Tatar yoke), Remizov remained for some years in Petrograd, working in the repertory section of the state Theatrical Department. After their departure from the Soviet Union in 1921, Remizov and his wife lived first in Berlin and then, from 1923, in Paris. Throughout the years of emigration, Remizov continued to write and publish prolifically.

There is hardly a more eccentric figure than Remizov to be found in the annals of Russian literature. To visitors in his later years he seemed half medieval bookman, half gnome, tirelessly reworking ancient legends and holy tales, dashing off Thurber-like drawings and curious watercolors, devising elaborate practical jokes and spinning fantastic stories from a private mythology based on Russian folklore. Those who won his particular approval might hope to be presented with a charter, written in exquisite seventeenth century cursive script, of the Grand Free Assembly of Monkeys—an order invented by himself.

Never popular in Russia, and all but impenetrable to the translator by reason of his intensely national quality, Remizov has remained a "writers' writer," and as such has had immense influences—together with Bely, he is the progenitor of the so-called "ornamental" prose of the twenties, with its lyricism and playfulness, its tendency to *skaz* (a distinct personal narrative voice), its abrupt shifts of tone and penchant for the grotesque, its attention to facture ("writing is made not with thoughts, but with words," said Remizov, echoing Mallarmé). Claiming to take his beginning from Gogol, Leskov and Dostoevsky, Remizov was at the same time a devoted antiquarian of the word, a kind of linguistic Slavophile who wished to restore Russian to an ideal pre-Petrine purity and vigor; he was a passionate collector of vivid, out-of-the-way words—dialectisms, archaisms, even neologisms if they suited his purpose. Paradoxically, this "anti-literary" language is itself an intensely bookish creation to which the author himself sometimes feels the need to supply a glossary (as with the work translated here).

Mirsky has remarked that in the drama "more than anywhere is Remizov a contemporary of the symbolists"; Remizov's plays were written during, and are undoubtedly part of, the brief flowering of the Symbolist theatre in Russia. Moreover, he was at this time very close to Meyerhold and had some influence (perhaps more than has generally been acknowledged) on the evolution of the director's thinking. Remizov's friendship with Meyerhold apparently dates back to 1896, when both were students at Moscow University. In a letter of that year, Meyerhold pays fervent tribute to his young mentor: "Yes, through him I have been reborn." A shared enthusiasm for Hauptmann led to them collaborating on a translation of A. Rode's *Hauptmann and Nietzsche* (published 1902). Later, when Remizov was exiled to Penza, Meyerhold's native town, the two studied Marx together and Meyerhold, by his own account, suffered some unpleasantness from the local police for association with an active dissident. During the years 1902 to 1905, when Meyerhold was touring the provinces with his Fellowship of the New Drama—the years when he was arriving at a new, anti-Stanislavskian aesthetic—Remizov was, in the words of Meyerhold's biographer Konstantin Rudnitsky, his "ally, comrade in arms and to some extent his theoretician." In his role of, effectively, "head of the literary section," Remizov encouraged the inclusion of work by such exponents of the "new drama" as Hauptmann, Ibsen, Maeterlinck, Schnitzler and Przbyszewski in the troupe's repertoire, himself translating Przbyszewski's *Snow* and Strindberg's *Miss Julie* for the Fellowship. Other plays translated by Remizov—Gide's *Philoctète*, the German naturalist Johannes Schlaf's *Weigand* and the satirical comedy *Scherz, Satire, Ironie und tiefere Bedeutung* by the German romantic dramatist Christian Grabbe—bear witness to his wide theatrical interests.

An article entitled "The New Drama" (1903) gives a good idea of Remizov's view of the theatre during these years with Meyerhold. Calling for "a search for new forms to express eternal mysteries," Remizov advocates a theatre of ecstasy and mystic communion in which "actor and spectator, as one, transfigured, will lose themselves in a single action, a single emotion," and where "the voices of the soul, which are to be heard only in fateful moments, will flame in tongues of fire." The siren voice of Nietzsche sounds as clearly here as it does in Viacheslav Ivanov and Sologub: "The theatre is not amusement and distraction, the theatre is not a copy of human wretchedness; the theatre is worship . . ."

Remizov wrote three original plays: *The Devil's Comedy* (1907), *The Tragedy of Judas, Prince of Iscariot* (1908) and *The Comedy of George the Brave* (1910); in addition, he reworked the traditional folk drama *Tsar Maximilian* (1918) and wrote three pieces for musical setting to which he gave the generic name *"rusalia"* (written about 1914, they were published in Berlin in 1923). The concept of the *rusalia* was an important one for the writer (he later attached the name to his three early plays as well); in its origin, he explained, the *rusalia* was a pagan rite, which after the Christianization of Russia had been transformed into a popular open-air show with buffoons and tumblers. Proclaiming that "the theatre is theatre," needing no justification outside itself, Remizov now called for a theatre of grotesque exaggeration with "hempen beards, dunce's caps, noses stuck on awry, harsh voices, loping strides, masks as terrifying and comic as can be" in which everything should be "strange, enchanted, excessive, as in a dream."

In his dramas Remizov attempted to revive the medieval mystery and morality play, in which biblical or allegorical scenes alternated with interludes of bawdy farce—a form which satisfied his antiquarian bent and also enabled him to convey a duality of vision entirely characteristic of the Symbolist aesthetic. *The Devil's Comedy* was based on the popular morality subject known in its English version as *The Pride of Life*—a struggle between Life and Death. First performed at Komissarzhevskaya's theatre in December, 1907 (with sets by Dobuzhinsky and music by Kuzmin), it caused a scandal comparable to the first night of Blok's *Puppet Show* a year before, and for much the same reason: the audience was bewildered and outraged by the deliberately unresolved dissonance between grotesque and serious elements.

Remizov's second play, *The Tragedy of Judas, Prince of Iscariot*, is based on an apocryphal tale that bears an obvious relation to the Oedipus myth. It is curious that the previous year had seen the publication of Andreyev's story "Judas Iscariot and Others," which, though it deals with the biblical rather than the apocryphal Judas, is also, in its way, an apologia for the betrayer of Christ. The play was accepted for performance by Komissarzhevskaya's theatre, designs were made by Nikolai Roerich and a "March of the Monkeys" composed by Kuzmin, but for reasons "outside the control of the theatre management" the project had to be abandoned. Possibly the presentation on stage of a biblical personage caused offence to the powerful church authorities who brought about the banning of Wilde's *Salome* in 1908 and the closing down of Andreyev's *Anathema* in the following year.

Like much of Remizov's work, *Judas* is permeated with Russian folklore; in writing it, by his own admission, he drew on "folksongs, incantations, Christmas songs (*koliadki*) and laments." There is an interesting connection (illustrative of the interpenetration so characteristic of the arts at this period) between *Judas* and the Stravinsky-Fokine ballet *The Firebird*. In his *The Birth of the Ballets-Russes* Prince Peter Lieven recounts how in 1909 Diaghilev decided to produce a genuinely *Russian* ballet to present at the Paris grand opera, and how in putting together a libretto "they sought information from the fashionable expert in this line, Remizov." The "Kingdom of the Unclean" presided over by the evil Kashchei in *Firebird* is a typically Remizovian fancy, and the magical golden apples of *Judas* appear once more in the ballet.

The monkey king Asyka and his kingdom were an invention to which Remizov was particularly attached, and one which appears elsewhere in his work. Though their creator compared his monkeys to Swift's Houyhnhnms, one suspects that he really meant the Irish writer's Yahoos—an obscene lampoon against mankind. The comic scenes in *Judas* have a wild, anarchic humor, verging on the surrealistic, that brings to mind the work of Alfred Jarry. Remizov, with his lively interest in the contemporary French stage, could hardly have been unaware of *Ubu Roi,* the opening night of which in 1896 had been the occasion of a great theatrical scandal. The two writers share a taste for elaborate mystifications that serve to thumb a nose at all the solemn nonsense of the world: Jarry's Science of Pataphysics (the "science of imaginary solutions") is close kin to the Grand Free Assembly of Monkeys.

ALEKSEI REMIZOV

THE TRAGEDY OF JUDAS, PRINCE OF ISCARIOT[42]

In three acts

DRAMATIS PERSONAE

JUDAS, *Prince of Iscariot*
STRATIM, *Prince of Iscariot*
UNKRADA, *Niece of the King of Iscariot*
PILATE, *Hegumen of Jerusalem*
SIBORIA, *Wife of Simon, the owner of the orchard where the golden apples grow*
KADIZHA, *Siboria's womanservant*
ZIF, *Retainer of Judas*
ORIF
MONKEY KING
MESSENGER

PLACE—*The first act is set on the island of Iscariot; the second and third in Jerusalem.*
TIME—*In the days of King Herod.*

ACT ONE

A secret door in the palace wall, leading to the sea.

SCENE ONE

Orif and Zif

ORIF. *He is sitting on a rock close by the secret door. He wears a half-mask. He croons.* "Dawn had not reddened, the sun had not risen, when a dark man came—his hair unkempt and bast shoes on his feet. And by the lily-white hand he took her, and to the green forest he led her. And there she saw a fine new palace with sunlit chambers. And he seated her at a table covered with a white cloth and loaded her with silver and gold.

— Oh for silver and gold I care not, for mother and father, for brothers and sisters care I only.

— Oh be silent, fair lady, do not weep—ten servants shall you have, troubles ten . . ."

A silence. Zif appears in the doorway; he too wears a half-mask.

ORIF. *Startled.* Who goes there?

ZIF. Fee-faw-fum.

ORIF. Oh! It's you. *Angrily.* You fidget-ass cat-catcher you!

ZIF. *Looking him up and down and laughing.* You sit under a bush and eat leaves!

ORIF. You would have to turn up. Did Unkrada send you?

ZIF. It's her business I'm on.

ORIF. You going to bump Stratim off?

ZIF. *We're* going to bump him off.

ORIF. We'll have to stew in this hellhole till the marrow runs out of our bones 'twixt flesh and hide . . .

ZIF. Looks like we will. *Bursts out laughing.*

ORIF. And what's so funny about it?

ZIF. Well, I've got a little fish, and anyone who looks at it will die laughing.

ORIF. To hell with you and your little fish! I'd like to lay a cudgel across your back—crawling out like a goblin from a stove.

ZIF. What an honor: the murderer of Prince Stratim! Judas won't forget us, you can bet on that. He'll reward us royally for such a service—bags of gold he'll shower on us. And Unkrada won't be stingy either—the undertaking's hers!

ORIF. Don't shout! You can shout your fill when the noose is round your neck. Don't think someone isn't keeping an eye on us too, you blockhead!

ZIF. The merchants from Jerusalem gave a fine feast: forty barrels of Ethiopian vodka alone!

The whole bank was spread with carpets, woven and embroidered, and on top of the carpets there sparkled precious stones. Pipers, balalaika players, roistering, music. A fine bonfire they made—the sparks showered like pearls in a red ringdance: hey boys, stamp it out!

Yes, they know how to live, those folks: free and easy—live it up and don't fret about anything. A friend of mine—a fellow who's been around—was telling me of the wonders to be seen in that Jerusalem. The ears of corn there spring straight out of the earth, the bees are the size of your fist, the men are fine strapping fellows, the beasts speak with a human tongue, the granaries are crammed with wheat and still there's some left over, and the River Jordan there, with its quiet creeks, rolls between steep red banks. They say the court of the Hegumen Pilate is more splendid than that of the Monkey King himself, the palaces are roofed with green Kozarian copper, more precious than fine gold! They're rolling in money, and they down their liquor at a gulp—and there's such an abundance of everything that you can drink it, sink in it, or douse yourself with it.

ORIF. Will the merchants stay long?

ZIF. They'll be on their way this very night.

ORIF. To Jerusalem?

ZIF. Straight there, by the sea route.

ORIF. That'll suit us fine. Pilate will receive us. Did you come to an agreement with the mariners? We won't get caught?

ZIF. What a coward you are!

ORIF. And you're a drunken oaf! A bow-legged loon! Do you want to go rushing straight into the lion's maw, devil take you! . . No, that won't do. We can't afford to take risks. They might seize us any moment, clamp us in irons and skin us three times over—it'll be too late for thinking then. What we should do is settle our little business and then creep aboard, quiet as mice.

ZIF. Heh-heh—you've really got carried away! So I'm a fool then, in your opinion?

ORIF. Prince Stratim is on his guard. Doesn't move a step by himself. Just now, as I was making my way to this deathtrap, I ran into a whole band of his creatures. I recognized them by their owl feathers.

ZIF. Stratim's on board ship. I had a chat with him—oh just a word or two. He's got wind of something. He keeps himself apart. He's proud—it's not for nothing he's called top dog around here. He's strong, mighty in battle, with a voice like thunder, and drunken as the earth . . . ha ha! . . I've been at the palace.

ORIF. Are you joking? Talk sense.

ZIF. I saw the king himself.

ORIF. Did the king summon you?

ZIF. With all the marks of honor: thirty-three dwarfs, two and seventy buffoons—a fine din and clatter they made. The king and I were alone together. We talked of this and that. The king declared that ever since the brothers' duel his disfavor had fallen on us too, as the chief retainers of Prince Judas. The king wants to make his peace with us. He recalled our campaign in Beormas. That loosened his tongue. The king loves to recall that cold, rich land: we spent not a few happy days on the white banks of those raging rivers—they saw our battles and our victories.

Ha!—the arrows stretched the taut bow-string—they flew like snow and rattled like thunder. Sharp lances, not the plough, turned the earth of the spring fields, the swift legs of our steeds furrowed them; not with rye were they sown, but with heads too rash, watered not with the rains of autumn, but with tears . . .

The king asked, had I remained loyal? I swore it. The year of our campaign was the year of Judas' birth. The king gradually moved the talk round to our prince: what places does he frequent, is he in good health, does he see his brother? Yes, and he asked about Unkrada too. I answered truthfully: as before, Judas doesn't miss a single meeting of the Council, sits over his books, goes down to the sea in the evening, he's sober and keeps to himself, and—what matters most—there's Unkrada . . . He's fallen so madly in love with her that he's as frisky as a regular stallion—and she's not unwilling either. To this the king said:

as long as the crown remained on his head and its cusps unbroken, as long as heaven and earth stood firm, this should not come to pass, just as much else would not come to pass that could very easily do so. He appointed an hour for me tomorrow: the lot has fallen to the two of us—an important undertaking is in store for us both. I agreed. Do you get his drift?

ORIF. Surely the king can't have decided to do away with our dear disgraced Judas? It's beyond me. I don't understand. I remember that I came to you as a messenger in Beormas.[43] The king, hearing from my lips that a son had been born to him, wept for joy, and never since that time has the dread Yumala[44] devoured so rich a sacrifice as he received from the king that night, nor has anyone hung anything more beautiful than the king's necklet about the idol's neck.

ZIF. Unkrada would not lie. It was she who first revealed the danger to us. Her word is stronger than granite; it is impossible not to believe her. I know the king well: he is capable of anything. You see that door—no one has passed through it alive. Much sorrow has been sown, many tears have fallen, the bones alone would fill a grave; dew will not settle here, nor hoarfrost; there is blood in every stone, and only the winds howl—so many winds. Afterwards not a word is said. The king's hints are clear.

ORIF. Surely the brothers' quarrel over Unkrada cannot be the cause of such anger! Can the old man have fallen in love with his niece in his dotage?

ZIF. Nonsense! He hasn't bothered with that for a long time.

ORIF. *Dreamily.* When she passes over the fields, she is like a dark stormcloud, when she enters the hall she is the sun, and when she takes her place at table she is the fairest of the fair. She has brought us spring and dawn and joy and merriment . . . A man might well lose his mind over her.

ZIF. You're talking out of the back of your head! The brothers' quarrel is just an excuse. There's a foolish tale the king can't get out of his head: you remember how the wisewomen foretold that Judas would kill the king his father, marry the queen his mother and become king himself? That foolish tale gives the king no peace.

ORIF. The king believed it? A son slay his own father, a son marry his own mother! A harebrained prophecy. A delusion of the prince himself. And where's the proof?

ZIF. The sea confirmed it.

ORIF. Who put the question?

ZIF. The king.

ORIF. The king. So that's how it is! Then the prophecy must be fulfilled, but if even the smallest part of it is open to doubt . . . Judge for yourself, is such a thing conceivable? The queen is so old. Have you spoken with the prince?

ZIF. Where should I find him? I passed it on to Unkrada.

ORIF. *Suddenly uneasy.* Look, isn't that someone's shadow?

ZIF. Where?

ORIF. Over there by the old well; do you see it?

ZIF. Could it be our prince? Wait a moment, I'll take a look. *Goes over to the well.*

ORIF. *Anxiously.* Go on then—quick. By the old well . . .

ZIF. *Offstage.* Halt, not a step further! You won't get away.

ORIF. Whew, that gave me a turn!

ZIF. *Returning.* No one there. But it seemed to me that someone struck me on the shoulder—a warm hand it was too.

Zif walks back and forth. Orif squats down. A brief silence.

ORIF. *To himself.* There's no getting away from fate. It must be true then. Yes, you just have to believe it . . . There have been ill omens everywhere, as if some great misfortune were hanging over us. Strange birds have appeared at sea that wail like wild beasts, fire has been seen over graves—it appears, flickers and vanishes—a candle burns in the forest, tables creak, an eagle owl has taken to perching on the palace dome, swallows fly into houses, the cock crows with its head down, dogs howl, pigs carry straw out of the yard . . .

ZIF. That's all nonsense! Dogs and pigs have nothing to do with it; if the arm be strong, the blow will tell.

SCENE TWO

Orif, Zif, Unkrada

UNKRADA. *Appearing from the direction of the palace.* Are you ready?

ZIF. *Baring his sword.* Right to the heart—and never misses.

ORIF. *Flashing his knife.* This will not tremble.

UNKRADA. And I . . . *As if suddenly bursting into bloom.* I will help with all my heart. The lights are out on board ship. The moon is going down. Night grows murky. The sails are spread. Stratim and his band are at the palace. Dead drunk. They were brawling. Now they're snoring. Stratim will come here alone. You'll have to guess the right time to strike. Then into the sea with the body. A wave will come rolling. And then there'll be nothing; no foam, no bubbles.

ORIF. The water is deep.

ZIF. *With an air of wisdom.* Seven years ago an axe was dropped into the sea and it still hasn't reached the bottom.

UNKRADA. Stratim is unprepared. He won't give you any trouble. Make no noise. As the grass cannot stand against the scythe, so will he not be able to stand against you. He must not leave here alive.

ORIF. Does Prince Judas know?

UNKRADA. No. I alone am answerable. *Hands them a purse.* Take this for the time being—it contains Arabian gold.

ORIF. We thank you. We shall leave nothing undone.

ZIF. Stratim's soul shall take leave of his body before the cock crows. But where are we to wait?

UNKRADA. Stand over here. That's right. No one can see you here.

Zif and Orif conceal themselves.

SCENE THREE

Unkrada and Judas

UNKRADA. *Pensively.* "Birch tree, my birch tree! Who has brought such sadness upon you, birch tree of mine? Was it the cold north wind? Or the cruel frost? Who numbed your leaves? Was it the angry flood that washed away the bulwark of your roots, the earth? It was not the frost that froze you, it was not water that overwhelmed you. No, they came . . ." *Suddenly throwing aside restraint.* If it be so, if the prophecy is to be fulfilled . . . Well, we shall see—I'll pull the heavens down about me! Shall we see who is the stronger then? Shall we find out who is the more powerful? *Becoming thoughtful.* "They came, they overwhelmed you, they bent your branches, birch tree of mine. They trampled the green grass, pulling it up by the roots. Sad is the fair sun's rising . . ." And you, wind, blow—waft my heart and soul to the land of my birth, with light wings tenderly enfold her, bring warmth to her white breast. Help me. O wind! Come to my aid, O wind! I shall return. I shall come to the white shores so dear to me. I shall bring with me a king—my king and yours—Judas.

JUDAS. *Appearing from the sea.* What kind of trap is this? You can hardly hear your own voice here. The sea wind carries half the words away. *Looking about him.* Memory does not play me false: here on this snaky path I met those terrible, all-seeing wise women. That accursed tower was the favored gathering place of witches. Unkrada!

UNKRADA. Prince.

JUDAS. You bring bad news?

UNKRADA. Sit here.

JUDAS. *Sadly.* Today my mother would not receive me. I no longer see my father.

UNKRADA. Malignant heavens! A pit is being dug between us. Your fate is being decided.

JUDAS. *Sharply.* By whom?

UNKRADA. Today, after having given audience to the merchants from Jerusalem, the king paid the queen a visit. I was in the adjoining chamber. At first I meant to leave. Your name was mentioned. I pricked up my ears. The king said that his patience was at an end and painted you in the most villainous colors to the queen . . . According to him, there is nothing you are not capable of: you have already attempted your father's life, and you will destroy your mother and your brother. And to protect himself against you, the king decided to name Stratim his heir and to condemn you to exile. Later, your retainer Zif told me that he had talked with the king and clearly understood from hints he had let fall that your life is in danger.

JUDAS. *Flaring up.* Deprive me of the throne? I—kill my father? Condemn me to death?

UNKRADA. Here, this is a letter from Stratim. I received it this afternoon.

JUDAS. *Rapidly casting an eye over the letter.* He knows of my father's decision! He begs you for a meeting. Have you replied?

UNKRADA. I consented.

JUDAS. Unkrada, will Stratim come here?! You should not have done that. He will think himself alone with you. No, this may not be.

UNKRADA. Stratim will come here—to the old well. It must be so, you must understand that. Your fate hangs in the balance. I shall be tender, affectionate with him. He will trust me. He will go anywhere I wish. I shall lure him here, to this door. You will see him. The two of you will be face to face. You will not need to raise your hand, to shed blood. Others will do that: their sword is sharp, their arrows swift. Such men are to be found. Then into the sea with the body. The sea holds many bones! Tomorrow they will say: the Jerusalem merchants killed him.

JUDAS. The Jerusalem merchants . . . Now I see it all!

UNKRADA. Your father is old. He will not wear the crown long. It will pass to you. It is yours by right. The island shall be yours and the sea also. We will subdue the west as far as the Ocean, the east as far as the Caucasus. We shall sail the sea from one end to the other. We shall press northward to the white land of my birth. By dawnglow, by moonlight, by starshine, I myself will lead you over the mountain ridges until we reach the mighty rivers with their still, deep pools, until we reach the many-branched willow trees. You will be greeted there as king . . .

As if weaving an incantation. Long and dark are the winters there. White the snow. When the savage north winds blow, winter will clamp iron fetters on the clouds and will set forth with his nails, chaining earth and water, throwing bridges of ice over lakes and rivers, rivetting them with nails. Windows then will bloom with flowers of frost, feathers of snow will whirl along the road, and bright hoarfrost will fly through the air, threading branches with smooth and perfect pearls. Then spring will come, the black north wind will fall asleep, and from the south a white wind will come floating, and soft will be its breath. The beasts will rouse themselves from sleep. The sun will let down his golden swing into the yard, standing day-long, night-long in the sky, spreading his crimson tapestries over the meadow, spilling gold. And along the river banks the guelder rose will dapple with white the dark thickets. Before you know it, summer has ripened. The night is filled with the glow of thornwood fires. Song echoes joyously. And the ringdance twists and turns like the tendrils of the hop. And so it goes from dusk to dawn. Then suddenly a storm gathers, ripping the sky apart and lashing us with rain; and after the downpour the rainbow comes. And the meadows sing and ripple. The bear goes foraging. The great wheel of the sun has dipped, the spider's web is spun and floats across the fields. The curly rowan wears red worsted, and icy is the dew at dawn. Autumn has come. All is melancholy, quiet, transparent. Clouds glide like swans about the sky. And the forest will be shaken, and in the groaning and the soughing nothing will be heard, save a solitary human voice—and that voice will be mine, singing you a lullaby . . . Further I shall lead you, to lands encircled with mists and forests. We shall sweep through the forests, pressing on past plains and bristling swamps—by mousehole and snake track we shall make our way—past sinuous shores, past mountains of iron, until we reach the land of sorcerers. The whole world we shall conquer, the whole earth shall be ours.

JUDAS. But the prophecy?

UNKRADA. There is no other choice.

JUDAS. Father, mother, brother—all are against me.

UNKRADA. I am with you. Do you love me?

JUDAS. I renounce the father who gave me life. I kiss the dust of your feet.

UNKRADA. I give you a kingdom. Do you love me?

JUDAS. I renounce the mother who gave birth to me in torment. I lay my hand upon your heart.

UNKRADA. I lead you into paradise. Do you love me?

JUDAS. I renounce the brother with whom I grew to manhood and learned to love sun, sea and earth. I embrace your soul.

A clock strikes from the palace tower.

UNKRADA. *With a start.* It is time. Wait for me. You will find friends here. They will help you.

SCENE FOUR

Judas, Zif, Orif

ZIF. *Coming forward.* Prince Judas.

ORIF. *Coming forward.* Prince Judas.

JUDAS. You were here? You heard? You know? You are for me?

ZIF. Prince, it was I who taught you to master a horse, it was I who forged for you your martial sword.

ORIF. It was I who sang songs over your cradle—songs that are sung in the white land of Unkrada's birth. To my songs you dreamed your first dream.

JUDAS. I trust you. But why are you dressed like this? Take off those masks. Why conceal yourselves? You are for me—right is on your side.

ZIF. Yes, but . . . the masks don't bother us. In our life it's the nose that counts.

ORIF. We can see better like this.

JUDAS. I can defend myself alone. You are prepared to die for me, I know. How rare in this age of wolves! Disloyalty and treachery should stand as laws among our laws. The spirit falters. There are no values, only prices. Words are worn out. It has become terrible to speak. Everywhere there is blood. And from blood the earth will take fire, and not a tree, not a stone will be left in the world—and the wind will blow away the dust . . . How am I guilty?

ZIF. Prince, someone is coming.

ORIF. It is he, your brother Stratim.

JUDAS. So be it—so be it then . . . my brother . . . Stratim.

He paces back and forth. Lost in thought, to himself.

The Bogeyman is on his way—
Fill the horses' bags with hay.
Lulla, lulla, lullaby—
Daddy's bringing fish to fry.

Opening the door slightly. Come down to me, O star! *As if trying to solve a riddle.* The shore is white with foam. Waves are breaking. The sea is dark. The horizon is gray. A star has fallen. If only I did not have to think! *Suddenly steps back, then tries to close the door—but cannot. In a whisper, to someone on the other side of the door visible to him alone.* I hear, I hear. Again you have come. You told me once—why repeat it? My memory is good, I have not forgotten, I remember your prophetic voice! *The door closes of its own accord, with a creaking sound. Slowly and distinctly.* "You will kill your father, you will marry your mother, and you will be king." *He stands for a moment in silence.* No, that shall not be. *To Zif and Orif, who have withdrawn to a safe distance.* Go to the ship. It has not yet sailed. I shall follow at once.

ZIF. Prince, to leave you here alone . . . Then you must make haste.

JUDAS. *Insistently.* I shall follow at once.

ORIF. It is against our orders. We have a duty. We swore to perform it.

JUDAS. *Impatiently.* Go! The ship has not yet sailed. I shall follow at once.

Zif and Orif go out in the direction of the sea.

SCENE FIVE

Judas and Unkrada

UNKRADA. *Appearing suddenly from behind some ruins.* Have no fear. It is I. I am alone. I left Stratim at the running spring. He is wandering about in the dark there. I wanted one more glimpse . . . Why are you staring like that?

JUDAS. *Pointing to the door; in a whisper.* They came again.

UNKRADA. What are you saying? Who came?

JUDAS. The three wise women.

UNKRADA. Calm yourself; all living things have long since abandoned this dead tower.

JUDAS. No, I recognized them. They repeated the prophecy to me word for word.

UNKRADA. It was the blood speaking in you. You mustn't think. Leave these thoughts. I am with you—now and forever.

JUDAS. I sent Zif and Orif away. They are on board the ship.

UNKRADA. Why did you do that? You will ruin everything.

JUDAS. I can't go through with it.

UNKRADA. You can't?

JUDAS. I'm afraid.

UNKRADA. Afraid! But tomorrow they'll kill you like the lowest criminal.

STRATIM. *Offstage.* Unkrada! Unkrada! Where are you?

UNKRADA. They'll tie you to a horse's tail and drag you through the fields. Birds will swoop down to peck at your body. The winds will arise and scatter your bones, and no trace or memory of you will remain. What of your empty prophecy then?

STRATIM. *Offstage.* Unkrada! Where are you, I say?

UNKRADA. I shall bring Stratim here. Steel yourself. For my sake. For the sake of our love. For the sake of our kingdom. You gave me your oath. *She goes out.*

SCENE SIX

Judas, Unkrada, Stratim

JUDAS. *Alone, meditatively.*

The Bogeyman is on his way—
Fill the horses' bags with hay.
Lulla, lulla, lullaby—
Daddy's bringing fish to fry.

STRATIM. *Appearing with Unkrada from the direction of the palace, addressing Unkrada.* What a godforsaken place! I've never been here before. I can't see my hand before my face. It's cold and damp. What's that, a beacon?

UNKRADA. Step out boldly! Through here you can reach the sea.

STRATIM. Through this cranny? I shall order this wall to be destroyed.

UNKRADA. We shall destroy it together.

JUDAS. *Without moving.* Ah, my brother. What a good thing you have come. See, I am still alive.

STRATIM. *Looking him up and down.* You bear the title of prince, but you hide yourself like a thief.

UNKRADA. Kings don't behave in that way, do they?

JUDAS. *Coldly.* Don't imagine you can insult me!

STRATIM. So you wanted to sneak up on me! I suppose you've got your informers hidden in the ambush with you? We know who they are. Unkrada, this rogue has been stewing like a toad in his hole, watching our every move . . . And a grave has been dug ready for me . . . He's in a hurry.

UNKRADA. *Flirtatiously, caressing Stratim.* Prince, you shouldn't say such things.

STRATIM. *Enigmatically.* No doubt.

JUDAS. *Flaring up.* Prince Stratim, the future ruler, the future king, ha! .. day and night from one tavern to another—riot and drunkenness. With that hot head of yours you'll bring the kingdom down, with you will come discord, hatred and malice, devastation, blood, ashes . . . the wild beasts will eat their fill of human flesh, the birds will drink their fill of human blood. You will dig a grave for all the people.

STRATIM. And what are the people to you? You have attempted your father's life.

JUDAS. A lie. Who bears witness to it?

STRATIM. Had it not been for me, the king would have perished. Regicide!

UNKRADA. Who is in the right? Resolve it!

STRATIM. *To Unkrada.* Look, he's foaming at the mouth. He would raise his hand even against you . . . There's nothing he isn't capable of. *Teasing Judas.* Your wings are clipped, your tail feathers are plucked.

UNKRADA. Do you hear him, Judas?

JUDAS. *Overcome with fury.* Be silent! It is you who are going to your death.

STRATIM. What are you doing here? Leave us. Use force, would you? A scoundrel, a beggarly wretch . . .

UNKRADA. *To Stratim.* Let's go, or he'll kill us . . .

JUDAS. *Reaching for his sword.* I'm ready.

STRATIM. Who are you? My dignity does not permit me . . .

JUDAS. *Unsheathing his sword.* Have at you then.

STRATIM. *Retreating.* I shall defend myself as I would against brigands on the highway.

JUDAS. What? .. Trembling, are you? .. One blow and that will be the end of you. You are in my power. *Silence. Handing Stratim his sword, regally.* Of my own free will, as a king, I yield to you my sword, my right, my island. Farewell. *He moves seaward. In the doorway.* The sea stretches to the clouds. I am free: never again shall I see my father, never again shall I see my mother, and my kingdom I have given over to my brother. *To Unkrada.* I shall be beyond the reach of fate—the wind bore it hither and the wind shall bear it hence.

STRATIM. *Throwing down the sword.* Unhappy man! For you there can be no salvation. You have taken leave of your senses.

UNKRADA. *After him, as if in her sleep.* Hour follows upon hour. Go. Seek out whom you will. Love whomsoever shall find favor in your eyes. I know what I must do. I shall wrap myself about with clouds; I shall gird myself with the dawn; the moon shall be my shield, the stars my spears, the sun shall light my way. No door or gate or path or road shall see me pass; in the sea's depths I shall find a key; I shall unlock the door; I shall raise the iron slab no man has raised, from under it I shall take all the grief and all the longing of the world, and I shall bear them in my hands, never letting them fall; for if I let them fall upon the earth, the earth would take fire, and if I let them fall upon the waters, the waters would take fire. All the grief and all the longing of the world shall pass from me into your feet, into your hands, into your heart, into your brows, into your eyes—you won't dance it out with dancing, you won't roister it out with roistering. And you, O moon—O moon of mine—you have deceived me! And you, O stars—O stars of mine—you have deceived me! But you, my trusty darksome night, you will not deceive me. You will cover him with darkness—he shall rend his garments, he shall suck his own blood. I will bide my time—and I will find you.

Curtain

ACT TWO

Outside Pilate's palace. A fenced-in orchard can be seen. In the orchard is an apple tree with golden apples.

SCENE ONE

Kadizha, Siboria, Orif

KADIZHA. *From behind the fence, to Orif.* Pray tell me, sir, what's the news from the palace? Is the Hegumen in good health?

ORIF. *Drawing himself up.* As before: no better, no worse—the same. What swarms of wasps there are here—my neck is covered with bites.

KADIZHA. Are you from the court?

ORIF. I serve the grand vizier—my person is inviolable.

KADIZHA. My mistress is called Siboria, and my name is Kadizha. I've seen quite different faces around here many a long year. What became of old

Carpius who used to be vizier?

ORIF. Well, you are out of touch, and no mistake.

KADIZHA. We've only just returned to Jerusalem. We were staying with my mistress's grandmother at Sokolinaya Hill—you know, not far from Sorochinskoye Field.[45] We helped her with making jam and fruit jelly. We arrived back home last night. Our lord, Simon, was keeping watch over the orchard and only had time to tell us that great changes had taken place at court and that when I saw things for myself I'd just gasp with amazement.

ORIF. The prince of Iscariot—he who fled the island of Iscariot with your merchants—has been appointed grand vizier.

KADIZHA. A prince! Well I never! It's news to me. A real prince, you say.

ORIF. *Gazing with satisfaction at Siboria, who is walking in the garden.* As real as you please. Only he doesn't have a princess.

KADIZHA. On the eve of our departure from Sokolinaya Hill I dreamed I was sitting alone in a dark room, and suddenly a peasant came in carrying a lantern; he lifts up the lantern and starts coming after me—black-haired he is, and shaggy too. I take to my heels, and he's right after me. Round and round we go: from window to bench, from bench to floor, from floor to door; then it's over the threshold into the lobby, through the lobby to the porch, through the porch into the yard, through the yard to the gate—on and on—then, bang, he grabs me by the arm and I'm caught. Grandmother says that Friday's dream will come true on Sunday . . .

ORIF. *Crossly.* I don't believe in dreams. Old folk grumble and believe in dreams because they have nothing better to do.

KADIZHA. *Laughing.* But why did the prince run away?

ORIF. Well, if he hadn't, they'd have done him in.

KADIZHA. The poor thing. How did all this come about?

ORIF. It's a dark tale. The king his father was very frightened by a certain prophecy. On our island we have these wise women who wander about; some call them Those Who Judge, others just witches. Simple folk talk all kinds of nonsense about them—they can do this and that, they can read the stars and know what's going to happen in the world for a thousand years to come; they are surrounded by snakes great and small, by vixens and owls, and they have webbed feet like geese—that I've seen myself. Well then, these witches somehow came across our prince and meted him out his fate—such a heap of nonsense they piled up, your ears would shrivel listening to it. And then the prince goes and blurts it all out to the king. And the king begins turning it over in his mind. And then there were all sorts of other things: there are two princes, you see—brothers—and they both fell in love with the same woman; had them both under her spell, she did, twisted them round her little finger. Then the old Adam began to rear its head. Once they nearly packed each other off to kingdom come.

KADIZHA. Sin always lies in wait! But who is this woman?

ORIF. Unkrada is her name. She's the Iscariot king's niece. Her father was a real king—our one's brother, but her mother, though of royal lineage, was a captive: from the north, she was, from the dense forests, from the distant land of the white sea. When they died, the king brought Unkrada to his island. And that's when it all began. Even a stupid woman will cause trouble, but this one—she's light and fire and beauty. Her eyebrows are long and thick, and so black you'd think two crows were perched there over her eyes. When the color rises to her face, it's slow to go away. And her voice is so rich and free—you'd think a swan was singing. When she sings, old men begin to dance, the stony-hearted weep, and the dashing young bloods are all afire.

KADIZHA. What about the new vizier—is the prince very terrible?

ORIF. You'll soon see: after lunch the prince will come here with the Hegumen to sit on the porch for a bit. How shall I put it? He's a favorite of fortune, he can turn his hand to anything, only he's terribly hotheaded: in the palace he's turned everything upside down—cleaned things up in fine style—even we got hauled over the coals. Well, at twenty that's understandable—the lad's got spunk in him. When he gets a bit older, he'll calm down.

KADIZHA. What's his name?

ORIF. Prince Judas.

SIBORIA. *Who has shown no interest in the conversation up to this point, is surprised, even thunderstruck.* Judas?

ORIF. Prince Judas. On our island such a name is given only to kings, but here in your Jerusalem it's as common as you please.

SIBORIA. Who gave him that name—Judas?

ORIF. Who gave it to him? His mother and the sea. He was the firstborn. The queen was advanced in years and childless. Days and nights together she used to spend on the seashore, always praying. Well, and her prayers were answered—she didn't have to eat elderberries any more. The king was away on campaign when his son was born.

Judas in our language means something like "sea king" or "water god."

SIBORIA. *With curiosity.* But wasn't the king suspicious?

ORIF. Why should he have been? The queen never showed her face anywhere, she lived like a nun—the only time she ever went out was to go down to the sea. And exactly a year later she gave birth to another son, Stratim.[46] He was called that after the great sea bird, the one that holds all the world under its right wing. A wise man gives a wonderful description of it.

In the blue sea it lives,
In the blue sea it multiplies,
At sea its eggs it lays,
Out of the sea its young it leads.

SIBORIA. *Lifts her veil. Agitatedly, through tears.* My servingwoman told me that a terrible old giant of a man was walking about in front of the palace, and when you began to tell your story, it suddenly came to me that he was the new vizier . . . the prince . . .

ORIF. A terrible old man . . . There are only two of those here: Zif and me. It couldn't be anyone else. *With certainty.* That was Zif.

KADIZHA. And who is this Zif?

ORIF. His person is inviolable. He's a bold one. Nothing will hold him back, be it bad weather, blizzard or autumn rains. And where in the world have the two of us not journeyed together!

We've visited the land of Mazaika—there is in the world such a land inhabited only by women; every year they take Ethiops as husbands; the boy children they send away to the Ethiops, and the girls they keep for themselves. We lived there for a month—as Ethiops, you might say; there was a goose girl there called Vasilisa . . . Well, and we also visited those strange folk who live under quenchless fire in Alyber land: they don't drink, they don't eat, and the wind carries them wherever it blows, like cobwebs; they never die, and there's no laying your hands on them. They're peaceable, god-fearing folk: you'll never hear a single swearword from them . . . Somehow or other we managed to make the time crawl by—lopped off a dozen or so heads by way of diversion—and then we set off for the Petrified land. There's nothing there worth speaking of, except that they burn nuts in their stoves; the place is at the back of beyond, and you can't get white bread there for love nor money. We promised to bring them some pea pie and got the hell out. At one time we landed up in Polivania[47]—a funny sort of land, I can tell you, where everything's like nothing you've ever set eyes on: the people there aren't people—they're half man, half beast, with one eye and one leg, and as for a head—not a trace; instead they've got something like a mouse's tail sticking up. We barely managed to escape. A hard time we had of it. *Without taking his eyes off Siboria.* Zif—he keeps his brains in his belly. Sleeps with one eye open. And here he is himself.

Kadizha rushes out with a cry of terror.

SCENE TWO

Siboria, Orif, Zif

ZIF. *Appearing from the palace gates.* Aha! My dear friend—so these are the local affairs you busy yourself with. Trust you to pick out the choicest morsel. Who is this?

ORIF. Siboria, the wife of our neighbor Simon.

ZIF. That snuffling old wreck with the spidery beard? What a surprise! *Bows to Siboria.* I am the prince's councillor, Zif, and this venerable elder is my comrade in arms, Orif.

ORIF. *Taking offense.* You can hardly limp along yourself with that gammy right leg of yours. Lame devil!

SIBORIA. You know my husband?

ZIF. *To Orif.* That baldheaded old coot! *To Siboria.* A fine, a remarkable man. *Noticing the apple tree with the golden apples; in amazement.* What beautiful apples! We don't have anything like that on the island of Iscariot. I would never have believed that such things grew on this earth. Golden apples—and very tasty they must be too. *Lifts a leg to climb over the fence.*

SIBORIA. *In alarm.* No, you mustn't do that. Those apples are sacred. We offer them up only as a sacrifice. In memory of our son. My husband trembles over every apple. He doesn't trust anyone. He doesn't sleep at night.

ORIF. *Drawing himself up.* We'll see how well he guards them . . .

ZIF. Well, I wouldn't mind, and that's the truth . . . Never in my life did I taste anything like those: as rosy as your lips and as golden as your hair.

Attempts to fondle Siboria.

SIBORIA. *Retreating.* Shame on you! At your age! . .

ZIF. *Jigging about.* I may be old, but I've still got potential—there are some things I've still got plenty of.

ORIF. *Snorting.* Not as much as I have.

Zif and Orif begin fooling around. They slap and nudge each other, giving little shouts, sly winks, knowing "h'ms." They speak in a rapid patter full of double-entendres aimed at Siboria. Dumb show.

ZIF. *With a sly wink to Orif.* A certain old man had ten sons, and all ten of them mounted the same nag to go a-ploughing.

ORIF. Smart fellows! And what did these ten lads get up to?

ZIF. Clever folk will always find something to get up to.

ORIF. H'm, and so will a hairy-legged nag.

ZIF. A-ploughing they went—oh how they sank that plough in!

ORIF. Ha-ha-ha! Get what we're driving at?

ZIF. You'll soon get it all right.

ORIF. I'll say.

ZIF. This way and that way.

ORIF. And the other way too!

SIBORIA. *Goodnaturedly.* Goodness me, you'd take them for devils, except that they don't have tails.

ZIF. You're wrong there: we do—and fine ones too! Orif, show her yours!

ORIF. *Coyly.* It's hard to get out.

ZIF. He's lying: it hasn't grown to full size yet.

SIBORIA. You should be ashamed of yourselves! I'll tell your prince. *Withdraws.*

SCENE THREE

Zif and Orif

As soon as Siboria disappears, Zif and Orif rush over to the fence without a second's hesitation. They search for a cranny. Having found one, they peer into the garden.

ZIF. *Breathlessly.* A toothsome morsel.

ORIF. I can't see a thing.

ZIF. The look she gave me . . . Did you notice?

ORIF. You're standing on my foot!

ZIF. Where do you think you're going then!

ORIF. I bet you I can pull it off. *Squeaking.* She's risen to the bait!

ZIF. *Wheezing.* The fish is hooked!

ORIF. Shine down on us, fair sun!

ZIF. Gleam away, little apple!

ORIF. Fair sun! Little apple!

ZIF. *Tenderly.* Siboria, ah why are you so beautiful? Siboria!

ORIF. *In a childish voice, carrying on a conversation with himself.* I am here. Do you hear?—No.—And where are you?

ZIF. I shall go out of my mind. Let me in!

ORIF. Just show me your little finger! Just let me touch your dear little finger!

ZIF. Lay off, she doesn't want to . . . Let me in!

ORIF. *Unable to contain himself.* Miaow-miaow.

ZIF. *Unable to contain himself.* Miaow-miaow.

Zif and Orif thrust their heads at the cranny like blind kittens after milk.

SCENE FOUR

Zif, Orif, Judas

JUDAS. *Watches them from the steps with great curiosity.* What are you two up to then?

ZIF. *Caught off his guard. With a grimness unusual for him.* Business.

ORIF. *Caught off his guard. Furiously.* Business.

JUDAS. *Quickly descending the steps. To Zif.* You've come back from the ship then. I've been looking for you everywhere.

ZIF. *Regaining his composure.* I didn't venture to disturb you, prince. I saw that lunch was being served, and so I came here and found Orif. We had a little argument: is it possible for a man to crawl through a crack in a fence or not? And so—hey presto—we began to try it out for size.

ORIF. And that's all there was to it.

JUDAS. An odd sort of a game! Well, what did the merchants have to say, what's the news?

ZIF. Things couldn't be worse. It looks pretty serious. The king's mind is clouded. No one is allowed to enter the palace. Spies swarm everywhere, anyone pointed to by an informer is seized. The king's got it into his head that you're back on the island, and an order has gone out that all redheaded men are to be put to death. As you know, there aren't any redheaded men apart from yourself, but the king's faithful servitors have done in more than a few whose hair was gray or black just to demonstrate their zeal. Unkrada . . .

JUDAS. Unkrada?

ZIF. Is to marry Prince Stratim . . .

JUDAS. *Incredulously*. Can that be true?

ZIF. As I'm standing here. Murder, looting, executions. Failed crops, stunted grass. Plague, famine, tempests. Trees torn up by the roots. Clouds have loosed their thunderbolts and the earth has been shaken. The sea has been in turmoil, day and night it roars unceasingly. Meadow and marsh are under water. Wolves prowl and snakes lurk everywhere. The sea is avenging you. They say that the sea will grow calm, ill fortune pass and the earth be at peace only when Prince Judas returns to the island.

JUDAS. *As if drained of all emotion*. I—return? I knew nothing of this! My heart is like night, the world is tottering about me, something has been overturned . . . Where shall I go? I can hardly see. Father, mother, brother . . . *He begins to spin around like a top, shouting*. Unkrada! Unkrada!

ZIF. *At the top of his voice, trying to shout him down*. The Hegumen!

ORIF. *Imperturbably*. Now is it worth getting into such a state over a trifle?

SCENE FIVE

Judas, Pilate, Zif, Orif

PILATE. *From the steps*. I have despatched messengers. They have left no stone unturned. It's as if the earth had swallowed him up. And here he is, lost in his daydreams. Bad. It's treason.

Laughs.

JUDAS. *To himself.* Unkrada . . .

PILATE. Judas! Prince! Have you lost your tongue or something?

JUDAS. *Incoherently.* Say it again—again—again!

PILATE. It's clear you've lost your hearing. I told you it was dangerous to bathe in the Jordan. Prince! *Pointing into the distance.* Look—the blue sea isn't far away.

JUDAS. *He gives a start. Approaching Pilate.* I have just received disturbing news. My native land is at war.

PILATE. There you go again. What is this "native land?" Spit on it. Is it musicians you want? Shall I order someone to crawl through a log from one end to the other to amuse you? Or we could rest for a bit and go for a ride on the elephants. I don't suppose they have white elephants on your island?

JUDAS. Only little white beasts of prey with long legs like fleas and quick, soft paws to guard their own. Apart from that, nothing.

PILATE. You're out of sorts today. Come on, laugh! Do you know what's on my mind?

JUDAS. I'm not God.

PILATE. Guess!

JUDAS. Why should I?

PILATE. You can't. All right, I'll tell you . . . Or shall I keep it to myself?

JUDAS. *After an awkward silence.* It's all the same to me.

PILATE. I want you to get married.

JUDAS. What nonsense! Why?

PILATE. What do you mean, why? You are a strange fellow. If I'm not mistaken, I just told you in perfectly clear Russian that I want you to get married.

JUDAS. I'm not in need of that.

PILATE. Then allow me to enquire what it is you *do* need. I received you as if you had been my own son. You were naked as a stripped linden and barefoot as a goose. I shod you and clothed you; you hung like a raindrop from a leaf—I gave you a home, I made you the first in the land. What kind of hegumen would I be if I didn't hold my subjects' welfare dear—especially the welfare of such a subject as yourself? Just look at you—I ask you, what do you look like? Sleep never touches your eyes, and then you're forever fidgeting about. Believe me: just get married, and everything will be as smooth as oil.

JUDAS. *Hardly able to control himself.* In that case I'd advise you to get a divorce—you look a bit too oily to me.

PILATE. Get a divorce? Ha-ha! Me! *Looks about him complacently, as if prepared to embrace everything that could possibly be embraced, and notices the apple tree with the golden apples. In amazement.* What wonders have we here?! Prince, do you see?

JUDAS. Apples.

PILATE. *Unable to believe his eyes.* Golden ones?

JUDAS. Golden ones.

PILATE. Pick me one.

JUDAS. Impossible.

PILATE. Impossible?!

JUDAS. They don't belong to us.

PILATE. *Just like a little boy.* I'll waste away! Pick me one! I want a golden apple!

JUDAS. The law forbids it.

PILATE. *I* am the law.

JUDAS. *Remaining motionless for a moment. Silence. Abruptly.* All right, I'll get you one. *Goes over the fence, tears the lock from the gate and disappears into the orchard.*

Zif and Orif, who have been skulking somewhere in the background, hurry forward at the clank of the lock and, shaking with laughter, stare inquisitively at Pilate. The autarch sits with mouth agape, filled with the consciousness of his unlimited majesty and lost in anticipation of the forbidden delight.

ZIF. The law!

ORIF. There's a maw for you—looks as if he just swallowed an ox.

ZIF. Life and Death.

ORIF. Now that's what I call a pretty face.

ZIF. He who knows all.

ORIF. See how his belly glows.

ZIF. The light that shineth in darkness.

ORIF. He's drooling.

ZIF. Destiny incarnate.

ORIF. *On his knees.* Rejoice, rejoice, O king!

ZIF. *On his knees.* Rejoice, rejoice, O king!

Zif and Orif conceal themselves at the sight of Judas, who emerges from the orchard with apples in his hands.

JUDAS. *Agitated.* The old fool . . . He came rushing at me from behind a bush and tried to hit me. *Threateningly, to no one in particular.* Well, you have only yourself to blame. You and your pilfering . . . *Hands Pilate the golden apples.*

PILATE. *Selecting an apple.* How splendid to sink your teeth into a golden apple. *Taking a bite.* As sweet as sugar!

JUDAS. *Examining an apple.* Not bad. I've never come across anything like them. It burns like a hot coal.

PILATE. *With relish.* You've really given me a treat. Simply delicious. *Sinking his teeth into another apple.* What a dimwit I am. How is it I never noticed them before?

JUDAS. *Tossing an apple from hand to hand.* You don't notice anything. A whole tree right in front of your nose.

PILATE. We'll bear it in mind. Oh, and I'd completely forgotten. We have visitors today: the Monkey King himself is to be our guest.

JUDAS. How interesting.

PILATE. An old and dear friend: a pood of salt we've eaten together. Our Jerusalem is the most ancient of all kingdoms; it stands at the center of the earth—the hub of the universe—and the Monkey Kingdom is just a stone's throw away . . . It's a land of dense forests, heat, riches undreamed of. As for the people who live there—rogues, the lot of them: you can't so much as sneeze without them knowing all about it. There's nothing the Monkey King doesn't know, and he doesn't mind handing out advice either. Heh heh, he comes in and everyone goes crazy, he gives out such a stench of monkey . . . it would raise the dead. Just wait and you'll see for yourself. Just have a chat with him. He's a remarkable fellow: he keeps his nose to the wind when he walks, knows all the back streets and alleys, doesn't do anything without some hidden reason, lies like a trooper—he'll shower you with words as if they were autumn leaves, will Asyka the First. What a stroke of luck this is! We have to entertain him. He's got a terribly sweet tooth.

JUDAS. Does he have many retainers?

PILATE. Ooo! There's no counting them! At first you think there aren't all that many, but then they keep on coming and coming, like fish in the River Jordan, and they'll be singing and clapping their hands—such a shrieking, whooping, pushing and shoving there'll be. They munch enough sugar in a day to last anyone else a year, and they make such a mess of the floor that there's no getting it clean afterwards, even if you scrub it for a week. But some of them are very amusing fellows.

JUDAS. Buffoons?

PILATE. What buffoons? *Abstractedly.* Wait a minute! . . What was that just came into my head? Ah yes! *Guffaws.* I'll marry off those old clowns of yours. By God I will! *Rubbing his hands with satisfaction.* We'll see, something will come of it . . . a man and a monkey . . . *Guffaws.* Do they go in for that in your country?

The faint sound of a woman's weeping is heard from the orchard.

JUDAS. *Suddenly alert.* I don't know.

PILATE. And we'll invest you with the monkey insignia. Have you ever seen such things?

JUDAS. *Listening intently.* No, never.

PILATE. I sent King Herod one not long back, and he was offended. The fool! As if there weren't all kinds of insignia: you know, some have stars, others have animals, others have . . . What's that noise?

JUDAS. *Tensely.* Yes, there does seem to be some sort of noise.

PILATE. It's not a fire, is it? *Brightening suddenly.* Ah! It must be him—the Monkey King! And here I was thinking Lord knows what. The gates must be thrown open.

JUDAS. *Trembling all over.* Someone is weeping in there.

PILATE. What will you think of next! You're imagining it. I am never mistaken.

JUDAS. Someone is weeping.

Knocking at the gates.

PILATE. *Getting up.* Hey, come out, whoever's there!

JUDAS. Someone in the orchard is weeping.

PILATE. *Impatiently.* What the devil is this! I'll poke your eyes out! I'll flay you alive!

Silence. Enter Orif.

PILATE. Well?

ORIF. Zif will find out right away. A fast one on his feet is Zif—he'll be there and back in a jiffy. Oh he's a sharp one—he'll find out quick as a wink.

Knocking at the gates. Fearful expectation. A messenger appears.

SCENE SIX

Judas, Pilate, Orif, Messenger, Monkey King

MESSENGER. His Majesty the King of the Monkeys, the Great Monkey Valakh-Tantararakh-Tarandarufa Asyka the First.

PILATE. Bid him welcome. *The messenger vanishes. To Judas.* There! You see, I'm never mistaken. *Goes toward the door.*

Music: march of the monkeys.

PILATE. *On the threshold.* Welcome, dear guest—we've been awaiting your arrival with impatience. The tables are set, the pies are baked, the honey is flowing, the kasha's cooked. Hey there, bring in the goose, the ram and the white swan!

MONKEY KING. A star with a flaming tail has appeared in the east. Its path is fiery. Day and night it gleams. It's moving toward Jerusalem.

PILATE. But we have golden apples.

MONKEY KING. *Staring at the wonder.* Shams. Fakes.

PILATE. Don't be afraid. Hold one in both paws. Take a good bite—and then sing their praises.

MONKEYKING. *Reluctant to take one. Suddenly recovering himself.* Well, we had a bear that flew through the skies—it flapped its legs and steered itself with its tail.

PILATE. But we have golden apples.

MONKEY KING. But we had an armless man who picked up an egg and slipped it into a naked man's shirtsleeve; a blind man saw it, a deaf man overheard it, a dumb man shouted hurrah and sent a legless man in pursuit.

PILATE. But we have golden apples.

MONKEY KING. But we had a blackamoor arrive. He doesn't ask to be fed—sits under a pyramid and eats sand.

PILATE. But we have Judas, Prince of Iscariot.

MONKEY KING. *Glancing at Judas in bewilderment.* But we have . . . *Stops short.*

PILATE. *Mimicking him.* But we have . . .

SCENE SEVEN

The same and Zif

ZIF. *Appearing from the gate.* A man has died.

PILATE. Well?
JUDAS. Who is it?
MONKEY KING. A man?
} *All at once*

ORIF. I knew it.

ZIF. Our neighbor Simon, the owner of the orchard.

JUDAS. Where?

ZIF. He was found dead beneath the apple tree.

JUDAS. Had he been dead long?

ZIF. Still warm.

JUDAS. What do they want then?

ZIF. They say he was killed.

JUDAS. Who killed him?

ZIF. They demand to see the Hegumen.

PILATE. *Flustered.* Tell them that I—I have nothing to do with it—I have guests. Please excuse me, Asyka, I'll be right back. *Takes refuge in the palace.*

JUDAS. *To himself.* An old man has been killed. *Harshly, curtly.* Who dares make such a demand? Who? Disperse the mob, bury the body; all property is forfeit to the treasury, and if he has a wife, let her be brought to the palace immediately!

ZIF. *Withdrawing.* Royally done.

ORIF. *Withdrawing.* So be it.

MONKEY KING. *Grabbing a golden apple, to Judas.* Good lad! Your hand . . .

PILATE. *Peering from the palace through a half-closed door.* It's starting. Now there'll be the devil to pay!

JUDAS. *Frenziedly, as if tearing himself loose from a chain.* Whether you be black or red or yellow or white—monster or the most hideous freak—it's all one to me; all women are one to me. The heart has no memory. The heart may not be judged. The heart may not be answered. You, O Sun, you, O Moon, you, stars, and He by Whose word the earth stands, give me the animal's power to forget! Arise, you stormclouds, rend my heart asunder: the heart remembers, the heart has not forgotten . . . My feet are pierced by nails, my hands are pierced by nails, my heart is transfixed—yet I am still alive!

The gate opens to reveal Siboria, accompanied by Zif and Orif.

SCENE EIGHT

Judas, Monkey King, Zif, Orif, Siboria

ZIF. Do not mar your beauty. Do not break your heart.

SIBORIA. Where are you taking me? What have I done to you?

ORIF. Do not grieve. Do not weep.

SIBORIA. Why have you taken me away? What do you want of me?

ZIF. Do not bow your head. Dry your tears.

ORIF. Our prince is not a vixen: he won't devour you, he won't tear you with his claws.

JUDAS. *Catching sight of the approaching Siboria.* Ah, there she is!

MONKEY KING. *Tossing up a golden apple with one hand and catching it with the other.* A star is coming! A star is coming!

JUDAS. *Gazing long and intently at Siboria.* Do you know who I am? I am Judas, Prince of Iscariot. *After a tense silence, to Zif and Orif.* Take her into the palace. *Goes on ahead.*

SIBORIA. I had a son called Judas.

Curtain

ACT THREE

In Simon's orchard by the bank of the River Jordan.

SCENE ONE

Zif and Orif

ORIF. *He is sitting on a bench not far from the wicket-gate. He croons.* "Dawn had not reddened, the sun had not risen, when a dark man came—his hair unkempt and bast shoes on his feet. And by the lily-white hand he took her, and to the green forest he led her. And there she saw a fine new palace with sunlit chambers. And he seated her at a table covered with a white cloth and loaded her with silver and gold.

— Oh for silver and gold I care not, for mother and father, for brothers and sisters care I only.

— Oh be silent, fair lady, do not weep—ten servants shall you have, troubles ten . . ."

ZIF. *Wandering about aimlessly like a drowsy fly.* All those damned monkeys—a fine state of affairs! And we have to grin and bear it. Well, it's true what they say: the Monkey King has only to appear and everyone goes crazy—he'd raise the dead, that devil would! I heard a story about one of them: in two shakes of a lamb's tail he grabbed hold of a sharp stick and walloped a sleeping woman over the head with it so that her skull split right in two. He just prodded her with the stick and went on his way as if nothing at all had happened.

ORIF. Did he do it out of jealousy?

ZIF. No, no special reason.

ORIF. Well, that's a monkey for you! Those monkeys could make mincemeat of any one of us.

ZIF. And you should have seen what they did with that slant-eyed wench—you'd have died laughing! One of them kept stroking her and stroking her—quiet as a mouse—then all of a sudden he stuck his knife in . . .

ORIF. And were they brought to trial?

ZIF. According to our law.

ORIF. They got what was coming to them.

ZIF. That's the only way—the death sentence for all of them, and no mercy. Prince Judas is not to be moved: he won't pardon a guilty man.

ORIF. If I had my way, I'd take that Valakh-Tantararakh-Tarandarufa, lay him flat on the palm of one hand and squash him flat with the other, just like that! He's behind everything. Yes, and he's not the only one who'd get it . . . there are one or two others beside . . . Fulsome flattery, honeyed words, airs and graces. He's human to the waist—a beast below. He's turned everything upside down, the swine!

ZIF. They'll get their comeuppance! Each according to his deserts: some will be stretched on the rack, some will have nails driven into their heads, some will be disemboweled, some will be burned to a cinder, some will be thrown into cauldrons of molten lead, some will be buried to their ears, some will have their heads chopped off. That'll teach them to fool around with us!

ORIF. *Sadly.* What's happening now on the island of Iscariot?

ZIF. There's been no news for ages. Gone to rack and ruin, you can be sure.

ORIF. In your own house even the corners help.

ZIF. When an ant crawls over the sea—that's when we'll return to our island. We shall no more see that island than we shall our own ears. Put it out of your head.

ZIF. *Mockingly.* What are you all bundled up for then? It's not winter. Why don't you unbutton?

ORIF. *Irritably.* Why don't you?

ZIF. All right, I will.

ORIF. *Teasing him.* Well then?

ZIF. *Turning his back on Orif.* Accursed Wednesday—unhappy day! What an idiotic whim—to make us wear these monkey insignia. And with treasures like these hanging round your neck you'd better not show yourself without something to cover them up. There's not a soul who wouldn't hold you up to mockery.

ORIF. Thank God we only have to wear them on Wednesdays. Or we'd have to swelter even more. *Whining.* I'm in a terrible state. They'll be the death of me, they will: you get limper than a rotting leaf. Oh to be somewhere a bit cool!

ZIF. So here we are—a laughing stock! That's what we get for all our services—a slap in the face! We've been led by the nose! And there I was thinking they'd be handing us gold by the bagful—three bags apiece. *Overcome with indignation.* What does he care about us, after all? A pox on these monkey insignia! I have my self-respect too! Call that friendship . . . The ingratitude!

ZIF. The prince is jealous of us where she's concerned.

ORIF. Sssh, he's here in the garden.

ZIF. With her?

ORIF. No, with the Hegumen.

ZIF. Where's Siboria then?

ORIF. She went to the palace. *Meaningfully*. She always makes sure that she walks past me. She's a real . . .

ZIF. You need to keep an eye on that kind or they'll cuckold you in a jiffy.

ORIF. *With satisfaction*. It's not so long since they were married and she's climbing the wall already.

ZIF. *Stroking his whiskers*. And that pipsqueak doesn't take a blind bit of notice. *Digging Orif in the ribs*. I'll wager there's something she'll be needing!

ORIF. Not worth getting mixed up in that.

ZIF. It *is* worth it—even very much so . . . *Bitterly*. So he gets himself a fine wench, and all we get are these . . . monkey insignia. And that's not all . . . Just think what he wanted us to do: marry a monkey, he says! *With a grimace of disgust*. Try it yourself, if that's your fancy.

ORIF. I still have nightmares about that filthy beast. I almost went out of my mind.

ZIF. And I got a black one with thick lips, absolutely repulsive . . . I spat right in her face.

ORIF. *Hissing*. Mouse tail—cockroach eye!

ZIF. It's clear what the trouble is: Prince Judas is jealous.

ORIF. Wolves' carrion—bag of hay!

ZIF. It's gnawing at his heart: and so he makes a mock of us.

ORIF. Don't even talk about it! What has this Jerusalem got to offer? Be it in love or soul or conscience—nothing makes sense. Now on the island things were different: eat your fill and push your plate away. But here you go hungry the whole year round. Back at home, you eat a bun, you feel like another one, you can't resist a third. They're monsters here, not decent folk. You struggle, you wear yourself out like a river between its banks. You're either numb with cold or baked alive. Something like eggshell is slowly spreading all over my body. I don't see how things could get worse.

ZIF. I tell you that there's going to be such a fine old to-do here that the feathers will fly—all hell will be let loose.

ORIF. *In alarm.* Not that Monkey again? I can't take any more of that. I'm clearing out.

ZIF. Nobody's seen hair nor hide of the Monkey King for ages: he knows when to make himself scarce. No, a strange kind of man has appeared: he raises the dead, gives the blind back their sight, has power over the winds and waves, and when he goes forth he is a shining light to all the world, the grass of the fields and beasts bow down before him, and there's nothing his eyes can't see through. They say that this man and no other will be king of Jerusalem.

ORIF. And the Hegumen will be sent packing?

ZIF. He won't be handled with kid gloves, that's for sure! He'll get a taste of his own medicine. A terrible time is at hand: such doings there'll be—death will follow on destruction, mark my words!

ORIF. *Sinking down.* I'm an old man now, two and seventy summers weigh me down; I don't need newfangled things, I don't need riches. No matter how you twist and turn, time will claim its own. Once I was otherwise—handsome, lithe, you could slip me through a ring. My strength has gone from me. There's no returning to the days of my youth. *Squats.* Nothing is sweeter than sleep.

ZIF. Sleep and death are brothers. There's a storm brewing, and here you are moping. I'm still a fine fellow: I can still cut a caper or two!

ORIF. *On the verge of tears.* Oh for a bite of something sour! Everything's lost its savor . . . I'm deathly afraid of that storm.

ZIF. Up with you then! *Chaffing him.* Let's go and get some goat-milk curds. *With a wink.* Or shall we feed you with honey pancakes? Oh you frog-spawn you! Softy!

Zif and Orif move away into the orchard. A storm gathers.

SCENE TWO

Zif and Unkrada

ZIF. *Coming back.* Everything's gone dark in front of my eyes. No, I couldn't be mistaken. It is she—Unkrada. There's nothing wrong with my eyesight.

UNKRADA. *Following him in.* You recognized me?

ZIF. I'd know you among a thousand. You haven't changed in the least, Unkrada!

UNKRADA. Shhh! No one must know. Where is Judas?

ZIF. Here, in the orchard. His wife is in the palace.

UNKRADA. He's married?

ZIF. The honeymoon year is over.

UNKRADA. Who is she?

ZIF. Siboria, the wife of our neighbor Simon.

UNKRADA. I knew nothing of this.

ZIF. The prince will soon be here.

UNKRADA. *After some thought.* Do you know the road to the quay?

ZIF. A merry road—of course I know it!

UNKRADA. Will you escort me there? No one must know. I do not wish it . . . Do you understand? Our ships have not all cast anchor yet. Will you escort me?

ZIF. Whenever you wish.

UNKRADA. I want to know everything.

ZIF. You won't stay?

UNKRADA. I shall return later. I shall come in a different guise.

ZIF. Quick, let's go! Do you hear?

UNKRADA. *Listening intently.* Judas?

ZIF. With the Hegumen.

Unkrada and Zif exit hurriedly.

SCENE THREE

Judas and Pilate

PILATE. *Emerging from the garden, to Judas.* You're always able to reason so calmly about everything. This man's teaching is absurd.

JUDAS. *Deliberately.* He is one of those who appear in times of oppression, when the hand of authority is strong and there's peace and quiet throughout the land. A fearful time is upon us. Cemeteries—graves scattered with earth—only seem to be at rest, and what they hide—all the stifled longing of the earth—still lives, and secretly in the silence it is forging a heart from the tears of men in the flames of their anger, and that heart, proud and fearless, it will set in one man's breast . . . He will fall like a thunderbolt, avenging thousands, and his vengeance will be more cruel than a thousand vengeances . . . No, he is greater than any avenger, he is more powerful than a prophet who brings down fire and pestilence upon the earth, he is higher than man. The winds bear him. Beasts, plants and stones talk to him and own him their lord; birds give heed to him. Life is beyond our understanding: men live, not knowing for what; they suffer torment, not knowing why. And truth is yours and truth is mine—truth is everywhere, yet nowhere to be found. He will justify life, he will give a new law.

PILATE. Law! He wants to be king? King of Jerusalem!

JUDAS. *Mysteriously*. Now he has halted where three roads meet. He awaits another . . . and a man must come to him, one who is tormented, who finds no comfort anywhere, who is willing to take upon himself the ultimate, the most terrible guilt, that the cup of sin may overflow and that by his sacrifice the way may be opened for him who waits . . .

PILATE. What sacrifice? As it is, we do everything we can for them.

JUDAS. *Not answering; to himself.* But the heart that has taken upon itself the ultimate, most terrible guilt, can that heart bear all the burden of that ultimate guilt?

PILATE. These rebels have done a great deal of harm.

JUDAS. The ultimate sin, the ultimate guilt . . . It will flood the heart, it will encompass the soul, it will enfold you from head to foot. Men will recoil from you in horror, the power of heaven will fly away from you shrieking, the earth will slide from beneath your feet, and you will remain alone—you will be suspended in air, you will hang alone between earth and heaven.

PILATE. *With growing irritation.* What more do they want, then? How dare they? My head's spinning. Of course we shall find ways. I shall look to you, prince, as a tower of strength. *Stopping short.* What a black cloud! Spring hail is flying. There will be ringing in heaven.

JUDAS. A storm is approaching.

PILATE. And how is your wife? Are you happy?

JUDAS. My wife? . .

PILATE. Is she ailing? You know, I told you, I warned you . . . Choose another one if you like. That's easily arranged.

JUDAS. No, I didn't mean that. We love each other. She's cheerful, calm, meek as the dew. At times she's moody. On sultry days at the end of the month—days like these.

PILATE. Do you know, that happens with me too.

JUDAS. Here she is.

Siboria walks through the orchard and stops by the apple tree.

PILATE. *Observing Siboria.* Not bad looking.

JUDAS. She stands by the apple tree and weeps.

PILATE. For the old man?

JUDAS. No, for her son.

PILATE. I didn't know they had children.

JUDAS. They had one son. On the night he was to be born, this apple tree with golden apples miraculously appeared. There is a great mystery in this.

PILATE. You haven't talked to her about it?

JUDAS. Never.

PILATE. She's melting away like a candle. Look, she's kissing the earth. She imagines herself to be at her son's grave.

PILATE. I'm going. I feel like a bite of something. Tears aren't to my taste, and graves sicken me. Let's go.

JUDAS. She feels better when she's alone. I'll come in a moment. You go on.

Pilate goes out in the direction of the palace. Judas remains behind.

SCENE FOUR

Siboria and Judas

SIBORIA. *She stands by the apple tree, lamenting.* Little did I think, little did I dream that I would live to this sad parting and be left to moan in sorrow and misfortune. I can no longer mourn in silence—the fierce grief that consumes me must be given utterance. My heart beats only in longing for you, wasting away with grief, and there is none to comfort me. Every hour, every minute, be it at noontide or midnight, I cannot eat, I cannot drink without shedding tears. O bitter weariness! Poor heart, morning to evening consumed with grief. You were whiter than white snow, ruddier than the flaming sun, more lovely than the silvery moon. Mountains close upon me—grief encompasses me. Draw breath and answer me! Or have you, forgetting your own mother, become enamored of damp mother earth? Blizzards arose, bringing with them snow—and that to my grief; black clouds emerged from white, bringing fierce storms—and that to my misfortune; they have carried away my precious darling, they have buried him beneath the earth. Dawn will come, but you will not arise: you have sworn brotherhood to black night. The great fiery tears of the stars will arise and gaze at you, and fall, but you will not stir. If I pluck flowers and lay them on your grave, my burning tears will keep them from fading. Who will drink my tears, if not the damp earth? O you, my unforgettable one! Dreaming and waking I weep and do not see you. Grief is wasting me away. Was it for this I conceived you, was it for this I loved you? Where are you? Has the blue sea swallowed you or lulled you to sleep, crooning, "Sing lullaby, blue sea, sing lullaby?" Where are you? O tell me, tell me truly. I stand here close to you, alone, and long have I waited for an answer. Or do you not know the voice of your own mother, choked with sobbing? I bow before you, I kiss your lips—whisper into my ear, bring a joyless woman joy, embrace her who embraces you . . . Awake, arouse yourself from your eternal slumber!

JUDAS. Siboria . . . *Siboria gazes at Judas, her arms extended. He goes up to her.* Siboria, tell me . . . I have stood here and listened to you. Your lamentation rends my heart. Have pity on yourself. Do you not love me?

SIBORIA. I love you!

JUDAS. My sweet, my lovely turtle-dove! We shall always love each other. We shall be together for eternity. The two of us—forever and ever. Neither snows nor frosts shall part us. *Caressing her, softly*. Open your heart to me. Have no fear. *Siboria hangs her head*. I shall help you.

SIBORIA. There is no help for me.

JUDAS. Does some sin weigh upon your soul?

SIBORIA. I am beyond all comfort.

JUDAS. With what do you reproach yourself?

SIBORIA. *After an inward struggle, bowing very low*. I have committed a grievous sin.

JUDAS. Does anyone know of it?

SIBORIA. Simon knew.

JUDAS. *Resolutely, after a silence lasting some moments.* Siboria, whatever your sin, be it even the most terrible, I swear to you that I will take it upon myself.

SIBORIA. I shall never find absolution. It is a sin that cannot be washed away with repentance. I have needlessly destroyed a helpless, innocent soul.

JUDAS. Whatever your sin, I take it upon myself.

SIBORIA. *Despairingly.* I have killed my only child.

JUDAS. Your son?

SIBORIA. My son . . . I shall tell you, I shall conceal nothing.

JUDAS. *Softly.* Tell me.

SIBORIA. *With an effort of will, calmly.* In the year of my marriage I dreamed a dream. A winged youth appeared to me and seared me as with fire, and he said to me that I would give birth to a son who would destroy all our house: "He will kill his father, marry his mother and be king, but woe unto his soul—woe exceeding woe, grief exceeding grief—it would have been better for him had he never been born." I told my husband, and Simon laughed and made a joke of it. That very night I conceived. And when our son was born we were seized with fear: we wanted to kill him—but we could not raise a hand for pity; to let him remain with us, to bring him up was fearful. I knocked together a little raft out of planks, sealed the little coffin with pitch and lined it with straw. I took the child, washed him with my tears, dried him with my tresses, wrapped him in swaddling clothes and laid the little one in the coffin; I inscribed his name on a parchment and put in a golden apple for him to play with. I carried the coffin to the River Jordan and let it float out to sea. I thought to myself: the waves will carry him away and the sea will surely swallow him. And the sea did swallow him. Simon lived to old age, no one laid a finger on him, and he died suddenly, without absolution. I married you. And my innocent child perished. No one can know the ways of fate. Yet I believed my dream.

JUDAS. Did all this happen long ago?

SIBORIA. Twenty years.

JUDAS. *To himself.* Twenty years. *Aloud.* And the apple was from this apple tree?

SIBORIA. The night he was born, the golden apple tree appeared by a miracle. There is not such an apple tree in the whole world.

JUDAS. And if a man were to appear with such a golden apple, he would be your son?

SIBORIA. He will never appear. The sea has swallowed him. There was a time when I waited for him: I would fall to the ground and listen for the clatter of horses' hoofs . . . My eyes are dim with weeping. I will never be released from torment.

JUDAS. And what was your son's name?

SIBORIA. Judas.

A silence. A messenger appears, and after him Zif.

SCENE FIVE

Siboria, Judas, Messenger, Zif

ZIF. *Holding the messenger back.* Stop! Wait a moment! Where are you going?

MESSENGER. I must deliver a message to the prince.

ZIF. It is not the time now.

MESSENGER. Unkrada has brought news of great moment from the island of Iscariot.

ZIF. What's that to you! She herself will come and tell it.

MESSENGER. The prince has no idea of . . .

ZIF. The prince has forgotten the world.

MESSENGER. Happy man.

ZIF. Look how his brow has darkened; it is darker than a stormcloud. Better stay clear of trouble: if he sees you you're done for!

MESSENGER. Very well then, let her come herself. That's what I'll tell her.

Zif and the messenger disappear. Shortly after, Unkrada appears from the direction of the river, unseen by Siboria and Judas.

SCENE SIX

Siboria, Judas, Unkrada

SIBORIA. *To Judas, whose silence is becoming unbearable.* But why do you say nothing? Give me an answer.

JUDAS. *Deliberately.* I killed your husband.

SIBORIA. *Not understanding.* Who killed?

JUDAS. I . . . I killed Simon.

SIBORIA. *Staring at him in incredulity and alarm.* You don't know what you're saying.

JUDAS. *Steadily.* At the Hegumen's command, I came here, came into your orchard, after the golden apples, but before I had time to pick one, an old man threw himself on me, intending to strike me. I pushed him away—the old man had a hard fall and never rose again. It was Simon, your husband. He didn't die a natural death, but by these hands. I killed him. Can you forgive me?

SIBORIA. *She has risen in silent horror.* Wait a moment . . . I don't know anything . . . I can't all at once . . . Let me collect my thoughts. *She walks away, into the orchard; suddenly she stops.* O God, how can this be? . . It cannot be possible . . . *Again she begins to walk.* I didn't know anything.

JUDAS. *Following her with his eyes.* You can't forgive—you can't forgive me? *He is crushed. Involuntarily he turns his head in the direction of Unkrada; his eyes widen and he staggers back as he recognizes her.*

SCENE SEVEN

Judas and Unkrada

UNKRADA. You've made your confession?

JUDAS. Who brought you here?

UNKRADA. The sea.

JUDAS. What do you want?

UNKRADA. I bring news from the island of Iscariot.

JUDAS. What has happened?

UNKRADA. You have broken your oath.

JUDAS. And you?

UNKRADA. You believed that . . . So that's the way you love!

JUDAS. You betrayed me.

UNKRADA. Your brother has been killed—Prince Stratim.

JUDAS. My brother killed?

UNKRADA. *Laughing.* The Jerusalem merchants killed him.

JUDAS. I don't understand.

UNKRADA. You have forgotten everything . . . But I, in the twilight hour, in that brief time when day and night merge—I would steel my heart, bow my head, hold back my longing . . . And the forest will be shaken . . . You have forgotten everything. And the forest will be shaken, and in the groaning and the soughing nothing will be heard, save a solitary human voice. It is I who sing—and the song I am singing sears my heart. O songs of mine, my swift-winged hawks, whither shall I send you? I loved you, Judas, and shall always love you, love you in defiance of wind and thunderstorm and blizzard. A year I passed without you and it seemed an age. There was no thought I did not think. And my longing grew like the evening dark at autumn time. *Moving toward him.* If I had forgotten you, I would never have come to you. Look, my head is twined about with gold. I am your will, I am your fate. I reach up my arms to place the crown upon your head. The crown I give will not be blown away by winds or washed away by rains or snatched from you by men. I have found you.

JUDAS. *Seized with foreboding.* Unkrada . . . Unkrada?

UNKRADA. Your mother has died.

JUDAS. *In confusion.* My mother?

UNKRADA. She is no mother to you. You are no son to her.

JUDAS. No mother to me? . .

UNKRADA. Come closer. I am not a walking fire: I will not burn you.

JUDAS. What are you saying! *Approaching Unkrada.* That cannot be.

UNKRADA. For twenty years your mother kept her secret, and only on her deathbed did she resolve to make confession to the king. She had long been sterile—everyone knew of it—and wanted a child. She went nowhere and prayed continually to the sea alone. One day she was praying at the sea's edge when she noticed a little coffin, sealed with pitch, that the waves had cast up; inside it on some straw lay a baby. There was also a parchment inscribed with a name and a curious golden apple—for him to play with. Here is the apple! It burns like a hot coal. *She gives Judas the apple.* Now you are a free man. There is nothing to fear. It is dark between earth and heaven. No one can know the ways of fate. All prophecies are false.

JUDAS. *Speaking with his lips alone.* Prophecies are false . . . And this apple?

UNKRADA. Golden as the sun!

JUDAS. The sun does not lie.

UNKRADA. The king awaits you, the king will yield his kingdom to you. The winds have grown calm in the field, the earth is at peace, the great wave has rolled back to sea. The lowering, salt, black sea, no longer churned by the ill weather, is at rest. Gently its water ebb and flow. The ship stands ready. *Reaches out her hand to Judas.* Why are you standing there? I am not a crawling serpent, I will not bite you. *Bitterly.* Or are you loath to leave your cosy nest, your shady garden? Your wife is meek, she will forget everything. You killed the old man, her husband—what of it? You have repented. She will forgive you. And you will live at peace together, and your lives will pass like a bird in flight! *Angrily.* Go, take your leave of her. *Judas continues to stand before her with eyes downcast.* King! You are king!

JUDAS. *Shuddering with an effort.* See how she fares—my mother . . .

UNKRADA. Your mother?! *Looks about her in bewilderment. Her eyes fall on the apple tree. She stands amazed.* Golden apples! *Suddenly recalling something.* Where have I seen them before? .. *Tormentedly.* Golden apples . . . *Quickly she goes over to Judas and examines the apple.* Give it to me! *She stares into his face.*

JUDAS. *Not letting go of the apple.* She is there, in the garden . . . my mother . . .

UNKRADA. *Drawing back* Your wife!

JUDAS. And mother.

UNKRADA. *Suppressing the shriek which rises to her throat, she retreats into the garden, moving uncertainly and looking about her as she goes; she quickly returns. In a whisper.* Sleep has overcome her—she lies beneath the apple tree. Her golden tresses are spread over the earth like the rays of the sun. It is as if the sun were sleeping in an apple orchard. Pink blossoms fall upon her eyelids. *Crying out.* Look! A black cloud is passing over us . . . A thunderbolt will strike her dead.

JUDAS. *Draws himself to his full height. Throws away the apple. Makes the sign of the cross over himself.* I am ready.

UNKRADA. *Blocking his path.* Where are you going?

JUDAS. To the crossroads.

UNKRADA. *As if in her sleep.* To the place where three roads meet.

JUDAS. To take upon myself for the whole world the ultimate, the most terrible sin.

UNKRADA. I shall follow you. We shall go together . . . Do you know the name of the ultimate sin?

JUDAS. *After a moment's thought; to himself.* The ultimate sin . . .

UNKRADA. *As if suddenly bursting into bloom.* Its name is—betrayal.

JUDAS. I am ready. *In a silence that presages storm, he begins to move.*

UNKRADA. *Rushing after him.* No! You are king. The sea is yours. The ocean is yours. *On her knees.* Stop! As earth falls upon earth—softly, tenderly—so I upon you . . . *Frenziedly.* Your shadow is leaving you. You have no shadow now! Judas! *Crawling after him.* Traitor . . . traitor . . . traitor . . .

Curtain

1908

LEONID ANDREYEV

Leonid Andreyev (1871-1919), short-story writer and dramatist, was born in the provincial town of Oriol, the son of a surveyor. As a struggling law student, first at Moscow and then at St. Petersburg University, Andreyev experienced great hardship. His bouts of heavy drinking date from this period, and an early suicide attempt left him with a permanent heart ailment. A failure as a lawyer, Andreyev entered literature by way of journalism, first as a court reporter and later as a feuilletonist. A story published in the *Moscow Courier* in 1898 caught the attention of Maksim Gorky, who was generous with support and encouragement. Although close for a number of years to the group of writers, realists in literature and socialists in politics, who had gathered about Gorky under the imprint of the *Znanie* ("Knowledge") publishing house, Andreyev remained fundamentally apolitical; his strength lay, as Gorky observed, in his "uncanny understanding of everything that concerned the dark aspects, the contradictions of man's soul, the ferment of the instincts." After 1905, during which he spent two weeks in prison for permitting his apartment to be used as a meeting place by the Marxist Social Democratic party, Andreyev's path increasingly diverged from that of his erstwhile mentor.

The publication in 1901 of his first collection of stories brought Andreyev fame, and he was soon established as the most popular and controversial writer of his generation. The year 1908, in the course of which he published his most famous story, "The Seven Who Were Hanged," and moved into a luxurious art nouveau villa on the coast of Finland, marks the apogee of his success; the ensuing years witnessed a catastrophic decline of his reputation among the intelligentsia. A passionate foe of the Bolsheviks, Andreyev remained in White-controlled Finland after the October Revolution, isolated, despairing and in conditions of worsening material hardship. In 1919 he addressed an S.O.S. to the allied forces, calling upon them to drive the Bolsheviks out of Russia. In the Soviet Union the famed writer's death passed almost unnoticed.

In his own day, the faults of Andreyev's writing—the rhetorical, careless style, the melodramatic effects, the philosophical pretensions—were overlooked or forgiven by many for the quality of the anguish it conveyed. In Blok's striking phrase, Andreyev had been the scream that a sick and insane Russia had let forth in the agonizing years immediately preceding and following the 1905 Revolution. Unfortunately, Blok added, he had continued to scream after everything had calmed down. Such an evaluation reflects the changing attitude of the Symbolists to Andreyev's work.

The relations between Andreyev and Symbolism were uneasy on both sides. Andreyev felt himself to be an outsider among contemporary literary groupings: "for the nobly born decadents, a despised realist; for the congenital realists a despised symbolist." He was drawn toward the Symbolist aesthetic, yet in the presence of the Symbolists themselves he had an uncomfortable sense of inferiority. For their part, the Symbolists, while admitting his talent, were patronizing enough: "an uncultured talent" (Briusov), "a Russian foreign to culture" (Gippius) are entirely characteristic comments. Blok, who sensed a spiritual kinship between himself and Andreyev ("the chaos in each of us called out to the other"), was at first inclined to defend him against snobbish detractors, praising him for posing the great questions of life "as children do, relentlessly"; but even Blok came at length to reject Andreyev as a kind of grotesque *Doppelgänger*—"an amalgam of horrors of a mystical order that are very close to me." It is certain, however, that no account of Russian Symbolism, and particularly of Russian Symbolism and the theatre, can leave Andreyev out of account—as a popularizer he played a unique role.

Andreyev's interest in the theatre dated back to his days as a journalist, when he had written enthusiastic reviews of the Moscow Art Theatre's productions of Chekhov and Ibsen. He shared Blok's dislike of the all-powerful director, and in 1909 attempted to organize an "authors' theatre" which would have no permanent director to impose his own interpretation on the dramatist's creation. A prolific playwright (he would often turn out a play in the space of a week), Andreyev wrote some twenty full-length dramas between 1905 and 1916 as well as eight shorter pieces. He was as much the dramatic voice of his own generation as Chekhov had been of the previous one.

Andreyev's plays occupy an intermediary position between Symbolism and realism; significantly, his first great success, *The Life of Man*, was staged by both Stanislavsky and Meyerhold, directors closely associated with realism and Symbolism in the theatre. In his early dramas *To the Stars* and *Savva*, Andreyev claimed to be "the continuator of Chekhov" in that he was "a hater of the naked symbol and of naked, shameless reality." Soon, however, Andreyev was calling for a "stylized drama," for "broad generalizations" that were "unthinkable in the drama of everyday life." In his attempt at a modern mystery play, *The Life of Man* (1906), Andreyev offered a model of just such a stylized and generalized drama, following it with others in a similar vein—*King Hunger* (1907), *The Black Maskers* (1908), *Anathema* (1909) and *The Ocean* (1911). In these plays Andreyev effectively reduced the complexities of Symbolism to a not too demanding allegorism, allowing the public the illusion of grappling with profound philosophical problems while offering them the strong situations and simplified characters of melodrama.

In addition to his "symbolic" plays, Andreyev produced a number of stage works in a more traditional manner, among them the dramas of student life *The Days of Our Life* (1908) and *Gaudeamus* (1910) and a cycle of dramas dealing with sexual problems in a bourgeois milieu. The late "myth-play," *He Who Gets Slapped* (1916), in which Andreyev attempts to "bury" the Psyche myth in a modern circus setting, is an attempt at a synthesis of his two styles.

Rather than one of Andreyev's plays (which have been widely translated), the present volume offers selection from his lively "Letters about the Theatre." While he is admirably sensitive to the peculiar quality of Chekhov's plays, Andreyev's general ideas about the present and future of the drama are not particularly original or profound: his actionless "panpsychological drama" has much in common with Maeterlinck's "static theatre," and his vision of a theatre absorbed into life clearly owes not a little to Evreinov's "theatricalization of life" and "theatre for oneself." The "Letters," then, present with characteristic panache a number of ideas current in "advanced" theatrical circles of the time.

Leonid Andreyev
Theatre and the Inner Life
(from "Letters about the Theatre—Letter One"[48])

Does the theatre need *action* in its consecrated form of deeds and movements on the stage—a form not only accepted by all theatres but even espoused as the sole and indispensable way to salvation?

To this heretical question I will venture to answer no. There is no necessity for such action, inasmuch as *Life itself* in its most dramatic and tragic collisions draws away from external action, retreating ever further into the depths of the soul, into the silence and outward stillness of intellectual experience.

Rereading Benvenuto Cellini's memoirs, I was struck by the enormous number of events in the life of this artist-adventurer: so many escapes, murders, unexpected turns of fortune, losses and discoveries, loves and friendships. Truly, the average man of today will not record as many events in his entire life as Cellini encountered in the short journey from his house to the city gates! And this is true not of Cellini alone, but of all who lived the life of that time, with its bandits, dukes and monks, its rapiers and mandolins. In those days a man was interesting only if he was a mover and a doer; and the man who remained in one place was deprived of experience, of life itself—he was like a stone by the roadside about which there is nothing to be said.

But just step forward a few centuries and you are confronted with the life . . . let us say, of Nietzsche, the most tragic of modern heroes. Where are the events, the movement, the deeds in his life? There are none. In the days of his youth, when he wore the uniform of a Prussian soldier, Nietzsche was at his least dramatic: the drama begins at the very moment that the stillness and silence of the study descend upon his life. It is here that we will find the agonizing reappraisal of all values, the tragic struggle, the break with Wagner, the seductions of Zarathustra. And what of the stage after this?

The stage is impotent and dumb. Submissive to the immutable law of action, it refuses to give us, it *cannot* give us the Nietzsche we find so important, so essential, offering us instead, in enormous quantities, the useless, empty Cellini, wooden sword and all, whom we have long outgrown. Life has gone inside, but the theatre has remained at the threshold. Understand this and you will understand why not a single drama of the last few decades has reached the heights of the modern novel or has been able to compare with it; why Dostoevsky did not write a single drama;

why Tolstoi, so profound in the novel, is primitive in his plays; why that cunning fox Maeterlinck dressed his thoughts up in breeches and set his doubts scurrying about the boards. Follow my thought to the end and you will understand why Ostrovsky, who relies on the externals of life, is so enchantingly theatrical (and thus no longer needed) and why Chekhov is so needed and so "untheatrical."

I am not saying that events no longer take place, that no one *acts*, that history has come to a standstill. No: the journal of events is crowded enough, there are plenty of murders and suicides, of complicated frauds, cunning intrigues and strenuous hand-to-hand combats, but . . . all this has lost much of its dramatic value. *Life has become more psychological*, if I may so express myself; a new hero—the intellect—has joined the ranks of the elemental passions and those "eternal" heroes of drama: love and hunger. Not hunger, not love, not ambition, but *thought*, human thought, with all its suffering and struggle, is the true hero of modern life, and consequently deserves primacy of place in the drama. Even the bad dramatists and the bad audiences of the present day have begun to understand that the external presentation of a struggle, however much blood may be shed on stage, is the least dramatic thing about it. The dramatic moment is not when the worker takes to the streets, but when word of the new life first reaches his ear, when his timid, feeble, inert thought suddenly rears up like a maddened horse and at a single leap carries its rider into a shining wonderland. The dramatic moment is not when the soldiers arrive in response to the factory owner's demand and are readying their weapons, but when in the silence of sleepless nocturnal self-communing the factory owner struggles with two truths and cannot bring his conscience or his tormented mind to accept either one. The same is true of modern love—here too, as in every profound manifestation of life, action no longer finds external expression, but has retreated inward to the depths, to the seeming immobility of emotional experience.

An interesting particular. For the hero's weightiest thoughts, pondered in solitude, there once existed the soliloquy; but today's realistic drama has done away with even this last possibility, pitiful enough, of withdrawal to the depths: the soliloquy has been abolished. It is curious to see the sly tricks resorted to by dramatists who feel the necessity for at least a brief soliloquy but dare not introduce one openly: talk to a deaf old man, to a stove, to a glove, anything as long as you don't talk alone on stage—it's unnatural, it isn't lifelike. In order to be lifelike you have to perform one action after another without stopping, to chatter away incessantly like an inebriated parrot and never once fall to thinking for more than twenty seconds!

They keep on painting the same old portrait of life, modeled on the old masters, and they fail to notice that any likeness has long since vanished and they are not painting a living face, but only *copying an old picture*.

1912

Leonid Andreyev

The Failure of the Symbolist Theatre (from "Letters about the Theatre—Letter One")

The impoverishment of dramatic literature . . . You know, of course, that there is in progress a desperate struggle for the theatre between the symbolists and the "healthy" realists; you know, of course, that at the present time—an extremely sad one for literature in general—"healthy" realism has won the day. But have you noticed that for some reason this victory *coincides* with the impoverishment of dramatic literature and the decline of the theatre? Like the landowner in Saltykov-Shchedrin who, as a result of a misunderstanding, conceived a hatred for peasants and killed them off to clear the air, only to sink into a hopeless state of misery and starvation—the public and the theatre between them have joyfully exterminated symbolism on the stage, and suddenly . . . misery, starvation . . . what has become of drama? Ah, how good it is to breathe the pure air of realistic drama . . . But what has become of drama? Where have the dramatists disappeared to? At all events, I'm starving—and bored to tears!

But what then was this dear departed symbolism of ours whose death has cleared the air but left us nothing to eat?

It's name was compromise. Only in a few cases has symbolism on stage been dictated by the absolute laws of individual creation; for the most part it has been no more than a *means* for living thought to reach the stage, performing the function of the Jewish smuggler who gets Brussels lace through the customs in the guise of a ram. Limited by the demands of "action and spectacle," the dramatist was unable to give theatrical *incarnation* to the manifold aspects of the subtle and complex modern soul, a soul suffused by the radiance of thought, creating precious new emotions and discovering wellsprings, unknown to the Ancients, of a new and profound tragedy. The dramatist was unable to give incarnation to these aspects because the new emotions of the soul are without *flesh*, and so the smugglers with their heavy load of contraband stretched across the stage in a neverending file—stylized figures, barefoot dancers, nameless enigmatic personages, galvanized (but not resuscitated) Pierrots and Harlequins, symbolic blind men, symbolic deaf and dumb, symbolic devils, gnomes, fairies and frogs. The blind men tripped over the sets, the devils sank without trace, Harlequin groaned like a living being, the barefoot dancers looked lugubrious, a very fat person tried unsuccessfully to turn into a shadow . . . And the whole naive masquerade meant only one thing: thought is suffocating in your theatre!—the soul is dying on those boards of yours!

Like all compromises, this self-conscious, Janus-faced contraband symbolism failed to satisfy either side and *had* to perish. Both author and public were squashed flat by the cumbersome, all too corporeal three-dimensional figure of the actor, clean-shaven and energetic. The actor was wrenched about like an india rubber doll, made to assume poses encountered only in geometry and plied with potions of bile and vinegar to make him sound like a real live corpse instead of a human being; he accepted this new yoke submissively, but in spite of all his efforts he was unable to transform himself into vapor, or air or into a real frog. The public sensed a sham, whistled and left, while the author sensed that the stronghold of the modern theatre would not be captured by trying to evade its laws: he had either to destroy the Bastille or perish in the Bastille!

For a time the theatre was spiritually enriched; it acquired inner significance, even importance, but outwardly its form became of such glaring absurdity, so disjointed, so creaky that its continued existence became impossible. And with a smile at once unctuous and malicious, that old bag, the realistic drama, arrived to reset the actor's bones and tighten the nuts and bolts. To drive out the unclean Maeterlinckian spirit she fumigated the theatre with Ostrovsky. The result: the impoverishment of dramatic literature—a Renaissance of a peculiarly Russian kind.

1912

Leonid Andreyev

Chekhov as Panpsychologist (from "Letters about the Theatre—Letter Two")

I return to Chekhov and the Art Theatre.

The special quality of Chekhov lies in the fact that he was the most consistent of panpsychologists. If Tolstoi could breathe life only into man's body, if Dostoevsky is devoted exclusively to the spirit, Chekhov brought to life everything he touched: his landscape is no less psychological than his people; his people are no more psychological than his clouds, his stones, his chairs, his tumblers and his apartments. All objects of the visible and invisible world make their appearance simply as component parts of one great soul; and if his stories are only chapters of a single vast novel, his things are simply *thoughts* and *sensations* scattered in space—action and spectacle is informed by a single spirit. He brushes in his hero's life with a landscape, recounts his past with clouds, depicts his tears with rain, demonstrates by means of an apartment that the immortality of the soul does not exist. Such is Chekhov in his fiction—and such he is in his drama too.

On the stage Chekhov must be performed not only by people—he must be performed by tumblers and chairs and crickets and military greatcoats and wedding rings. In *The Cherry Orchard* Chekhov suddenly introduces the mysterious sound of a bucket falling in a distant mineshaft, a sound which it is impossible to reproduce but which is essential because it is an essential part of the soul of the characters in the play—without it they are not the same, without it there can be no Chekhov. If we bear this in mind we will understand why theatres where people perform, and things do not, to this day cannot play Chekhov and do not love and understand him. (In the provinces his plays are hardly ever given). We will also understand not only why the Art Theatre is able to perform Chekhov, but where its strength, its originality and its distinction lie: at the Art Theatre things perform as well as people. It is a psychological theatre. More than that—it is a theatre of that very panpsychology of which Anton Chekhov was the perfect example in literature.

Returning now to the beginning of the Art Theatre and of my article, we will understand what was attractive and touchingly novel in the fur-trimmed caftans worn by the boyars in *Fiodor Ivanovich* was psychologism: not historical accuracy, not faithfulness to an era of which we have no more than an approximate notion, but a *vital spirit* that brought them close to the profoundest truth of life. The apartment of the Prozorov sisters, Ivanov's study, the half-eaten cucumber that Shabelsky-Stanislavsky carries off with such pain and resentment, the cricket, the rings and the military greatcoats which the actors practiced wearing at home all had one thing in common: psyche. Things are *not* things, but the scattered thoughts and sensations of a single soul.

Not only things, but *time* itself Chekhov, and the Art Theatre after him, has shaped not as a clockmaker does, but as a psychologist: time is simply the thought and sensation of the characters. And when there are no miraculous pause-thoughts, pause-sensations, when merely talented people, and not time itself, are performing—there can and will be no Chekhov. Recall how Germans without any knowledge of Russian wept when from the stage of the Art Theatre the *living* time of Chekhov's plays spoke to them in its international language of pauses! The feat of compelling subtle time to submit to the force of its artistry is enough in itself to win for the Art Theatre eternal glory!

Living time, living things, living people—herein lies the secret charm of Chekhov's plays, plays which remain in the Art Theatre's repertoire to this day. Whether a servant plays his balalaika at the gates, bringing to the stage the sound—barely audible, almost guessed at—of the "Siskin" (*Ivanov*) or a cricket starts chirping, as in *Uncle Vanya*, or dogs bark, as in *The Cherry Orchard*, or sleighbells jingle or shouts carry from a fire or Natasha walks through the darkened rooms with a candle in her hand or Yepikhodov eats an apple, it all comes to one thing: the panpsyche. These are not the objects, the sounds and voices of the real world, but the thoughts and sensations of Chekhov's characters scattered in space. How curious, for example, that at the end of *The Three Sisters* all the characters in the play *think and feel by means of the military march* that the soldiers play, as if by chance, as they march past; and the discord in their souls is expressed, again, not by the direct, naked word, but by the apparently incidental figure of the girl with the harp, by her absurd and out-of-place ditty: I have loved, I have suffered.[49]

Turn your attention to the dialogue in Chekhov's plays: it is improbable, people do not speak that way in life; it is full things half-spoken, it seems the continuation of something already said, it lacks the clearly marked inception with which any speaker in a play by another writer would make an entrance: Chekhov's characters never begin and never end their speeches, they only continue them. For this reason Chekhov's plays seem difficult, not very interesting and even lacking in life when read: from this point of view, Tolstoi was right when he roundly condemned a play by Chekhov which he was too bored even to finish reading. But he was wrong because he had not seen Chekhov, had not seen Chekhov's performing things and pauses—all that the Art Theatre has brought to life with such profound understanding. After all, if Chekhov's dialogue always *continues* something, must there not be someone or something that it continues? This enigmatic being who is always absent when the play is read is composed of living things and living time. The dialogue never, in a manner of speaking, stops: it jumps from people to things, from things back to people, and from people to time, to silence or noise, to a cricket or to shouts carried from a fire. Everything is alive, everything has a soul and a voice: oh how far the Art Theatre was then from the intolerable naturalism which has been foisted on it and which knows only *things*. Who needs things?

But here is a very interesting and important question: who led the way, Chekhov or the Art Theatre? Who brought whom into being: Chekhov the Art Theatre or the Art Theatre Chekhov? Who was the psychologist (or rather panpsychologist) first? To this I will venture to reply: neither one nor the other, but both together and at the same time; but Chekhov was so always and in everything, while the Art Theatre became a psychologist gradually—the moment of meeting only confirmed the fate of both. It is possible that without the Art Theatre Chekhov would have given up writing plays—vain is the writing of laws if they be not observed; and without Chekhov the Art Theatre might easily have lost its way among all the naturalisms, realisms and symbolisms, and perhaps would never have found its true path.

1914

Leonid Andreyev
The Theatre of the Future
(from "Letters about the Theatre—Letter Two")

In the theatre of the future there will be no audience: that is the first and fundamental requirement of the new theatre; it is essential, as it is essential to society to eliminate the situation whereby some dine while others look on—let everyone come to the feast! The abolition of the audience will, it seems to me, be brought about in two ways, ways that are at once logical and inevitable.

The audience at the performing theatre will disappear because the performing theatre itself will gradually fade away, becoming absorbed by life itself; it will no longer be a special building with policemen at the main entrance, but will become a joyful element in the individual's everyday life. People will perform for themselves, without an audience and without actors. All these eurythmics and dances, these mock trials, these funny Futurists[50] on Tverskaya Street with their painted faces and fancy dress—all this and much else that the reader will be pleased to call to mind tells us one thing: life has been plundered, it has been divested of play as the cream is skimmed from a pitcher of milk, leaving people a thin, insipid potation to drink; life demands that play should return to the ancestral house of life like a prodigal son from his reluctant wanderings. How this will be brought about in practice I don't, of course, know, and I don't even give it very much thought—life is developing and growing at such a rate that all kinds of miracles become thinkable. And is it really such a miracle?—to become ourselves in some degree creators and artists, writers and musicians; not only to look and listen but to create with our own hands something for our own joy! The trouble, after all, is not that there is any lack of talented people, but that there is too little soil for them—vital seed is going to rot in damp warehouses. Who would have said before the aeroplane that the world had so many men of extraordinary courage and determination, of such physical and spiritual perfection? We complained of degeneracy—and then this! Consider this miracle: yesterday man was jolted about like a peasant on a carriage seat, sleepy, jelly-like, utterly passive, while today he drives an automobile, that fast and furious machine with its demand for superhuman concentration and for the utmost sharpness of eye and wit.

Of course, there will always be people with no capacity for play and there will always be people with a special capacity for and love of play—and the first will look on, if they wish, while the second perform with particular skill. But it won't be theatre, with its obligatory division into actors and audience: it is not, after all, theatre when old men look on, laughing and sighing, as children play! The development of social life gives promise of new ground for this non-theatrical play: there will be processions in which the masses will take part; perhaps the mystery play will be revived on a somewhat altered basis, but with the indispensable condition that everyone will participate in the performance. From this point of view, the future promises so much that is new that it would be a vain labor to look to the old and outworn for answers. For example, we are still quite unacquainted with the social drama: it was impossible under the conditions of the old life, the old theatre. We do not yet have plays in which the *people*, the *masses* would be the protagonist, and not an individual personality against the background of a couple of dozen extras. The entry of the masses into the arena of history—for which the present century will be remembered in centuries to come—will lead the performing theatre out of its dark alleyway into the open freedom of streets and squares; and, who knows, perhaps scenarios, if that is the right name, will be written for productions in which the entire many-millioned city will participate . . . What can we know of this, we who are subject to the law of "assembly" and cannot even gather in groups of four without someone immediately dispersing us?

1914

NOTES

A note on transliteration.

My rendering of Russian names is a traditional and "literary" one, involving certain inconsistencies. For example, I have conveyed the softness of a consonant preceding a vowel by means of an "i" (Briusov rather than Bryusov), but between two vowels I have preferred to use a "y" (Komissarzhevskaya rather than Komissarzhevskaia). Certain names have been given in their more familiar western forms (Diaghilev, Chaliapine, Alexandrinsky). Russian names of foreign origin are given in their original form (Benois, Roerich rather than Benua, Rerikh). However, in the titles cited in the following notes (which will be of interest primarily to readers of Russian) I have adhered to a stricter system of transliteration.

1. "Unnecessary Truth." First published in *Mir iskusstva*, 1902, no. 7.

2. Rubek and Irene: Characters in Ibsen's *When We Dead Awaken*, first produced by the Moscow Art Theatre in 1901.

3. *Tsar Maximilian*: The most popular example of Russian folk drama. The play's blending of tragic and grotesque elements and its remoteness from "realism" attracted the Symbolists. Remizov made a highly personal version of *Tsar Maximilian* (1918).

4. "On the Theatre." First published in *Zolotoe runo,* 1908, nos. 3-5.

5. "The hero striding forward in his winged helmet, sword slung over shoulder": Blok put these words into the mouth of German, the hero of his play *The Song of Fate*, which dates from the same year as this article.

6. "Vera Fiodorovna Komissarzhevskaya." First published in *Rech'*, 1910, February 12, and subsequently in *Sbornik pamiati V. F. Komissarzhevskoi* (St. Petersburg, 1911). Komissarzhevskaya died of smallpox while on tour in Tashkent on February 10, 1910. She had been forced to undertake a prolonged tour in order to recoup the losses her theatre had suffered as a result of the last-minute banning of *Salome*, and her premature death had an aura of martyrdom about it. Blok composed two "obituaries" for Komissarzhevskaya: the one offered here, and another which he delivered at an evening dedicated to her memory on March 7, 1910.

7. *The Puppet Show*. First published in the almanac *Fakely* in April 1906, and subsequently, together with *The Stranger* and *The King in the Square*, in *Liricheskie dramy* (St. Petersburg, 1908). The Russian title (*Balaganchik*) has sometimes been rendered, with greater literal accuracy but less poetic truth as "The Fairground Booth." A *balagan* (*-chik* is a diminutive suffix) was a gaily painted booth at a fair, inside which the spectator could expect to see conjurers, jugglers, acrobats, clowns and a pantomime, as well as a *Petrushka*—the Russian equivalent of a Punch and Judy show. *Balagan* has acquired an additional metaphorical meaning of "tomfoolery," "buffoonery."

8. "At her back a scythe": In Russian *kosa* means both "scythe" and "braid," and Blok takes advantage of this double meaning to make both verbal and visual puns.

9. *The Rose and the Cross*. First published in the literary almanac *Sirin* in August 1913. Blok's special fondness for this last major dramatic work of his (and perhaps a deep-seated doubt as to its theatrical viability) is witnessed by a number of secondary writings of an elucidatory nature. After reading the play to Stanislavsky (who pronounced it unstageworthy) in April 1913, Blok composed "Bertrand's Memoir, Written a Few Hours before His Death"—a kind of autobiography of the play's hero. When in 1915 the Moscow Art Theater did at last decide to stage *The Rose and the Cross*, Blok wrote an "Explanatory Note for the Art Theatre." Finally, for the play's publication in his collected plays (*Teatr*) in 1916, Blok added extensive notes that demonstrate the thoroughness of his research into historical background. Although of interest in themselves, these writings "around"

The Rose and the Cross add little to the understanding of the play as theatre, and considerations of space have made it impossible to include them here.

10. To ***: The dedication (which first appeared in the 1918 edition) was intended for the singer Liubov Delmas, to whom Blok had earlier dedicated his lyrical cycle "Carmen."

11. "You pay me in Toulouse gold": The gold of Toulouse has been proverbial since pagan times; it signifies riches that bring misfortune (author's note).

12. "Presentiments and Portents." First published in *Zolotoe runo*, 1906, nos. 5-6, and reprinted in *Po zvezdam* (St. Petersburg, 1909).

13. *Meon*: "Unbeing" (Greek).

14. "Rapture at the grim abyss's brink": A quotation from a song in Pushkin's "Little Tragedy" *A Feast in the Time of the Plague* (1830).

15. *Orchestra*: Russian makes a distinction in spelling between "orchestra" in the sense of the part of ancient Greek theatre reserved for the chorus and its modern sense of an instrumental ensemble. Since the word is used in both meanings here, it has been italicized in its archaic sense.

16. "The poetry of Innokenty Annensky." First published in *Borozdy i mezhi* (Moscow, 1916).

17. "He loves his song": A quotation from a short lyric by Pushkin (1827), itself adapted from a poem by André Chénier, in which the poet compares himself to a Venetian gondolier.

18. "Olympus is the smile of the god": A verse cited by Nietzsche in Section Ten of *The Birth of Tragedy.*

19. "The Cherry Orchard." First published in *Vesy*, 1904, no. 2, and reprinted in *Arabeski* (Moscow, 1911).

20. "The Theatre and Modern Drama." Published in *Teatr: Kniga o novom teatre* (St. Petersburg, 1908).

21. Schuré: Edouard Schuré (1841-1929), French music critic and contributor to the *Revue Wagnérienne.*

22. "That beefwitted oaf Siegfried, waving his cardboard sword": Apparently an attack on the heroic Wagnerian imagery favored by Blok at this time (see note 5).

23. "The Theatre of the Single Will." Published in *Teatr: Kniga o novom teatre* (St. Petersburg, 1908).

24. E. K. Vizener. *The Silence of the First Bride*: I have been unable to trace any such author or novel, and both may well be the author's invention. The fake epigraph is a well-established tradition of Russian letters.

25. "Children, only children live": The opening lines of a poem by Sologub (1897).

26. " . . .the capricious Aisa . . . the strict and consoling Ananka": *Aisa*—"fate"; *Ananka*—"necessity" (Greek).

27. Simply in order that "the people should congregate": Apparently a dig aimed at Viacheslav Ivanov's notion of *sobornost'* (a kind of mystical communion), which Sologub made fun of elsewhere (for example, in his play *Night Dances*).

28. "In reproach to the unjust day": A quotation from one of Sologub's best known poems (1902).

29. Whether Shuisky or Vorotynsky is bustling about on stage: A reference to Pushkin's historical drama *Boris Godunov*, which opens with a dialogue between the boyars Shuisky and Vorotynsky.

30. "With mystery he veiled": A quotation from a poem by Sologub (1894).

31. "No—the sufferings of a self-aware schoolboy": A reference to Moritz in Wedekind's play *Spring's Awakening*. Sologub edited the translation of the play made by G. Feder for production by Meyerhold at Komissarzhevskaya's theatre in September 1907.

32. "How sweet to know another life is with us": A quotation from Briusov's poem "Myshi" (1899).

33. *The Triumph of Death*. First published in *Fakely*, 1908, no. 3.

34. *Charodeika*: Russian for "enchantress".

35. Death: "Automobile" and "death" do not rhyme in Russian any more than they do in English.

36. Living and dead water: In Russian folklore, "dead water," if sprinkled upon parts of a dismembered body, will cause them to grow together again, while "living water" will bring the body back to life.

37. *The Comedy of Alexis, Man of God*. Published in *Tri komedii* (St. Petersburg, 1908).

38. Saints Gurias, Samonas and Abibus preserve us: Fourth-century Christian martyrs of Edessa. According to *Butler's Lives of the Saints*, "they had the curious distinction of being venerated as the 'avengers of unfulfilled contracts.'"

39. *The Venetian Madcaps*. Published in Moscow, 1915.

40. *Thamyris Kitharodos*. Published posthumously in Moscow, 1913 (in an edition of one hundred copies).

41. By the Cretan cavern, king: According to myth, Zeus passed his childhood on the island of Crete, where his mother, Rhea, hid him from the wrath of his father, Cronos.

42. *The Tragedy of Judas, Prince of Iscariot*. First published in *Zolotoe runo*, 1909, nos. 11–12, and subsequently in *Sochineniia*, vol. 8: *Rusal'nye deistva* (St. Petersburg, 1912) in a revised version. It is this later version (which the author pruned somewhat of folk idioms) that forms the basis of the present translation.

43. Beormas: Perm the Great, which extended, according to the conjecture of learned men, from the banks of the Northern Dvina to the Ural Mountains (author's note).

44. Yumala: The idol stood near the White Sea on the Northern Dvina, where the town of Kholmogory now stands (author's note).

45. Sorochinskoye Field: Not the field near which Gogol's Sorochinskaya Fair took place, but the field close to Jerusalem into which the *Golubinaya kniga* fell from the clouds (author's note). The *Golubinaya kniga*—which may be translated "Book of Wisdom," "*golubinaya*" derived from "*glubina*" ("depth") rather than "*golub*'" ("dove")—was a popular cosmogonal treatise.

46. "He was called after the great bird": According to the *Golubinaya kniga*, "the stratim bird is the mother of all birds" (author's note).

47. Polivania: The land of the great sinners, laid waste for its sins; mentioned in Russian scriptural verses (author's note).

48. "Letters on the Theatre." "Letter One" was first published in *Maski*, 1912, no. 3, and reprinted in the literary almanac *Shipovnik*, 1914, vol. 22, where it was followed by "Letter Two."

49. "I have loved, I have suffered": This will not be found in the text of *The Three Sisters*, and is clearly a Stanislavskian interpolation.

50. "These funny futurists": The Futurists, in that movement's early phase, found that studied outrageousness of public behavior brought them useful publicity; to this end, they wore odd clothes (Mayakovsky's famous yellow blouse) and painted their faces.